# The *Wild* Woman's Guide to Traveling the World

# The *Wild* Woman's Guide to Traveling the World

*A Novel*

## Kristin Rockaway

**CENTER STREET**

New York   Nashville

Copyright © 2017 by Kristin Rockaway
Reading group guide copyright © 2017 by Kristin Rockaway and Hachette Book Group, Inc.

Cover design by Diane Luger. Cover copyright © 2017 by Hachette Book Group, Inc.

Center Street
Hachette Book Group
1290 Avenue of the Americas, New York, NY 10104
centerstreet.com
twitter.com/centerstreet

First Edition: June 2017

Center Street is a division of Hachette Book Group, Inc. The Center Street name and logo are trademarks of Hachette Book Group, Inc.

The publisher is not responsible for websites (or their content) that are not owned by the publisher.

The Hachette Speakers Bureau provides a wide range of authors for speaking events. To find out more, go to www.HachetteSpeakersBureau.com or call (866) 376-6591.

Library of Congress Cataloging-in-Publication Data has been applied for.

ISBN 978-1-4555-9753-6 (trade paperback)—ISBN 978-1-4555-9754-3 (ebook)

Printed in the United States of America

LSC-C

10  9  8  7  6  5  4  3  2  1

*To April, for igniting the spark,*
*and to Audrey, for fanning the flame*

# The *Wild* Woman's Guide to Traveling the World

# chapter one

S o I think I'm going to go home."

Elena said this to me as I swigged from my bottle of San Miguel. She wouldn't look me in the eye. Instead, she stared down at her bowl of wiry brown noodles, jabbing at them with the fork she had procured from her purse. The emergency fork should have been my first indicator that she wasn't comfortable in Hong Kong.

"What do you mean you think you're going to go home?" I forced the words from the back of my throat, suppressing a cough from the mouthful of beer that I'd gulped. The bitter aftertaste burned the edges of my tongue. "We just got here eight hours ago. Our flight's not for another week."

"Well, when you were in the shower before, I called the airline and changed my return flight to tomorrow morning. So I think I'm going to go home." She twirled the noodles repeatedly around her fork, watching them glisten, but never brought them to her mouth. It was the most perfect noodle I'd ever tasted, firm and salty, but here she was, wasting them with her mindless fiddling. I wanted to grab the fork from her pale, bony hand and stab her in the eye.

"What about me?"

"Oh, I didn't change your ticket. You should stay," she said.

"You should definitely stay and enjoy the rest of your vacation." It was now my vacation, not ours.

The din around us at the Temple Street Night Market began to fade and I felt a dull ache behind my eyes. Jet lag was descending. I had expected to spend this meal reviewing our itinerary for the rest of the week. The itinerary I'd so carefully and painstakingly planned. Instead, I was being abandoned by my best friend, seven thousand miles from home. The earmarked guidebook I had placed on the table mocked me.

An overburdened waitress deposited two plastic plates in front of us, each laden with food fresh from the makeshift sidewalk kitchen four feet away. Spicy fried pork piled atop a thin layer of shredded white cabbage, dotted with nickel slices of fiery red peppers. Razor clams heaped with green vegetables, sopping in a thick brown sauce. Steam rose from them in fragrant, gray plumes. A grimace passed over Elena's face.

"Help yourself," I challenged. "It's probably your last chance for a meal in Hong Kong."

The fork stood upright in her bowl, tangled in the cooling noodles. Her hands were clasped around the purse in her lap, signaling that she was done with this meal. I picked up my chopsticks and pinched a narrow, tubular clamshell from the serving dish.

"What is that?" she asked, recoiling slightly, the clam a potential threat to her well-being.

"It's a fucking clam, Elena." I tore the chewy flesh from the shell with my chopsticks and popped it in my mouth, getting a burst of sweet fishiness as I bit down. "Why don't you try one instead of sitting there feeling sorry for yourself?"

"Why are you being so cold to me?" she said, her face twisted in disbelief, as if my aggression had been unprovoked. We'd known each other since grade school, but her Little Miss Innocent act still managed to astound me.

"As soon as we buckled ourselves in on the plane ride over here," I said, "you started crying about how much you miss Roddy, and you haven't let up since. I planned this whole trip for us, and now you're ditching me without even giving it a chance."

"If you were in love, you would understand."

My eyes reflexively rolled to the back of my head. "Is this what love is? Being so obsessed with someone that you can't be apart from them for a few days to have fun with a friend in a new country?"

"When it happens to you, you'll see," she said, turning her nose up. I expected her to storm away in her usual theatrical fashion, but I could see in the way her eyes darted that the crowd was intimidating her. She was too afraid to get up from this table and take the subway by herself back to our hotel in Wan Chai. So I held her hostage while I ate, taking my time to savor the flavors before me, the meal that I'd looked forward to for so long. Hong Kong had a reputation for delectable street food; at least one of us was going to enjoy this once-in-a-lifetime experience.

It was my own fault, really, for suggesting that we go away together. Elena rarely left the tri-state area; her idea of an exotic getaway involved tanning on the Jersey Shore. I, on the other hand, was on a mission to fill my passport with as many stamps as I could. I'd stood atop the Eiffel Tower, I'd sipped warm Guinness in a Dublin pub, I'd sunbathed on the balmy beaches of Ibiza—and I'd done it all alone. As a traveling IT consultant for an international firm, I'd found myself on the Tube in London one week and soaking up the sun in LA two weeks later. There was no denying that I had the travel bug. Life on the road was so much more interesting than staying at home in New York.

So when Elena came to me two months earlier, devastated by her breakup with Roddy, I took her out for an exorcism by alcohol and told her that a trip was what she needed to clear her head. And this time, we should go on vacation together.

"It'll be great," I said, still tasting the sweetness of the Jägerbomb on my lips. "We'll sightsee and shop and drink and eat all this awesome food. And pick up hot foreign guys! Let's do it!"

"I don't know, Sophie," she said. Her eyes were swollen from hours of crying and were growing increasingly glassy with each shot she threw back. "I don't even have a passport."

"We'll get you one; that's not a problem at all."

"There's no way I could afford it. Not all of us can be a bigshot IT consultant with a fat paycheck like you, Soph. I'm a receptionist. I'm not exactly rolling in dough."

"Then you don't have to worry about the plane ticket," I said, unwilling to take no for an answer. "I've got plenty of frequent-flyer miles. It's my treat!"

She smiled for the first time that night. "Really?"

"Of course!" I squealed, the booze turning up the volume on my enthusiasm. "I'm going to book this now before you change your mind and chicken out."

Three weeks later, she and Roddy reconciled and started talking about moving in together. I felt that the makers of Jägermeister now owed me a refund for the 120,000 hard-earned frequent-flyer miles I'd blown on her plane ticket.

Looking back on it, I should've planned a weekend in Miami or Vegas, someplace closer to home and more familiar for her. Someplace where the restaurants laid a fork on every table. To be honest, I wasn't really thinking about what would be most comfortable for Elena when I booked those tickets. Hong Kong had been next on my list of places I wanted to visit, and her breakup just happened to coincide with a trip I was already planning to take. My first vacation that wasn't incidentally tacked on to the end of a business trip.

But I also wanted to give her the opportunity to see something different, to introduce her to new experiences, to show her there was more to life than Roddy and New Jersey. So far, she'd lived a very sheltered life; she still lived at home with her mom, still slept in the same bedroom in which she'd grown up. Meanwhile, I'd struck out on my own and moved into the city. It had been so long since we'd spent any quality time together. I thought a foreign country would be the perfect place for us to rekindle our bond. Now, as we glared at each other over these Chinese delicacies, I realized I had made an error in judgment.

Elena pursed her lips. "You travel alone all the time. I don't see what the big deal is."

"Yes, I travel alone all the time, but this was something we planned together. A girls' trip. I wasn't expecting to be on my own here." I tore into a pork chop, the peppery juices stinging my soft palate, trying not to think about all the business trips I'd have to go on to recover those lost frequent-flyer miles.

"I thought you'd be happier this way."

"What's that supposed to mean?"

She tossed her long blond hair over her shoulder and took a deep breath. "It's clear I'm annoying you. I've been annoying you all day. I'm sorry I'm not comfortable here, but I'm not into traveling like you are. You'll have a better time without me."

"I really want us to have a good time together," I said. And despite that momentary fantasy about gouging her eye out, I meant it, sincerely. "I think if you just let go and forget about Roddy for a minute, you'll be able to relax and enjoy yourself."

"I don't want to forget about Roddy!" she cried. "I feel empty without him, like part of me is on the other end of the earth."

Tears pooled in the corners of her eyes and her fair skin flushed pink. Her display of melodrama elicited no sympathy from me.

"For God's sake, Elena, two months ago, you swore you'd never speak to him again. Now you suddenly can't live without him? This seems like the definition of a dysfunctional relationship."

She broke out in a full-force sob, salty streaks streaming down her splotchy cheeks. The waitress gave a sideways glance as she hurried past us with a stack of empty bowls. I covered my face with my hands, embarrassed to be a part of this performance.

"When did you stop being my friend?" she wailed. The couple at the table next to us paused their meal to gawk at the spectacle we were creating, the chopsticks in their hands suspended midair.

"Would you please stop making a scene?" I muttered this quietly, trying not to make eye contact with her, hoping that my body language would send the message to onlookers that I was not a willing participant in her tantrum.

"Oh sure, Sophie, let's not make a scene!" she said, waving her arms about in a very scene-making gesture. "That is so typical."

"Typical of what?"

"Typical of you!" she spat. "Controlling and judgmental. You have no emotions, no passion. You don't understand how I feel because you don't even know how to love someone! And no one could ever love you because you're so closed off and miserable!"

I reached inside my wallet and threw a wad of cash on the table, a rainbow of strange bills. I had no idea how much it was, if it was even enough to cover the cost of the meal. I had no time to convert the currency; I just needed to get away from her.

"I'm sorry you feel that way." I chugged the last of my San Miguel, snatched my guidebook off the table, and pushed my way out through the tent and into the tangle of people beyond.

"Sophie, I'm sorry! Please wait!" I heard her call behind me, but I was busy weaving among a pack of moving bodies, trying to lose her in the floodlit night. "I don't know how to get back to the hotel!"

*Passionless. Closed off, unlovable, and miserable.*

"Figure it out!" I yelled over my shoulder, and stalked

through the narrow aisles of the market, past tables piled high with plastic trinkets and irregular counterfeit T-shirts. I fumed, hoping she'd get lost trying to make her way back to the hotel. Perhaps I was being cold and spiteful; maybe Elena was right about me. Then again, I wasn't the one who'd secretly booked an early flight home while my unsuspecting friend was shampooing her hair.

It was hard to imagine that after all these years, our friendship was now deteriorating thousands of miles away from Garden Avenue, the tree-lined New Jersey street on which we'd grown up together. It was true we'd drifted apart in recent years, with me constantly traveling for work, and her relationship with Roddy taking precedence above all else. But I hadn't realized exactly how different we'd become. I felt like we didn't even know each other at all anymore.

If Elena really thought I was cold and emotionless, though, why did she even agree to come to Hong Kong with me? Considering our history, everything we'd been through together, her attack seemed vicious and, frankly, untrue. I had always been there to support her. The day her father packed his boxes and moved out of their house, I sat with her for hours in my room, reading *Seventeen* magazine on the pink bedspread, pretending that we couldn't hear the rumbling of the moving truck down the street. On prom night, I held her hair back as she hung her head out of the open limo door, the effects of too much blackberry schnapps splattering in the gutter. Lately, our only interactions had consisted of me listening to her mourn each of the breakups she'd endured with Roddy—three breakups in three years. After this, I didn't intend to be around for the fourth.

The night was still young, and I didn't intend to waste it seething about Elena, or worse yet, watching her pack her bags back at the hotel. Feeling suddenly energized, I slipped into an alley and opened my guidebook to the "Nightlife" section. Near the top of the list was Lan Kwai Fong, a district packed with bars and clubs, popular with tourists and locals alike, described as "a party in the streets." It seemed like it might be a good place to find company on what had turned into a solitary Saturday night in a strange town.

As I ducked into the entrance of the Jordan subway station, a sour gust of air rose up from its depths and washed over my face. I breathed it in, immersed in the unfamiliar sensation of this bustling city. Even if Elena was right, even if I was unlovable, in that moment I thought I didn't need to be loved. I was Sophie Bruno, international adventurer, and tonight I was flying solo.

# chapter two

Saturday night in Lan Kwai Fong wasn't just a party in the streets; it was an explosion of steam and voices and fluorescent light. Pennant banners fluttered above me as I made my way down and around the pedestrian-only curve of D'Aguilar Street. Bars lined the pavement with their front walls retracted, seats spilling onto the sidewalk. People congregated around tables with openmouthed grins, their hands wrapped around sweating glasses, cigarettes propped between their fingers. Women perched on stools, their bare legs emerging from the hems of short skirts. Men with damp shirt collars hovered over them. Music pumped out of invisible speakers, a bubble of beat enveloping the street. The night was on fire.

My anger began to evaporate and swirl away over the rooftops. There were people here who weren't armed with contingency forks, people who knew how to have a good time. Why was I so upset about Elena leaving me when there was a city full of folks like this? I stopped in front of a pub, the words BITTER SPOT shouting at me from the neon sign above the door. Pushing through bistro tables and flailing arms, I made my way inside, where the bartender set a napkin down in front of me.

"San Miguel, please," I said.

As I gripped the bottle and brought it to my lips, someone snickered softly behind me.

"You're at the best German pub in Hong Kong, and you're ordering a bottle of San Miguel?"

I turned around and saw his blue eyes glinting in the low light, plump pink lips curled in a playful smile.

"I mean, I know it's the local beer of choice," he said, "but you should get a Bitburger. This is the only place on the island that has it on tap."

He lifted his glass, half full of golden lager, emblazoned with a Bitburger logo, and tipped it in my direction with a wink. His sandy hair was perfectly tousled atop his head like a wheat field in a windstorm. Instinctively, I touched my dark curls. I was sure they were out of place; the Hong Kong humidity had laid claim to them the moment I disembarked the plane. I made a mental note to buy some serious hair product the next day.

"I'll pass," I said, willing my mouth to form words in the midst of my aesthetic crisis. "I get to drink plenty of German beer at home. San Miguel is a treat."

"Do you live in Germany? From your accent, I figured you were a fellow American."

"No, I live in New York, in a tiny apartment above a German restaurant called Zum Bauer. So sometimes I like to end the day there with a nightcap. Or two."

"The Germans know how to brew a fine beer."

"That they do."

"Ever been there?"

"Last year, for Oktoberfest," I said.

His eyes lit up. "Get out of here. I was there, too. Maybe we saw each other."

"Maybe," I said. But there was little I remembered of my hours in the Hofbräuhaus tent. After I finished my first stein of *festbier*, details of the evening grew fuzzy. It was possible I'd seen this handsome stranger but had no recollection of it. He could've even been that guy I made out with at the end of the night, when the crowds were shuffling into the streets. I never did catch his name.

"You travel a lot, then?" he asked.

"Yup. Always got a flight booked somewhere."

"That's the best way to live, I think." He tipped his head back and drained his glass, his Adam's apple bobbing with each swallow. I stared at the long curve of his neck and spotted the corner of a tattoo peeking out from under the collar of his shirt before he put his glass down on the bar and ordered another Bitburger.

"And a San Miguel," he said, before looking at me. "You want another one?"

"Sure." I had only taken two sips of the bottle in my hand, but I wasn't about to turn down another drink before I found out this guy's name. I started chugging.

"I'm Carson, by the way," he said, extending a hand toward me for a shake. It was slightly moist, radiating heat. I felt soft calluses along the heel of his palm.

"Sophie."

"So, Sophie, what are you doing in Hong Kong?"

"Taking a much-needed vacation."

"Alone?" He looked past me, over my shoulders, suddenly aware that he could be encroaching on some other guy's territory.

"Well, I *was* here with my friend, until she decided to go back home because she missed her boyfriend. So now I'm here alone."

"What?" He laughed. "She just picked up and left you here?"

"Her flight's tomorrow morning. Right now I guess she's packing her bag, or calling her boyfriend for the fifteenth time. But yeah, she's just picking up and leaving me here. Nice, huh?"

He shook his head. "That's unbelievable. I don't know if you can really call her a friend now. A friend wouldn't desert you like that."

I wanted to feel smug. Here was someone who was shocked and appalled by Elena's decision to leave, someone declaring *her* as the bad friend, not me. But I only felt an ache in my chest and a sense of dread, like I'd forgotten to pack underwear or lost my credit card.

"What are you gonna do now?" he asked.

"Enjoy myself," I said. "She was kind of a wet blanket anyway."

"What made you decide to come to Hong Kong with her, then?"

"I don't know. I wanted to reconnect with her. And I thought it might do her some good to see a different part of the world." I picked at the label on the bottle, peeling it back in thin, soggy shreds. "I'm sick of thinking about it."

"Then let's change the subject. What do you do back in New York, aside from drink German beer?"

"Sometimes I enjoy a schnitzel platter."

He laughed, revealing a dimple in his stubbled cheek. "Do you work?"

"I'm an IT consultant."

"What does that mean?"

"I work with computers, doing strategic planning for big businesses. Goal setting, scheduling, resource allocation. That sort of thing."

"Interesting." The blank stare on his face made it clear he hadn't spent much time in a corporate environment. "Do you like doing...that sort of thing?"

Shrugging, I took a sip of my beer. "It's all right. I'm good at it and it pays well. It looks good on my résumé, too."

"So the short answer is no," he said. "How did you get into it?"

"I went to college, got a business degree," I said. "Landed a job right after I graduated three years ago, and I've been there ever since."

The full story? I attended college on a full-ride scholarship, completed my degree a semester early, with honors, and had three companies clamoring to employ me. Even though I wasn't necessarily gung ho about working for McKinley Consultants Worldwide, I accepted their generous offer of employment. McKinley was one of the world's most prestigious firms; if they offered you a job, you'd be a fool to say no. Now, at twenty-four, I was routinely working a minimum of twelve hours a day, on the fast track to making partner. My career was, more or less, my life.

"The best part of the job is that I get to travel a lot," I

said. "My company has offices all over the world. The payoff in frequent-flyer miles alone is worth it."

"That's great." He took a long drink, his eyes fixed on the flat screen behind the bar showing closed-captioned commercials.

"What about you?" I said, trying to reel in his attention. "What do you do for a living?"

"Ah, you know," he said, still looking at the television. "Nothing like what you do. Just . . . artsy stuff."

"So you're an artist?"

"I mean, kind of," he said, clearing his throat. "I dabble here and there. I'm twenty-five. I've got time to figure it out, you know?"

In the real world, if I had asked a guy about his career aspirations and received this kind of vague, evasive response, I'd politely excuse myself and run for the exit. I needed a man with a plan, someone who was responsible and goal-oriented, who had his head screwed tightly on his shoulders—a tall order for guys in my age bracket. But this wasn't real life; this was life on the road. Who cared if Carson had no direction or discernible career path? After tonight, I'd probably never see him again.

"Where do you live?"

"Well, I'm originally from San Francisco," he said, his gaze finally focused back on my face, "but right now, I'm kind of living on the road. I've been traveling around Asia for the past month, been in Hong Kong for a week. I bounce around a lot. My home is where I lay my head. Know what I mean?"

"Totally." In truth, I didn't know what he meant. I definitely understood the feeling of restlessness, the need to pick up and fly somewhere new. But I always had an anchor grounding me at home, a place to come back to, with an organized closet full of clothes and a fireproof box to safeguard important paperwork. I also had a steady job with a paycheck, something I doubted Carson treated with priority. He struck me as someone who got by on his good looks, perhaps a playboy from a rich family who never had to save up his frequent-flyer miles to book a trip half-way around the world. Unlike me, working hard for every dime I spent.

"So, no boyfriend?" he asked me.

"Nope."

"Why's that?"

"Are you asking what's wrong with me?"

"No, no!" he said. "I'm just wondering how a cool girl like you is still single. Well traveled, educated, beautiful. I thought for sure someone would've scooped you up."

"Does that line usually work for you?"

"Sometimes." He flashed a smile.

"I'm not really into the idea of a relationship right now. Especially after seeing my friend with her boyfriend. They can't even be away from each other for a week. I travel a lot. I work long hours. I need room to breathe."

"Relationships don't always have to be that way, though."

"I don't know." After what Elena told me earlier that evening, I didn't feel I had the authority to speak on this subject. I'd never been in a serious relationship; hell, I'd never even made it past a third or fourth date. There'd only been fling after fling, heated but meaningless sexual encounters, most of which were on the road, one-night stands with guys I'd never spoken to again. Some guys whose names I never even knew. As far as I was concerned, men were only good for one thing. I'd always considered myself fiercely independent, a woman who didn't need a man to be happy. But maybe Elena was right. Maybe I really was incapable of love.

"I believe that when you really love someone," he said, "when it's right, it's always with you, even when you're apart. It's like a fire, burning in your heart. It needs air to live and breathe; if you smother it, it'll die."

"That's very poetic."

"I'm a poetic kinda guy. Ruled by my heart."

"Is there a girlfriend pining for you back in the States?"

"No, I'm a free agent right now. No fancy job, no home, no girl. Nothing tying me down anywhere."

The beer I'd guzzled started swimming through my head, softening Carson's features and endearing me to his carefree life of wanderlust. I wondered what it must be like to live without responsibility or obligation. How different would my life be if I didn't have to show up for work every morning, pay the rent on time, or board a flight back to New York in seven days?

"So, since you've been here for a week, any suggestions on where the best nightlife is?" I asked. "The guidebook led me to Lan Kwai Fong, but I know there's gotta be some other stuff I'm missing out on."

"Have you been to Wan Chai yet?"

"I'm staying in Wan Chai," I said.

"Finish your beer and I'll take you back there. There's a place I want to show you."

I took a long, slow sip from my San Miguel, peering over the bottle to study Carson's face, deciding if I should follow him. For all I knew, he could be a grifter, conning his way around Hong Kong. But his eyes were electric. And I wanted to see more of that chest tattoo. *I'll go. I just won't let myself get too drunk. I'll definitely stop drinking right after I'm done with this beer.*

# chapter three

I was dancing on top of a scuffed mahogany bar. How I got there was unclear. The sign on the wall proclaiming it "Jäger Night" at Charlie's may have had something to do with it. Impulsive decision-making brought on by overconsumption of Jägermeister was beginning to be a theme of mine.

My hand gripped a brass pole, steadying my body as I swayed to the sounds of a wailing guitar. There were moments when I could tell I was off by half a beat, where my hip popped when it should have swiveled. But I wasn't sober enough to correct myself, and ultimately, I didn't really care. My self-consciousness had disappeared, all thoughts of Elena banished. My unruly hair ceased to exist. The only thing I cared about right now, the only thing I saw amid the sea of people below me, were two blue eyes glinting in the low light.

The past few hours had been a blur. Memories came in hot flashes—Carson's hand on the small of my back as he guided me through a busy street, his lips brushing my cheek as he leaned in close to make himself heard over the roar of the crowd. Suddenly, being on top of this bar felt too far away from him. I needed contact.

He offered his hand to help me down, and I stumbled into his arms as he steered me to a safe landing beside him on the sawdust-covered linoleum. I stood for a few seconds in his embrace, the people around us falling away as we locked eyes.

"Let's get out of here," he said, hot breath in my ear.

Outside, the predawn air was warm but fresh, and we laced fingers before ambling down the sidewalk. I let him lead me, unsure of where we were, willing to follow him anywhere. We turned left on Fleming Road and headed toward the waterfront, toward the pale glow of the convention center with its curved roof, hanging out over the bay like a flying saucer. His thumb stroked the back of my hand as we strolled without a sound.

At the edge of the promenade, we stopped and stood still in the shadow of the city beyond the bay, the lights of Kowloon reflected on the water. Soft, briny breezes brought me back to sobriety, planted me firmly in the present. There was no one else around, and for an instant, I felt uneasy, like maybe I'd made a bad choice coming to this desolate corner alone with a complete stranger. Then Carson slid his hand around my back, pulled me close, smiled at me. My worry dissolved, and we stared at the skyscrapers, side by side.

"It makes you feel small," he said. "These big buildings. Think about all the people that are out there, living all their different lives."

"Makes you realize how meaningless your existence is."

"Or how we're each part of something so much bigger than any one of us. How our actions affect everyone else in this world."

"Maybe."

"No man is an island, Sophie."

"Again with the poetry."

"I told you, I'm a poetic guy," he said, then turned to face me, his hands resting on my waist. "Seriously, though. Everything everyone does affects someone else's life, somehow. Like if your friend didn't ditch you, you probably never would've come to that bar by yourself, and we never would've met."

"And you wouldn't be standing here reciting poetry."

"And I wouldn't be doing this."

Carson inched his hands up my sides, caressed my cheeks, and buried his fingers deep in the tangle of curls at the nape of my neck. He pressed his body against mine, pinning me against the railing. Sea spray raised goose bumps on my bare arms and I wrapped them around his midsection, absorbing his warmth. His blue eyes were fixed on my face as he bent down and kissed me. His tongue was in my mouth, thick and hungry, and I opened wide to let him explore. Every part of me swelled and tingled. I wanted to rip my clothes off on this pier and give my-self to him, for all of Hong Kong to see.

Time paused and stretched as I lost myself in the spice of his aftershave, the tang of his lips. Finally, he pulled back, brushed his thumb over my bottom lip and under my chin.

"Where are you staying?" he asked, his eyelids heavy.

"On Jaffe Road," I said. "I'm not sure how far that is from here."

"I know where we are. Let me walk you back."

We left the harbor with our hands in each other's back pock-ets, and I took a quick mental inventory, assessing my prepared-ness for the inevitable next step: cute panties, shaved legs, fresh pack of condoms in my suitcase. Whether he was a grifter or not, I wanted him. Then I remembered the one thing that would prevent me from inviting him up to continue the fun.

"Elena."

"I'm sorry?"

"My friend," I said. "The one who's abandoning me. She's probably still in the room."

"Oh, right. When's her flight?"

"I have no idea. At some point tomorrow." I looked skyward at streaks of lilac and baby blue, a sign of the sun's impending arrival. "I mean, today. What time is it anyway?"

Carson shrugged. "I haven't been keeping track of time lately."

"What about you? Where are you staying?" The moment was slipping through my fingers, and I was desperate to hold on to it.

"At a shitty hostel in Causeway Bay," he said. "Sharing a room with three snoring Aussies. Not the most comfortable digs, but it's dirt cheap."

With nowhere to unload our pent-up desires, the heat hanging in the air between us began to dissipate as we walked on. Daylight peeked over the tops of the buildings, and the streets slowly awakened with early morning commuters. When we reached the hotel and stopped in front of its glass doors, my heart deflated like a leaky balloon. The night had lasted forever but was over too soon. I'd never had the chance to see that whole tattoo.

"It was really great to meet you," I said.

"Likewise," he said. "So, what are you doing today?"

"I think I'm going to Man Mo Temple," I said. "Or was it Lantau Island? I can't remember what I had listed on my itinerary for today."

"Itinerary?"

"Yeah. I have everything planned out. Where I'm going, when I'm going there, how I'm gonna get there."

"Like, down to the day?"

"Down to the hour, more or less. I don't know if I'll ever get back to this part of the world again. I don't want to miss anything."

Carson looked at me like I had suddenly sprouted an extra head. "Okay. Well, if you're interested in deviating from your schedule, I'm thinking of taking the tram up to Victoria Peak this afternoon, see the city from up high. Wanna come?"

"Sure." Even though I hadn't planned to see Victoria Peak until Thursday, I figured it wasn't a big deal to swap out the days on my itinerary. Man Mo Temple—or Lantau Island—could wait until the end of the week, but who knew if I'd ever get another chance to hang out with Carson?

"All right, I'll come back in a little while. Try to get some rest."

He kissed me gently, leaving a wet spot on my bottom lip. I licked it off, swallowed his flavor.

"And good luck with your friend!" he called, before walking off toward Lockhart Road.

I sailed through the revolving door and floated across the lobby, my feet operating on autopilot. As I stood in the elevator,

I envisioned Carson's mouth on mine, his hand slipping under my shirt. Hours ago, he'd been a stranger; now his scent lingered on my skin. After my fight with Elena, I never would have expected the night to turn out like this. Traveling was full of pleasurable surprises.

Maybe it wasn't that I was incapable of love but merely that I wasn't interested in it. There was no feeling like the thrill of the chase, the fulfillment of a conquest. It was the unknown that bred desire—wondering how a new man tasted, what I would find beneath his clothes. Familiarity grew tiresome. What drew me most to Carson was that I hardly knew him at all.

Was there really anything wrong with that? Elena spoke of love as if it was something I should aspire to, but love didn't seem to offer her anything but misery. These were the best years of our lives, and she was squandering them in a relationship that stifled her independence. Her fear of being without Roddy paralyzed her, and she denied herself the chance to explore new terrain, to have fun and take advantage of her youth. She accused me of having no passion, but this evening with Carson proved her wrong.

The elevator doors rumbled open on the twelfth floor, and my mouth went dry at the thought of another confrontation. I didn't want to fight with Elena, but I also couldn't forget about the hurtful things she said. Standing in the hallway with my keycard in my hand, I paused in front of the door. *Deep breaths. She'll be gone soon, and you'll deal with this when you get home.*

Inside, the room was cool and dim. The only noise was the hum of the air-conditioning unit, blowing gusts up and under the curtains, making them dance against the window. My suitcase sat at the foot of an untouched bed, where I'd left it before we set out for dinner. The other bed had been slept in. Sheets pulled back, pillows askew, towels balled up and tossed in a heap on the mattress. There was no trace of Elena's belongings. She had already left.

The clock on the nightstand announced 5:45 in bright red digits. *She must have taken the first available flight out of Hong Kong. Couldn't get away from me fast enough.* I closed the door, kicked off my shoes, collapsed facedown on the fresh linens. It was nice to have the place to myself, like I usually did when I traveled, the freedom to hog the shower or walk around naked or bring back a guy at the spur of the moment. But as I lay there in the quiet, empty room, I felt loneliness creeping in. For the first time on one of my journeys, I wished I had a travel partner, someone with whom to share this experience, to reminisce with later on.

Fatigue settled in like a heavy weight. I sat up and pulled my shirt over my head and was contemplating whether to dig through my suitcase for pajamas or to sleep in the nude when I saw the note. It was folded in half, resting on the nightstand, "Sophie" written neatly in Elena's loopy script. I opened it and read:

*Dear Sophie,*

*I'm really sorry to be leaving you this way. This was not an easy decision for me to make. I never meant to hurt you and I'm sorry for the mean things I said.*

*I truly hope that you can understand how I'm feeling one day and will learn to forgive me. You deserve to love someone and to be loved as deeply as Roddy and I love each other. I know you will find it one day, when you're ready.*

*I hope you have an amazing time and enjoy the rest of your vacation.*

*Love,*
*Elena*

I crumpled it in one fist and tossed it toward the garbage can. As far as I was concerned, I would never be ready for the type of relationship Elena and Roddy had—codependent, unstable, and dysfunctional. As I peeled off my jeans, I thought about all the good things that were going on in my life. I had a successful career, a lease on a studio apartment in New York City, and a well-worn passport with plenty of room for more stamps. The last thing I needed was a boyfriend to mess it all up. And my grandmother always told me, when you let men get too close, that's what they do: make a mess of things.

Exhaustion, anger, and Jäger descended en masse, causing the walls to start spinning around me. I had to close my eyes and focus my breath to steady myself. Somehow, my head found the pillow. Behind closed lids, all I saw were chest tattoos and blue eyes, dimples in a stubbled cheek. *Men may make a mess of things, but some of them sure are gorgeous.*

# chapter four

The unfamiliar ring of a phone on my bedside table stirred me from a sound sleep. I fumbled with the receiver, disoriented, the way I always was when I woke up for the first time in a strange hotel room.

"It's me," said the guy on the other end.

I couldn't place the voice. I scanned my memory for a sign of recognition and croaked out a noncommittal, "Hi."

"Sounds like you had a rough night," he continued. I thought back to last night. Had it been rough? Suddenly, it flooded back to me: Carson smiling at me, touching my face, kissing me in the moonlight. *Did I really dance on top of a bar?*

"How'd you get my room number?" I sat up in bed, gripping the duvet to my chest, feeling exposed.

"I asked the front desk to connect me to Sophie Bruno."

Squinting my eyes shut, I tried to recall the events of last night as I fought against the pain shooting through my temples. I remembered our walk from the harbor back to the hotel. But when did I tell him my full name? And why was he calling me now?

"You ready to head over to the Peak?" he said.

"The Peak?"

"You said you wanted to go today," he said, his voice wavering with uncertainty. "But if you're not into it, it's no big deal."

I looked over at the clock: 12:40. My first morning in Hong Kong had come and gone while I slept off a hangover. This routine was getting old: the headaches, the vertigo, the sagebrush tacked to my tongue. I vowed not to drink for the remainder of my trip. Or possibly ever again.

"No, I'm still up for it," I said. Enough of the day had already been wasted. As far as I was concerned, today's itinerary was ruined, so sightseeing with a hot guy who had a destination in mind seemed like a reasonable way to pass the rest of the afternoon. "When do you want to meet?"

"I'm here."

"Where?" I surveyed the room, confused, thinking for a second he might be lurking behind the bathroom door.

"In the lobby. Ready when you are."

He hung up the phone, leaving me listening to dead air while I considered the situation. This was highly unorthodox, a vacation hookup coming back the next day. Usually I would kiss a man good-bye at the end of the night and never see him again. What was Carson's motivation? I pieced together fragments of the previous evening. His blue eyes, his glass of Bitburger, his penchant for poetry, his breath in my ear. As far as I could tell, he seemed harmless. And gorgeous. And we'd never had an opportunity to seal the deal.

I sprang to my feet. Grooming was required if this day was going to end where I hoped it would. Powering through the pounding in my head, I showered in a tizzy, nicking my ankle with the razor as I balanced on one leg in the narrow stall. I searched the contents of my suitcase for my least wrinkled and most thigh-revealing item of clothing: a sundress the color of lemons. Standing in front of the foggy bathroom mirror with a toothbrush hanging out of my mouth, I willed my curls to cooperate but quickly surrendered, pinning the wild frenzy up in a bun on the top of my head.

Twenty minutes after his call, I spotted him lounging in a leather club chair next to the concierge desk, immersed in a book. He stood when he saw me, tucking the book away into a canvas messenger bag he had slung across his body.

"I brought you breakfast," he said, handing me a white paper bag. "It's a pineapple bun."

Inside was a sugary pastry with a crunchy, egg-colored crust. I bit into it immediately, not realizing how ravenous I was until that moment.

"Thank you so much," I said, my mouth full.

"No problem." He dipped down to kiss the crumbs off my lips and raised his eyebrows when he saw what I was wearing. "You look amazing in that dress."

I thanked him again, and we set off. But when we arrived at the top of Victoria Peak, I was regretting my decision to wear a paper-thin, thigh-revealing sundress. The air was lighter up here, free of the humidity that hung over the rest of the city below. A crowded tram had carried us up the side of a mountain, climbing eighteen hundred feet above sea level at a forty-five-degree angle, until all of Hong Kong unfurled beneath us like a postcard. When I stepped out onto the platform at the summit, I shivered as a crisp wind blew directly through the lemon-yellow fabric.

We funneled out of the tram station into typical tourist hustle: the coin-operated binoculars; the street vendors hawking souvenirs; the massive, pristine shopping mall with the Häagen-Dazs outside. I fell blissfully into the trap.

"Want to go there?" I pointed to a sign for the Peak Tower, an observation deck mentioned in my guidebook. "It's supposed to have great three-hundred-sixty-degree views of the city, from the skyline to the outlying islands."

"I know a much better place to take in the scenery," he said.

"You did your research," I said, impressed that he'd come prepared.

"I was here the other day. Scoped it out already. Found a perfect vantage point, not so many people around."

*So this is why he brought me here.* How many times had he been to the Peak over the past week, and with how many different girls? I mentally prepared myself for a scripted experience, rehearsed lines, and a staged kiss in a picturesque spot. Then I thought, *Had the night before been a repeat performance as well?* If it had been, why did that suddenly bother me? Carson grabbed my hand and steered me to the right, toward a stone trail that led up and around a leafy hill. At his touch, I dismissed the thought of previous travel companions he may have known. In this moment, anyway, I was all that mattered.

"Besides," he continued, "those tourist traps are no fun. They're overpriced and overcrowded."

I pictured my guidebook and my carefully planned itineraries, reflections of my affinity for the tourist traps. As we walked beneath a canopy of tree branches, I wondered if I would have chosen this path had I come here alone.

"So how'd you sleep?" he asked, pebbles crunching beneath our feet.

"Seems like I closed my eyes and two minutes later the phone was ringing. But aside from a headache, I feel well rested."

"Wish I could say the same."

"Still tired?"

"Yup. Aussies were snoring all night. I should've just sprung for a damn hotel. Must be nice to have a private room, huh?"

The pang of loneliness I'd felt the night before shot through me again. "It has its downsides."

"I've been staying in hostels for months," he said. "You'd think I'd be used to it by now."

"I thought you said you'd only been in Asia for a few weeks."

"I have been, but before that I was backpacking through Europe. Oktoberfest, remember?"

"That was six months ago," I said. "It's April now. You've been traveling nonstop this whole time?"

"Yeah," he said. "Well, longer than that. I started last summer, camping around the States."

To think that Carson had the free time to travel for months on end made me envious, maybe even a little resentful. My trip to Oktoberfest had been a hasty two-night detour on my way back from a two-week stint in the Zürich office. The forty-eight-hour respite from work had been a real treat, though when I wasn't in the tents, I still found myself chained to my smartphone. If I had my way, I would've spent two whole weeks touring Bavaria. I'd always wanted to see Neuschwanstein Castle and drive through the Alps. This trip to Hong Kong was my first extended vacation since spring break of my senior year in college, when I hadn't yet strayed from the shores of Cape May. Carson's lengthy escapades made my weekend touring seem tame.

"How long do you plan to keep going?" I asked.

"Till my money runs out. At this rate, about another five or six months? I'm not totally on top of my cash flow."

"Wow." I was flabbergasted. "Where to next?"

"I'm considering Macau," he said, then smiled. "Maybe I can double my money at a casino, make this trip last even longer."

The idea of completely draining my assets, or worse yet, risking them on a game of chance, was dangerously out of my comfort zone. I maintained a spreadsheet of my personal finances, carefully balancing my monthly income with expenditures. My bills were paid in full and on time, and at every opportunity, I siphoned off excess cash for both a nest egg and a travel fund. My vacation was just as strictly budgeted as the rest of my life. I contemplated our fundamental differences, me and this guy I'd met less than twenty-four hours ago. *I doubt he's ever seen a spreadsheet in his life.*

We walked on through a thickening tunnel of trees, slivers of sunlight piercing through the branches and casting shadows that danced with the breeze. The steep, curving pathway was more of a hike than I'd been expecting, and I was happy that I'd had the good sense to wear comfortable shoes. Even my dress seemed appropriate now that I was working up a sweat. My breath deepened, and Carson placed a comforting hand on my back.

"Almost there," he said.

We turned a corner, and green gave way to blue. Victoria Harbour burst into view, with buildings on top of buildings, competing for space, reflecting the sun off their mirrored façades. Gray, glassy water bisected the land before snaking off into the horizon. In the distance were mountains, the farthest ranges fading into the far-off sky, their crests disappearing into clotted cream clouds.

"This is what I was talking about," he said.

"It's breathtaking."

"Worth the walk, no?"

He ran his fingertips in light circles between my shoulder blades, leaned down and kissed the tip of my earlobe.

"Come sit." He pulled me by the hand toward a bench at the railing. I joined him, pressing my hip against his as I sat. We kissed gently, a light, lingering caress of our lips. I felt myself sink into the romance of the scene: a foreign city, a sunny day, a handsome man leading me through a forest toward our own private view of the skyline. Carson may have rehearsed this, may have even been here with other girls, but for me, this moment was spontaneous, pulled straight from the pages of a fairy tale, not a guidebook.

I could have spent the entire afternoon kissing him on that bench. But after a short time, he pulled away and looked out into the distance.

"The light is perfect right now," he said, then produced a

spiral-bound sketchbook from his messenger bag. "Would you mind?"

"Of course not."

As he flipped through the pages, I caught glimpses of charcoal faces, flowers, food, and landscapes, until he stopped at an exact replica of the vista below us, sketched out in shades of gray. He pulled a pencil from the binding and poised it tentatively over the drawing, his gaze alternating between the paper and the sky.

"That's incredible," I said. And it was. The night before, Carson said that he dabbled in the arts, which I brushed off as the pie-in-the-sky daydream of an aimless slacker. But the piece he held in his lap was the work of a genuine artist with undeniable talent.

"It's shit," he said.

"No, it's not. It's amazingly realistic. It looks like a black-and-white photograph."

"I did this the other day, when I came up here," he said. "But it's missing something. So that's why I wanted to come back, to try to fix it."

He bit his lower lip, scrutinized his sketch with a furrowed brow, set to work on making changes. We sat in silence as I watched him draw, maneuvering his pencil on the page as if conducting an orchestra: up and down, side to side, light touches alternating with broad strokes. As I compared his rendering with the real world before us, I couldn't understand what he needed to fix or why he thought it was "shit." The details were impeccable, down to the smallest ripple trailing the wake of the Star Ferry as it crossed the bay between Hong Kong and Kowloon. I noticed the gentle white curve of the convention center roof peeking out from behind a skyscraper; what seemed so huge and ethereal last night was now reduced to a tiny blip in a vast expanse. I thought about what Carson had said the night before, how we were part of something bigger in this world, how we were all intertwined, no matter how distant we may seem from one another, how lonely or independent we may think we are.

"When you're done with this trip," I said, "when your money runs out, what's your plan?"

"Haven't thought that far ahead yet."

"Well, are you going to go back home to San Francisco?"

His jaw flexed and released, his eyes never leaving the page. "No, I don't think so."

"What about a job?" I pressed on. "You really have an obvious talent here; you could go far as a designer or an illustrator."

Carson stopped sketching, met my eyes, formed his mouth into a tight, thin smile. "You're full of questions."

"I just don't understand how you have no idea what your next move is gonna be. I've had a five-year plan for as long as I can remember."

He raised his eyebrows, looking amused. "And what does this five-year plan entail?"

"I revise it every year, but right now, I'll have earned an MBA and worked my way up to senior associate at my firm."

"That's it?"

"I'd also like to live abroad at some point, have a home base in a foreign city instead of New York, just for a little while. But I'm not sure if that's realistic. I have to go wherever my job decides to send me."

"Nothing else?"

I paused to think. It sounded ambitious enough as it was. What else could I possibly fit in there?

"No," I said.

"Sounds extremely practical."

"I'm a practical person. A planner. What's wrong with that?"

"Nothing," he said. "I just think that life's not worth living without a little passion, which your five-year plan has very little of. There's that whole living abroad thing, which is cool, but you don't seem really committed to making it happen. It seems like your whole life plan revolves around your job."

"I have career goals, and there are very specific steps I need to take in order to achieve them."

"And that's great. I'm just saying, you can't always control everything. Some things you have to leave up to the roll of the dice. If all you're concerned with is following a practical plan, you'll wake up one day, old and alone, and discover the world has passed you by. And then you're dead."

Controlling. Passionless. Where had I heard this before? I frowned, thinking of the words Elena spat at me over the dinner table the night before. Maybe she wasn't the only one who thought I was miserable.

Carson placed a hand on my bare thigh and turned toward me. "I'm sorry," he said. "I shouldn't have said that. It's great that you're so focused and responsible. You don't see that very often, especially in people our age. I wish I had some of that my-self."

His fingertips caressed my skin, sending electric shocks through my system. He hesitated, as if weighing whether to say the next words out loud.

"You just sound so much like my aunt and uncle," he said. "For a minute I was thinking, did they plant you here to whisper in my ear? Ridiculous, I know."

"How do I sound like them?"

"They're just always on my case to get a 'real' job and forget about my art. 'Get your head out of the clouds. Don't be dumb. Buckle down. Life's not a joke.' You know, that kind of thing. Nothing's ever good enough for them."

"Well, who cares what they say? What about your parents?"

"They died," he said. "When I was three."

"I'm sorry."

"It's okay. I don't really remember much about them. I know I was born in San Diego, and I kind of remember the house I lived in there, with this huge old tree in the backyard. After they died, my aunt and uncle moved me up to San Francisco. So I grew up with them and my perfect, genius cousins."

Carson's face grew hard; his normally soft, open features were now wrinkled and stiff. He took his hand off my leg, started tapping his pencil nervously against the bench. I regretted putting him on the spot with these pushy, prying questions. *What happened to what I thought last night, about attraction being driven by mystery?*

"As soon as I could," he continued, "I got the hell away from them. I had no money, so I couldn't get very far, but I bounced around on friends' couches for a while, until I could earn enough to afford the rent on my own little hovel in Oakland. I took the most random jobs to get by: waiting tables, painting houses, anything really. For a while, I was doing caricatures in Fisherman's Wharf."

He smiled at this last revelation, a good memory popping up unexpectedly among the bad.

"Must've been a high-paying gig," I said. "I mean, to fund this trip."

"No, that was a gift from my parents," he said. "Last year, I got a letter out of nowhere from this lawyer. Turns out they left me a trust fund, but I wasn't allowed to have it until I turned twenty-five. So on my birthday, it all sort of fell in my lap."

"Whoa."

"Yeah, I know. It didn't make me some mega-millionaire or anything, but it was enough to get me out of San Francisco. I wanted to get as far away as I could. So first thing I did was buy myself a little camper and a national parks pass, set out on a cross-country drive. But then I wanted to keep going, so I sold it off and bought a plane ticket over to London. I haven't been back since."

"So you're just blowing through all your money?" The words rushed out of me before I could stop them. I thought about all the ways in which I would have handled this financial windfall differently. Real estate purchases, long-term investments, Roth IRAs. So many ways to secure my future.

"What else would I do, save it?" he said. "That's what my parents did with it, and look what good it did them. What did they even do with their lives? They worked hard, they hoarded their cash, they had me, and then they died. What kind of shitty existence is that?"

He was looking into the distance now, searching for answers in the mountain ranges, in the rippling water, in the thousands of windows of the hundreds of buildings with millions of people inside.

"I get it," I said. "I do. I always think that about my own mom. How shitty her life was. Just in a different way."

Then I told him about my mother, things I'd never told any other guy before. How she had me when she was in high school, and how because of me, she never graduated. How she refused to tell anyone who my dad was. How she abandoned me with my grandparents when I was still in diapers. How we never heard from her again.

"I'm not sure if she's dead or alive, but at this point in my life, I don't care. I just always knew that I never wanted to be like her."

"Where are your grandparents now?"

"My grandfather died when I was in junior high, but my grandmother still lives in New Jersey, in the same house I grew up in. I try to see her on the weekends when I can, if I'm in town. She's pretty lonely out there by herself."

I'd been avoiding eye contact as I spoke, afraid of what I might see in Carson's face. When I turned to glance up at him, his expression had softened, and I saw myself reflected in the blue of his eyes. It was as if we were looking at each other for the first time.

"It's funny," I said. "Up until this point, I didn't think we really had anything in common."

"I told you, we're all a part of something much bigger than us. The universe has its reasons for bringing people together."

We kissed gently before he returned to his drawing. I listened to the scratch of pencil on paper, the wind whispering through the trees. There wasn't much more for either of us to say. All I kept thinking, as we looked out on the city, was how I never could have factored this moment into my five-year plan.

# chapter five

"What do you think this one is?"

"I'm not really sure. A meatball?"

"Maybe. This one's definitely an organ of some kind."

Bamboo baskets of dim sum were spread before us on a crowded table. With his chopsticks, Carson plucked a soft, white hunk of flesh from a serving tray and popped it into his mouth without hesitation.

"It's good," he said. "Try it."

He snatched up another one and held it out toward me, cupping his hand underneath to catch drips. I parted my lips and he placed it on my tongue. The sting of salt and vinegar made my taste buds tingle. As I chewed, his eyes were on me, waiting for my verdict. I swallowed and said, "Delicious."

We kissed with salty lips, the world moving slowly inside our cocoon, while the bustle surrounding us at Lin Heung Tea House zoomed along at triple speed. Steel carts filled with food rattled and crashed as servers navigated the narrow aisles between large communal tables, where patrons sat elbow to elbow with strangers. People raised their voices to make themselves heard over the clink of teacups and clatter of spoons, but Carson and I huddled together, so close that we could hear each other whisper.

·

After our conversation on the Peak, the rest of the afternoon rolled on swiftly. We walked hand in hand around the mountaintop, stealing kisses as we watched the sun cross the sky. On the bus ride back to sea level, a wave of hunger struck us, so we wandered the streets of Central until we found a dim sum place nestled beneath some scaffolding on Wellington Street.

We ordered our dishes at random, taking whatever was offered on the carts that passed us by, the contents of our dinner left up to chance. We didn't even bother to peek under the lids until our payment card had already been stamped. The result was an eclectic mix of sweet pastries, doughy steamed buns, crispy fried dumplings, and the occasional unidentifiable animal part. We ate them all, giddy with the thrill of a new flavor when we took our first bites.

"Let me get a picture of you," Carson said, taking what looked like a little cardboard box from the pocket of his cargo shorts.

"What is that?" I asked.

"It's a disposable camera," he said. "Haven't you ever seen one before?"

"No." I laughed. "What year are we living in? Why don't you just use your phone?"

"I don't have a phone," he said. "I prefer to live my life unplugged. Technology's destroying our creativity as a species. Besides, these little disposables take great pictures."

For a moment, I considered showing him all the selfies I had stored on my smartphone. Personally, I found the art of selecting an Instagram filter to be a highly creative endeavor. But

before I could reach for my purse, Carson was already squinting through the viewfinder, aiming the lens at me. "Come on,
strike a pose."

I struggled to balance a slippery chicken foot between my
chopsticks and smile at the same time. As the flash went off, the
foot fell with a splatter in my small ceramic bowl. I felt a tap on
my right shoulder and turned to see the older man seated next
to me smiling broadly at us.

"Would you like me to get one of the both of you?" he asked
in a British accent.

"Thanks, that'd be great." Carson handed him his camera and
swiveled me around in my chair, throwing one arm around my
neck as he pressed his cheek to mine. I felt my face flush as the
man snapped a photo, his female companion looking on with a
grin.

"Are you honeymooners?" she asked.

I snorted, about to break out in laughter, when Carson said,
"Actually, we just got engaged."

"Congratulations!" She clapped her hands. "How lovely. My
husband and I just celebrated our thirty-second anniversary last
month."

"Goes by fast," the man added. "Cherish the time now, when
you're young."

"Before the kids come along," she said, patting him on the
shoulder and flashing him a knowing glance.

"We're soaking it all in while we can," Carson said, his arm
still around my neck. I felt frozen to my seat, unable to speak
for fear of saying the wrong thing and blowing the cover off his

little ruse. "Though you certainly both look like marriage has treated you well."

"Smartest thing I ever did was marry this one," the man said, and kissed his wife on the back of her hand as they got up from their seats.

"When's the big day?" she asked.

"We haven't decided yet," Carson said. I sensed him looking at me but I couldn't turn my head; eye contact would send me into a fit of giggles.

"Well, best of luck to you," she said. "You're a beautiful couple, so in love. We've been watching you the whole time—the way you look at each other, it's easy to see you're a perfect match."

"When it's right, it's right." Carson kissed my cheek and I struggled to maintain my straight face.

"Good night, now," they said, before walking off toward the cash register. A waiting couple slipped into their empty seats, and I whipped around to glare at Carson.

"What was that about?" I said, letting my nervous laughter finally escape.

"We're a beautiful couple. You don't agree?" He flashed a smile and revealed that dimple, the one I discovered the night before when he smiled at me for the very first time. *Have we really known each other for only one day?* I felt my blood bubbling all through my body, rushing through my heart and flooding my head, my hands, my belly, my legs. He grabbed the bill from the table and said, "Let's go."

We strolled east along Queensway, toward Wan Chai, with our arms wrapped around each other's waists.

"So when do you think would be a good time?" he asked.

"For what?"

"Our wedding," he said. "I've always pictured getting married in the summer, on the beach, our toes in the sand."

"Tempting," I said, playing along. "But I'm a city girl. What about the Brooklyn Botanic Garden in the fall? Or a summer sail around Manhattan on a yacht?"

"Sounds like it could work, but I'd have to see it first. I've never been to New York."

"You've been all over the world, but never to New York? What about on your cross-country drive?"

"I headed farther south, flew out of DC. Maybe I should let you give me a tour someday. I can book my return flight to JFK, come stay with you."

"Lucky for you, I'm very intimately acquainted with New York City. But my apartment's awfully small." I envisioned Carson's naked body enveloped in my sheets. "I don't have a guest room or anything. We'd have to share a bed."

"I don't mind if you don't." His hand massaged my side and I felt the warmth from his touch spread down from my torso and into my hips.

Neon lights from nightclubs cast pink and green reflections on the pavement, where hostesses beckoned us to come in for a drink. We turned them all down with a polite wave of the hand. There was no discussion about where we were going; the destination was understood. At my hotel, we entered the lobby without a word and headed toward the elevator bank. I pressed the button for the twelfth floor, and the doors closed us in.

Immediately, Carson pressed my back against the wall, wrapped one hand around my neck, and kissed me deeply. I clutched at his shirt as he slid his other hand underneath my dress, running his fingers slowly up the front of my thigh. Briefly, I considered the camera mounted in the corner of the ceiling, the security guard who was most likely getting a free show. Then the elevator jerked to a halt and the doors rumbled open. We spilled into the hallway, where I sprinted to my room and let us inside.

We were on each other before the door clicked shut, inching blindly toward the bed, hands searching and tongues entwined. Seconds later, his shorts and my dress were tangled in a mound on the floor. As he fingered my bra clasp, I opened my eyes, fixing my gaze on his chest, remembering what I'd been aching to see. I carefully unfastened each button on his shirt, peeled it back and down over his shoulders, ran my palm over the tattoo on his left pec. A leafless tree, shaded in gray, its ropy braided roots winding down the length of his torso. Carved in its stout trunk were the words *Carpe Diem*. I kissed the tip of each branch before returning to his waiting mouth.

He ran his hands over my skin, his fingers blazing a trail around my body, then reached up to loosen my bun from its clip. I stopped him, but he tried again.

"Let your hair down," he said between kisses.

"It's a mess." I thought of my untamed mane, how crazy I would look with it kinky and loose.

"Let it down," he insisted. "I want to see it."

I hesitated, my insecurity threatening to stifle the mood. Carson reached up again and nimbly removed the clip from my hair before I could stop him. Curls tumbled over my bare shoulders like ribbons, and he sank his thick fingers deep into them, tugging softly until I released an unwitting moan.

"You look so good like this," he said. "Wild hair. No clothes. You're so hot."

Our breaths came in short, pleading gasps and I felt myself melt into him as we dropped backward onto the bed, two bodies in one motion. We made intense, satisfying love, releasing all of our pent-up sexual tension. When it was over, he collapsed beside me, catching his breath. Damp strands of hair fell across his forehead; I brushed them away, felt his blue eyes bore into mine. He reached behind my head and pulled me down to his face, kissed my nose, my cheek, my lips. I thought of how different this was than my usual encounters, how I didn't have an urge to run away.

Nuzzling my head in the crook of his armpit, my ear to his chest, I listened to him inhale and exhale, traced my fingertips along the boughs of his tree.

"Did you draw this?" I said. "The tattoo, I mean."

"Yeah," he said. "It's my design."

I caressed the intricate lines of his artwork, expecting the ink to feel rough or raised. But it was smooth and flat, ingrained deep under his skin. I wanted to know its meaning. *Carpe Diem* was obvious—Carson's life seemed to be all about seizing the day. But the tree, and the carving, and the wandering roots. Why this particular sketch? What did it symbolize? I waited for him to explain, but he didn't offer answers, and I'd already asked him too many questions that day. If he wanted to tell me, he would. Perhaps some things were better left to secrecy anyway. Though suddenly, I wanted to know everything about him, all the details that I possibly could.

We lay there in silence, his arm wrapped around me, his fingers twirling through my hair, splaying my curls out on the pillow. I had done this countless times before. The whole dance was familiar: the flirtation, the chase, the relief of the catch. The quickness with which it all unfolded. So why did this feel so new, and why was I so anxious?

Crazy thoughts raced through my head, feelings of desperate yearning. I envisioned myself crawling behind the carved-up tree on his chest, burying myself in his warmth and his scent. I started imagining his previous lovers, what they looked like and how they touched him. How many women had there been so far on his trip around the world? And how many more would there be after me?

The idea sent me spiraling into a panic. This was a fling, nothing more, scheduled to expire when I boarded that flight back to New York. So why was I going down this road of pointless thinking? Where was this coming from anyway? It wasn't like me to become so suddenly infatuated with a guy. My grandmother definitely would not have approved.

Carson stirred, turned over, kissed me down my neck and over my breasts, his hands moving from my hair to my stomach. The panic in my chest was consumed by desire as he swept his tongue over my navel. And then I decided, for once in my life, I was not going to overthink a situation. I wouldn't force life to adhere to a predefined schedule or tell myself how I was supposed to feel. Instead, I would allow life to happen. Let my hair down, let the dice roll.

I opened my body, relinquished all reason, and writhed around with him in that hotel bed all night.

A	t some point, I must have dozed off, because I cracked one eye open to find pale morning light pouring in through the sheer white curtains. Carson was awake beside me, still naked, lounging against the headboard and fully engrossed in a sketch. I took a moment to admire his physical beauty: the lean definition in his chest and biceps, the angular cut of his jaw, the way he narrowed his deep-set eyes in concentration as he worked. It was hard to believe someone so gorgeous had just spent the night in my bed. *He may be my hottest conquest yet.* And even though it was the morning after, the time when I usually shuttled a guy out the door with his shirt in his hand, right now I didn't want Carson to leave. I wanted him to stay all day, to make love to me again and again, to tell me what was going on inside his big, artistic brain.

I shifted my gaze from his body to his pencil, eager to see what he was drawing with such intense concentration. When I craned my neck to steal a view of the page, he smiled down at me and slapped his book shut in one fluid motion.

"Hey there," he said. "How was your nap?"

"Good." I stretched my arms overhead. "I don't even remember falling asleep. How long was I out for?"

"I think we both zonked out around four." He looked past

me, at the clock on the bedside table. "So probably about seven hours."

"It's eleven o'clock?" I popped up, disappointed in myself for sleeping away yet another morning in Hong Kong. Experience had taught me it was best to get an early start on sightseeing, before the streets got too hot or crowded. If I wasn't careful, this vacation would pass me by while I lazed around in bed.

"Yup," he said, unfazed by the way we were wasting the daylight. He stood up and casually crossed the room to tuck his sketchbook into his messenger bag. As I studied the curve and flex of his perfect round ass, I remembered the promise I'd made to myself the night before. I would not be bound by a schedule or obsess over an itinerary. I would take each moment as it came and immerse myself in the present, without worrying about what I should or shouldn't be doing. I would follow my feelings wherever they led me, acting out of desire instead of fear.

"Feeling hungry?" he asked me.

"Yes," I replied.

Within minutes, we'd thrown on our clothes and followed our appetites out the door and onto the sidewalk, in search of sustenance. We headed south and turned right on Hennessy Road, holding hands like it was second nature. Like it was something we'd done a thousand times before.

"I'm in the mood for something sweet," I announced. "What was that thing you brought me yesterday?"

"A pineapple bun?"

"Yes. I want that."

"Then let's get you what you're craving."

Carson planted a soft kiss on my temple, and we set off toward a bakery on Tin Lok Lane. Inside, the walls of the tiny shop were lined with glass cases containing crusty yellow buns and glazed brown tarts, and I could taste the thick sugary air on my tongue. Despite the crowd of patrons inside, it was orderly, and Carson blended right in, like a seasoned local who knew the routine and not a clueless American tourist. He silently grabbed a tray and a pair of plastic tongs, selected two pastries from the bins, and paid using coins he plucked from the pockets of his shorts.

On the way out, he took my hand again, and I followed his lead through a maze of side streets without asking him where we were going. It wasn't like me not to ask questions or to blindly surrender control of a situation like this. I always knew precisely where I was headed and exactly how I was going to get there. But the day before, high on Victoria Peak, he'd led me along that leafy green path toward that hidden view of Hong Kong— those were wonders I'd have never discovered if I hadn't allowed him to guide me. So I had faith in him to show me something new, something great. I knew it was foolish to trust someone I'd known for less than two days, but I'd vowed to let my feelings lead the way, and right now, I felt a burning desire to trail him through this city toward whatever he had in mind.

We wound up in Wan Chai Park, sitting under a palm tree on the pink stone bleachers beside a soccer court. On the far end, a few young men in basketball shorts were playing an informal pickup game around a single goal. In the midfield, some toddlers were kicking a ball to each other, tripping over their own chubby feet while their smiling mothers chatted and chased after them. Next to us, two office workers in business suits munched on sandwiches, trading hushed bits of conversation between bites. It was a slice of daily life here in this city, a reminder that, though this may be my vacation, there were plenty of other people who called this place home. This was real life, and it was happening now.

Carson handed me my pineapple bun, wrapped in a thin sheet of waxed paper. It was still warm from the oven, and my salivary glands tingled when I sunk my teeth in. I closed my eyes, letting the sweet dough dissolve in my mouth, losing myself in the sensation.

"You look like you're enjoying that," he said.

I waited until I swallowed to open my eyes. Carson looked ravenous, but the pastry in his hand remained untouched. From the way he fixed his eyes on me, I knew what he was hungry for.

"What's your plan for today?" he asked.

"I don't have one," I said, before taking another bite.

"No plan? I thought you were a planner. What happened to that itinerary you had?"

"I've gotten sidetracked." I licked the sugar off my bottom lip. "What are you up to today?"

"Not sure. I was gonna wander around, see where the day takes me," he said. "Wanna come?"

"Sure."

Carson looked down at his shirt, wrinkled from spending the night in a heap at the foot of my bed. "I should probably put on some clean clothes first. Why don't I go back to the hostel and change real quick? I can meet you in your room in a half hour."

"If we go back to that room," I said, "we may never leave it."

"Sounds like a fine way to spend the day, actually." He ran his hand along my thigh, and I recalled how it felt to lie next to him in that queen-sized bed with the pillow-top mattress, snuggled underneath the fluffy duvet, with his arm wrapped tightly around my body and his stubble gently scratching the nape of my neck.

"Here's an idea," I said. "How about you pack your bags, check out of the hostel, and bring your stuff over to my hotel?"

"What?"

"Come stay with me."

I didn't know where those words came from. They fell out of my mouth before I could stop them. And they kept flowing, directly from my heart to my tongue, with no filter.

"I mean, what happened last night, that needs to happen again. It just seems silly to, you know, keep going back and forth to get your clothes when I've got this big room all to myself now. It's all paid for and everything. So, I mean, why don't you just stay with me?"

Carson's mouth hung open, looking as shocked as I felt. He swallowed audibly, and his fingers tightened around the soft brown bun in his palm. I held my breath, and for a moment, I was certain he was going to say no. My heartbeat battered my rib cage and I felt the pineapple bun working its way back up my throat. *You shouldn't have been so impulsive. He's not interested, and now you look like a fool.*

"That would be awesome," he said, a smile slowly spreading across his face. "Are you sure?"

"Absolutely." I exhaled.

He gobbled down his bun and crumpled the white paper bag. Standing up, he reached his hand out to me and said, "Let me walk you to the hotel."

"Not just yet." I tilted my head back to look at the treetops. "I want to sit here a bit longer, finish my bun and enjoy the morning. This is a nice little park."

"Bet it wasn't in your guidebook."

"Actually, it was. I believe it was described as a 'peaceful oasis in which a traveler can rest her weary feet while watching some local patrons practice tai chi.'"

Carson leaned over to kiss me, and I tasted the grainy remnants of red bean paste on his lips. "See you soon," he said.

I watched him walk away, up the steps and through the wrought-iron gate, and the confident swagger in his shoulders warmed my insides. While I savored the rest of my pineapple bun, life continued around me: friends playing soccer, moms trailing toddlers, coworkers sharing stories. All of them smiling. Everyone belonging to a group. Then there was me, flying solo. I swallowed the last of my pastry and stood up to leave.

Walking back to the hotel, I pondered the downside of my five-year plan. Organization was my forte; it's why I was so good at my job. I had a knack for carefully laying the groundwork to ensure a successful future, whether I was considering the long-term goals of a Fortune 500 company or plotting out the details of my personal life. Considering where I'd come from—raised in a loving but modest home by grandparents who couldn't scrape together a college fund—I thought I'd done pretty well for myself. Certainly I never would have gotten this far if I hadn't set specific, attainable goals: professional success, financial independence, freedom to travel the world. I had it all planned out.

But with my focus on the future, I rarely immersed myself in the right now. My life was reduced to a series of check marks, ticking off each goal I achieved without taking the time to revel in my accomplishments. As soon as I hit one target, I was already reaching for the next one and contemplating the one after that. I rushed full speed ahead, my sights pointed sharply forward, never stopping to take a look at what was around me. If I did, I'd see exactly how alone I was. I'd always described myself as restless and consumed by wanderlust, but deep down, was I really just unhappy?

Now, in Hong Kong, I'd slammed on the brakes. I stood still, submerged in my surroundings. With my eyes wide open, I began to see all the possibilities for living life outside the narrow vision of what I deemed acceptable. There was no script for a successful life. We all had our own paths to wander, our own desires. Some people preferred the familiar comforts of home, while others found comfort in the unfamiliar. In the end, everyone had the same goal: to find peace, to be content. I thought I needed a plan to find happiness, so it surprised me to admit I was happy here, living in the moment. Happier than I could ever remember feeling before. And when I was with Carson, for the first time, I didn't feel so alone.

When I arrived back at the hotel, I stripped and showered,

reluctantly washing Carson's scent from my skin. As I toweled off my hair, I thought about how nice it was to be on vacation for a change. How relaxing it was to have abandoned my carefully planned itinerary and be completely unplugged from work. I couldn't remember the last time I'd gone this long without checking my e-mail.

*Work.*

*E-mail.*

*Am I forgetting something?*

I felt the blood drain from my face.

My boss had only approved this extended vacation on two conditions: that I stay in daily contact with her and that I attend a meeting with the head of the Hong Kong office, Martin Chu. I'd already failed the first requirement, and seeing as how I'd totally lost track of time these past few days, I wasn't sure if I'd failed the second one, too. Because even though I could remember how to take the train to Po Lin Monastery and the name of the restaurant that served the famous roast goose I'd read about online, I could not, for the life of me, recall the date and time of my meeting with Martin.

I just hoped I hadn't missed it already. Blowing off my boss was not the way to ensure a successful future.

# chapter seven

*Where the hell is my phone?*

I upended my purse on the rumpled bedspread, then started tearing apart my neatly packed carry-on. My smartphone was the slickest device on the market, a slim and sexy touchscreen with full international connectivity and an unlimited data plan. It weighed less than five ounces, but it contained my whole life: to-do lists, schedules, years of archived e-mails. It was also company-issued, and the last thing I wanted to tell my boss upon returning to New York was that I'd lost it while I was screwing around on vacation. That kind of irresponsible behavior would never earn me a promotion to senior associate.

Under normal circumstances, my phone was always within arm's reach, secured in my coat pocket or tucked away in my briefcase. I jokingly called it "my ball and chain," binding me to work obligations around the clock. Now, two whole days had passed, and it never occurred to me to check my e-mail or look at my calendar. And, obviously, I'd completely forgotten about this meeting with Martin Chu. I had no clue what I was expected to discuss with him, and I couldn't remember why Elizabeth even wanted me to see him in the first place.

*Never mind my phone. Where the hell is my mind?*

The contents of my tote were scattered haphazardly around the room, but my phone was still nowhere to be seen. Just as I was about to reach for my rolling suitcase to begin rummaging through my clothes, I finally remembered what I'd done with it. On the night I arrived, right before Elena and I headed out to Temple Street Night Market, I'd been scrolling through my e-mails when the power icon began to blink red; it seemed the four hours of Sugar Smash I'd played on the flight over had drained my phone's battery down to nothing. So I opened my carry-on to look for my charger, only to discover it wasn't there. Then I had the sickening realization that I'd never unplugged it from the wall beside my bed at home. It was still curled up on top of the nightstand, back in my New York apartment.

Seeing as my phone was incompatible with Elena's charger, and I was itching to sink my teeth into some street food, I powered it down and locked it inside the room safe, figuring I'd deal with the whole mess in the morning. Only I hadn't been expecting to be abandoned by Elena that night. Or to get distracted by a handsome stranger I picked up in a bar in Lan Kwai Fong. Now, here I was, two days later, completely out of touch with reality. A reality that included a no-nonsense boss who was undoubtedly going to be pissed.

When I'd initially called Elizabeth to ask her for a week off, she was hesitant to say yes. "I'm not sure we can afford for you to be on vacation at that time," she'd said, her monotone voice droning through the phone. "It's one of our busiest months."

At that point, it occurred to me I should've cleared the dates with my boss before purchasing those nonrefundable plane tickets. Then again, at the time, Jägermeister had been booking that flight for me.

"Well," I'd said, "the problem is, I already bought my tickets to Hong Kong."

"Hong Kong?" Her voice perked up. "You know, we recently opened an office in Kowloon. I'd love for you to drop in and meet with Martin Chu. He's a senior partner overseeing our Asia division, and it'd be good to touch base with him on some of his projects. Let me give him a call to set something up for you two."

"Okay," I'd groaned. Scheduling a business meeting in the middle of what was supposed to be a fun, adventurous girls' trip didn't exactly make me giddy. But I agreed, because what other choice did I have in the matter? Elizabeth was my boss. If she said, "Jump," it was my job to ask, "How high? And at what time? And do you have a detailed agenda for me to peruse beforehand?"

Which were questions I'd only just realized I'd failed to ask.

Still wearing a towel, I pulled my phone from the safe and sat on the floor, waiting for the little silver circle on the start-up screen to stop spinning. I felt that old familiar feeling creep into my chest, an encroaching panic about everything I was missing back at work, all the events I should be planning and preparing for. As soon as the phone finished booting, my thumb tapped the icon of the little golden envelope emblazoned with the giant letter *M*—the McKinley logo—and the next thing I knew I was scrolling through fifty-eight new e-mails.

I started to respond to them, one by one, until the power icon blinked red again. The battery was at 10 percent; it would never last long enough for me to clear out my inbox. So I decided to skip straight to the most recent message from Elizabeth.

> To: Sophie Bruno
> From: Elizabeth Fischman
> Subject: Hong Kong Office
>
> Please confirm status for meeting with Martin Chu at 9AM HKT this Thursday.

I sighed, relieved that I hadn't missed the meeting yet. In fact, I had three whole days to prepare. The timing seemed all right, too—nine in the morning was early enough that my whole day wouldn't be ruined. I'd undoubtedly be out of there with plenty of time to spare before lunch. Maybe Carson and I could even head to Tai Po in the New Territories to check out that famous roast goose. Or maybe we'd just wander around and find something delicious at random. I still had no clue what the point of this meeting was, so I shot off a quick e-mail.

> To: Elizabeth Fischman
> From: Sophie Bruno
> Subject: re: Hong Kong Office
>
> Confirmed. What will be the topic of our discussion?

My battery life was hovering at 9 percent. *If I shut it down now, I'll still have enough juice left to turn it back on later tonight so I can see what Elizabeth responds with.*

I slid my thumb up the screen, quickly surveying my inbox for any other important messages I may have overlooked.

And that's when I saw this:

To: Sophie Bruno
From: Elena Yardley
Subject: so so sorry

soph, i am so sorry about everything. for leaving you and for all the awful things i said. i really hope you can forgive me and eventually we can move past this.

one thing you should know—when i got home, i ran into your grandmother. so she knows i left hong kong and that you're by yourself. you'd think she'd be okay with you traveling alone by now, but she seemed really worried. she seemed pretty pissed at me, too.

anyway, i know you said you weren't checking your e-mail, but just in case you see this, you might wanna give her a call to let her know you're all right. i tried to tell her you were fine, but you know her. she never listens.

again, i'm really really REALLY sorry. i hope you can forgive me. and i hope you're having an amazing time.

please give me a call when you get home?

love,

elena

"Shit."

I said it out loud, to the empty hotel room. The biggest disadvantage of Elena still living at home with her mother, on the tree-lined street we grew up on, was that she ran into my grandmother all the time. My stomach tightened when I pictured Grandma, pacing around her kitchen and wringing her hands, worrying where I was and if I was okay. After all she'd done for me over the years to keep me happy and healthy and supported, I felt guilty for causing her distress.

At the same time, I didn't want to have to call and explain to her—for the thousandth time—that I was a big girl who was quite capable of traveling the world by myself. I'd been working on the road for several years now, hopping on an airplane every other week and living out of suitcases in dozens of different foreign cities. Not to mention, I leased my own apartment in the biggest, baddest city in the world. When was she going to realize I had grown up?

The clock read 12:45 p.m., which meant it was already past midnight back at home. Grandma would be sound asleep, with her hearing aids turned off and placed on her nightstand. If I called her now, she'd never hear the phone ringing. Which meant it was the perfect opportunity for me to leave a message reassuring her of my safety, without getting roped into an irritating conversation or draining my battery down to zero. I scrolled through my contact list, pulled up her number, and hit SEND. I knew the phone would ring six times before her ancient answering machine would click on. I leaned back against the foot of the bed and closed my eyes while I counted the rings. One . . . two . . .

"Hello?"

My eyes sprang open in surprise. Grandma didn't sound like I'd woken her from a deep sleep. Her voice wasn't hoarse or groggy. On the contrary, she seemed energized and a little on edge. As if she'd been chugging coffee for hours.

"Gram," I said.

"Sophie, is that you?" The edginess in her voice exploded to full-fledged frenzy. "Oh thank God. Thank God you're safe!"

"What are you doing up?"

"What am I doing up?" she screeched. "I can't sleep! I've been worried sick about you, alone out there on the other side of the world. Finally, you called. Are you all right?"

"I'm fine, Gram." I rolled my eyes, suppressing the urge to ask, *Why wouldn't I be all right?*

"So when are you coming home?"

"I get into JFK late on Saturday night."

"You're staying?"

"Of course I'm staying," I said. "I used my entire balance of flight and hotel points to come over here. I'm not going to give that all up and leave."

"For God's sake, be careful, Sophie," she said. "All alone like that and so far away, you could get yourself killed!"

I took a deep breath to steady my voice before saying through gritted teeth, "Gram, I travel everywhere. All over the world. All the time. By myself. I know what I'm doing, and I'm not going to get myself killed."

"I know." Her voice softened. "I wish you'd stop gallivanting, though. I worry about you all the time; you're always so far away.

I just love you so much, I don't want anything to happen to you."

"I love you, too, Gram," I said. "Nothing's going to happen to me."

"That Elena is a piece of work," she said, getting louder as her anger began to resurface. "What the hell's the matter with her? Leaving you like that. She should be ashamed of herself. And for a boy!"

"Roddy's twenty-seven, Gram. He's not exactly a boy."

"He's a boy! He's got nothing going for him."

"He's got a good job," I said. "He's a personal trainer."

"Doing jumping jacks all day? You call that a good job?"

"Trainers make good money, Gram. Besides that, he loves what he does." *Am I really defending Elena's relationship with Roddy right now? And to my grandmother, of all people?*

"It's not dignified," she sniffed. "Elena shouldn't be wasting her time with him. You should talk some sense into her."

I decided I didn't like where this conversation was going, nor was I interested in spending any more of my precious limited time in Hong Kong engaged in the same discussion we always had across her kitchen table. Stop traveling. The world is dangerous. No man is ever good enough.

"Listen, Gram, my phone's about to die," I said. "I just wanted to let you know I'm okay. I'll give you a call when I get home."

"Fine. But don't talk to any strange men. And don't ever put your drink down and walk away! You never know what they'll slip into it. Men are wild nowadays."

"Okay, Gram. Bye."

I hung up before she could squeeze in any more helpful advice. I knew my grandmother meant well and that all her fretting and nagging came from a place of love. I was also growing exasperated with pretending it didn't annoy me. My whole life, I'd followed her directions, taking her suggestions and opinions as gospel. She told me to be independent, to never rely on a man, to always have a plan. It was true that if it weren't for her, I never would've made it this far. After all, she was the one who'd encouraged me to work hard, establish a distinguished career, and earn a steady income. I'd done it all to make her proud. But once I became the successful, independent woman she'd groomed me to be, she seemed intent on keeping me close by, in some futile attempt to shield me from the rest of the world. Maybe she didn't want me to be independent after all.

Of course, I knew where this all came from. I knew she only acted this way because she didn't want me to turn out like my mother. A pregnant teen, a high school dropout, a deadbeat absentee mom. By now, though, wasn't it clear I had chosen a different path? I'd followed Grandma's advice; I'd done everything I could to make her happy. I hadn't turned out like my mother, and I would never be anything like her. What else did I have to do to prove to my grandmother that I was a completely different person?

Sneering down at my phone, I regretted ever turning it on to begin with. Only 3 percent of the battery life was left. Just as I was about to shut it down to conserve what precious power remained, the tiny blue light in the top right-hand corner started to flash, signaling a new message had arrived.

From Elizabeth.

At one in the morning, New York time.

*Does this woman ever not work?*

To: Sophie Bruno
From: Elizabeth Fischman
Subject: re: Hong Kong Office

See attached agenda for discussion topics.

The attached document contained five pages of bullet points organized under six different subheadings. It would take hours to touch on them all. Was I expected to spend the whole day with this guy?

To: Elizabeth Fischman
From: Sophie Bruno
Subject: re: Hong Kong office

How long is this meeting scheduled to last?

My thumb hovered over the SEND button, but before my skin made contact, the screen went dark. The battery was totally drained. I stared at the lifeless gadget resting in my palm and felt simultaneously grateful for the disruption and panicked about what to do next. *I suppose I'll have to buy another charger now.*

A knock came at the door. Carson had returned already. In my haste to check on things back home, I'd forgotten all about the here and now, the present I'd vowed to stay planted in. I was still wrapped in a towel, I hadn't done my hair, and on the other side of that dead-bolted door was the most gorgeous man I'd ever hooked up with. *Get it together.*

I tossed my phone back in the safe, and, rushing to the entryway, I paused to check my reflection in the mirror. *Shit.* I desperately tried to arrange my air-dried, frizzy hair into an aesthetically pleasing arrangement, but it was useless. Another knock, this time a little louder.

With one hand gripping the towel closed around my chest, I swallowed hard and opened the door. Carson stood in the hallway with a huge backpack perched upon his shoulders. When he saw me, he said, "What's wrong?"

"Nothing, why?"

"You're scowling. Am I too early? Or did you change your mind? Because if you did, it's not a problem. I can go check back into the hostel."

"Oh." I touched my fingers to the center of my brow, massaging away the frown. How had I not realized I'd been scowling? "No, come in," I said, moving aside to invite him in before shutting the door behind him. "It's not you. Work's just driving me nuts."

"Work?" He stepped into the foyer and placed his bag on the floor beside him. "I thought you were on vacation."

"My boss doesn't really believe in vacations."

"Well, that doesn't sound like much fun." His eyes traced my body from the top of my head to the tips of my pink-polished toes. "Let's see if we can get a smile back on your face."

Wordlessly, he reached for my hand and loosened my grip on

the towel. As it dropped to the floor, he ran his fingertips down my body, starting at my shoulders. His touch on the curve of my breasts gave me goose bumps. When he slid his hands past my hips, he said, "I think I figured out what I want to do today."

Just like that, our plans were made.

# chapter eight

Three days later, it was Thursday and my phone was still locked in the hotel safe, the battery still totally dead. I never did bother to buy that charger. I'd made a half-hearted attempt to find one when we passed by a shopping mall in Central on Tuesday afternoon, but the two stores I visited didn't have it in stock. Searching through electronics stores for a hard-to-find cable got old fast, especially when there were so many more exciting things to be doing with my time.

Like lolling in bed, naked, beside Carson. That morning, like every other, I opened my eyes and drank in the same scenery: his muscular body stretched out on top of the fluffy duvet, his blue eyes fixated on the sketchbook in his lap, his pencil dancing across the white vellum.

In that moment, I felt so content and comfortable. Nothing could bring me down off my high. I wasn't even worried about the fact that I'd just slept through my meeting with Martin Chu.

It happened accidentally. The night before, it had crossed my mind to call down to the front desk and arrange an early morning wake-up call, to make sure I arose with plenty of time to get to the 9:00 a.m. appointment in Kowloon. Before I picked up the phone, Carson suggested we take a sunset cruise across

Victoria Harbour to watch the Symphony of Lights from the Tsim Sha Tsui waterfront. If we wanted to get there for the eight o'clock showtime, we had to leave immediately. So I grabbed my purse and followed him out the door without hesitation. By the time we'd returned, it was after midnight, and my head was so fuzzy from those two cocktails I drank at the Lobby Lounge after the show that the only thing I had on my mind was stripping off my clothes and tumbling into bed with him. At some point, I drifted off, without ever having called down to the front desk.

So maybe it happened accidentally on purpose.

I knew Elizabeth wouldn't be happy, but somehow I'd rationalized my decision to blow it off. Technically, I wasn't on the clock. I had earned my paid time off. Legally, she couldn't make me work on vacation, right? Either way, I couldn't stand the thought of wasting an entire day in Hong Kong cooped up in a stuffy office, poring over spreadsheets and talking about strategic long-term IT planning. Not when there was so much else to explore.

Those past three days, every moment of touring Hong Kong with Carson had been a thrill. We'd smelled incense burning in tranquil temples, watched a laser light show illuminate the night sky with a swirling kaleidoscope of color, and sampled enough delectable street food at *dai pai dong* across the city to more than make up for my abbreviated first meal at Temple Street Night Market. We made decisions at the spur of the moment, following our feelings wherever they took us. Without an itinerary, I was able to relax and unwind for a change. And spending my days with Carson made me feel better than I ever could have planned for. When this trip was over, I intended to buy Elena a drink to say thanks for ditching me.

For now, I lounged in bed listening to the scratch of pencil on paper and the rhythm of Carson's even, focused breathing. *Only two more days of this,* I thought, then immediately shook the idea out of my head, preferring to live in the state of timeless limbo we'd created for ourselves. I'd stopped thinking about Elena, my grandmother, my five-year plan. I was living in the moment, fully immersed in the right now. As far as I was concerned, I could while away the rest of my days in the comfort of this temperature-controlled hotel room, lazing on this pillow-top mattress, inches away from the sexiest man I'd ever known.

"What are you drawing?" I asked, my voice still rough with sleep.

He closed his sketchbook and placed it on the bed beside him, then picked up a white paper bag blotted with translucent grease stains.

"I got you a pineapple bun," he said, placing the bag under my nose. The sweet smell aroused me.

"You went out?" I plucked it from his hands and peeked inside.

"I took a stroll down by the harbor to sketch," he said. "There's great light on the water in the early morning."

"But you're not wearing any clothes."

"I took them off as soon as I got back." He rolled onto his side, narrowing his blue eyes at me. "Clothes have no place in this room."

I smirked and raised the pastry to my lips, causing thick

crumbs to fall onto my exposed chest. Carson leaned over and licked them off, one by one. I dropped my bun back in the bag and tossed it aside as he reached his hand beneath the sheets and slid his fingers slowly across my thigh. Waking up had never felt so good.

After a leisurely romp, we rolled out of bed at half past ten and into a steamy shower. The water trickled over our heads and down our bodies while we soaped each other's backs.

"Where do you feel like going today?" My voice echoed off the tiles. This was how we made our plans: on a whim, while we washed.

"I was thinking about Macau," he said.

I'd definitely dog-eared the page on Macau in my guidebook—wherever it was by now. Macau was the world's wealthiest gambling territory, even bigger and richer than Vegas, but there was more to it than casinos. There were ruins and restaurants and a black sand beach, and I wanted to see as much as I could. But it was over an hour away by ferry, so even though it wasn't our usual style, I figured some forethought was necessary in order to make the journey worthwhile.

"I'd love to take a day trip there," I said, "but I think it's a little late by now. We probably should've gotten up four hours ago and caught an earlier boat. Maybe tomorrow? If we can get a TurboJET at Sheung Wan station by seven o'clock, then I bet we'd arrive with enough time for a quick spin by the Ruins of St. Paul before catching a bus over to Hac Sa Beach. I read all about a great little Portuguese restaurant on the water there. We can grab lunch and then head to—"

"Whoa, slow down." He smiled, perhaps a little shocked by my sudden transformation into a tour guide. "I don't mean a day trip. I mean pack up, leave Hong Kong, and go to Macau."

My heart thumped and dropped to my gut. I'd envisioned saying good-bye to Carson at the airport two days from now, not spending tonight in an empty bed, waking up tomorrow without him beside me.

"When are you going?" I asked.

"What? No, Sophie, I want you to come with me." He rolled his eyes and laughed. Leaving without me, I guess, was not something he'd even considered, but it was the first thing that popped into my mind. It seemed I had some abandonment issues; maybe I wouldn't be so quick to buy Elena that drink.

Still, checking out of the hotel early didn't seem like a reasonable option. I had booked it through the end of the week, and the nights were nonrefundable. Not to mention, my flight home was in a little over forty-eight hours, departing from Hong Kong International. I had promised to be more spontaneous, but this was a drastic change in my agenda.

"I can't."

"Why not?"

I ran through my list of excuses, which Carson swatted down like gnats.

"We'll get you back here in plenty of time for your flight. I'll pay the bill for our stay in Macau. And for this one, too. I hope you didn't think I planned on mooching off you the whole time."

"It was prepaid with hotel points," I said, sliding my hand

down his chest. "Besides, I think you've been earning your keep."

"So let's go."

"Do you have reservations somewhere?" I shuddered at the thought of staying in a hostel, sharing a bedroom with snoring strangers.

"I don't make reservations," he said. "It's off-season now; there are vacancies everywhere. Don't worry; we'll get a nice hotel. Someplace private. Okay?"

A sojourn in Macau meant another stamp in my passport, which definitely sounded alluring. More alluring, however, was the idea of following Carson wherever he went. There were so many questions I could ask, so many reasons why I could say no, but there was no denying the pleasure and passion I'd experienced these past few days. And it had happened because I'd stopped overthinking and surrendered to impulse.

"Okay."

He kissed me, shut off the faucet, and pulled back the shower curtain. I stood there for a second with the towel in my hand, water dripping from my chin, looking at my reflection through the mist on the mirror. Who was this naked woman with the sopping curls, dropping her plans to chase after some guy? I wasn't sure I recognized her.

We took our time getting dressed and packing up. After I slipped my phone from the safe, I jammed it way down in the bottom of my tote bag. My new motto for this trip was, *Out of sight, out of mind.* Before we left, I gave the room a once-over, combing the closets and dresser drawers in search of misplaced items. It was a habit I'd formed after leaving my favorite pair of shoes behind in a Munich hotel room. Carson said I was being neurotic, but when I found his sketchbook underneath the bed-sheets, I felt vindicated.

"See?" I waved the book under his nose. "You forgot this."

"Leave it," he said. "I don't have room in my backpack. The zipper on the front pouch is already busted from trying to over-stuff it."

I thumbed the pages, glancing at the artwork within. Some scenes were unfamiliar, drawn before we met or perhaps in the very early mornings, while I was still asleep. But I recognized others, like the impressive Hong Kong skyline he'd sketched at the top of Victoria Peak.

"You can't just leave this here."

"I do it all the time. There's nothing in there I want to keep anyway."

My fingers clenched the notebook, unwilling to let it go. How could he not want to keep something on which he'd worked so hard and spent so much time? The talent poured into his sketches, the exquisite results, the memories attached to them: Did he consider these all disposable?

"I'll put it in my bag," I said. "I've got room. I can carry it for you."

"What about after you leave? Then what do I do with it? I'll have to leave it behind anyway."

The words stung, even though I knew they were true. We only had two more days together. After that, I would return to New York, to my studio apartment, to my next job assignment, while he would continue on to wherever he felt like going. Our time as travel companions was only temporary. Carson was simply being practical. Didn't I pride myself on practicality?

"Can I keep it?"

He squinted his eyes, hinting at a smile. "If you want."

I tucked it in the front pocket of my suitcase and wheeled it out the door.

* * *

The Sheung Wan ferry terminal was mobbed. Upon walking through the doors to find a swarm of scowling faces, I began to regret our last-minute decision-making. I imagined arriving in Macau amid a crush of tourists, all the hotels alight with NO VACANCY signs. When the clerk behind the counter informed us that the crowds were due to weather delays, as opposed to overbooked boats, I realized even advanced planning couldn't have accounted for limited visibility on the high seas. We bought our tickets for the next departing ferry and waited for the fog to lift.

After fifteen minutes of hovering around the departures lounge, we managed to stake out a free bench, where we sat side by side with our feet propped up on our luggage.

"Looks like we'll probably be here awhile." Carson slipped a fresh sketchpad from the side pouch of his backpack, along with a black marker, thick around the middle with a fine, tapered tip. He opened to the first page of his book, crisp and blank, then rolled the marker back and forth between his thumb and index finger as he studied the woman sitting across the aisle. She was fast asleep, with her face turned toward us and her head resting on a duffel bag in the adjacent seat. Her mouth hung open, and I could hear her rumbling snores over the din of the crowd.

Carson traced broad black lines across the page, from which an image quickly materialized. It was the sleeping woman, in exaggerated detail. Her nose was bulbous, her lips protruded, her forehead took up half of her face. Droplets of drool hung from the corner of her mouth. Behind her, a boat sailed away toward a distant island, obscured by patchy fog. A thought bubble emerged from the top of her head, revealing her dream about striking it rich in Macau: a slot machine with three matching cherries, shooting out coins and dollar signs from all angles.

"Hilarious." I laughed. "I can't believe you finished that so fast."

"I've had lots of practice," he said. "Could probably do these with my eyes closed."

I'd forgotten about his job drawing caricatures at Fisherman's Wharf. "How long did you work there?"

"A couple of years. I gave up my stand when I started this trip. But I loved it. I can see myself going back to it someday."

He flipped to a fresh page as he scouted for his next muse among the sea of people, settling on an elderly man picking his teeth by the window.

"This is how I'd pass the time on slow days." He drew as he spoke, his pen strokes driven by muscle memory and instinct. "There were always a bunch of tourists hanging out, stuffing their faces with shrimp sandwiches or feeding the seagulls or whatever. I whipped up their pictures while they stood around and then tacked them up on my board. So when they walked by, they'd see themselves and do a double take. You'd be surprised how many extra sales I made that way."

"I didn't know you were such an enterprising businessman."

"The key is to get inside their heads. In the five minutes you're sitting there drawing them, you have to read their faces and figure out what it is that belongs in that little thought bubble."

"So, an enterprising businessman and quasi-psychic, then."

He finished with a flourish and showed me the sketch: a stooped gentleman, attacking his oversized overbite with a comically enlarged toothpick, dreaming about a gaggle of curvy young women in bikinis.

"Sometimes," he said, "people don't know they want something until you draw it out for them. Then when they actually have it, they wonder how they ever lived without it."

His words rang through my body like an alarm. I looked toward my feet, at the front pocket of my suitcase, where I sensed Carson's sketchbook burning a hole through the fabric.

"Are you really not saving any of your artwork?"

He turned the page, started over. "You sure know how to beat a dead horse."

"I just don't understand," I said. "Why spend all this time creating these beautiful pieces if you're not going to do anything with them?"

"Who's going to buy my shitty sketches?"

"I keep telling you, they're not shitty. They're amazing."

"Fine. Who's going to buy my amazing sketches? It's not exactly like there's a market for pencil drawings from random unknowns."

"I wouldn't necessarily expect you to sell them. But doesn't it mean something to you to look back on what you've accomplished? To see the end product of all your hard work?"

"The meaning is in the process, Sophie. Not in the results."

Carson's philosophy was foreign to me. My whole job—hell, my whole life—revolved around results. Evaluating metrics. Achieving specific, measurable, realistic goals. Perfectly balancing the numbers in the spreadsheet. If the outcome was not what I'd hoped for, it meant I had probably failed.

"What about memories?" I asked. "Isn't there anything in the sketches that's important enough for you to keep for sentimental value?"

"Sometimes," he said. "The stuff I think is really important I make room for, but there's not a whole lot of those."

Then it became clear: the memory of our afternoon on the Peak was not important enough for him to make room for. He discarded it in our rumpled sheets, and, like a fool, I retrieved it. I stared at my bag with blurred vision, swallowing hard against the lump forming in my throat.

"Here." He ripped a page from his notebook and held it out to me. "Something for sentimental value."

Two cartoonish faces peered out from the textured paper: one with a glint in his eye and a dimple in his cheek, the other with a wild mass of curls atop her head. They sat on a bench, holding hands at the edge of a mountain, the Hong Kong skyline behind them. Their thoughts converged in a single bubble, inside of which floated a solitary heart.

So maybe that day meant something to him after all. Or maybe he was just giving me what he thought I wanted to see.

"Cute." It was the only word I could muster without losing my composure. This was supposed to be a short-term fling. So why was I letting myself get so worked up over this man? Or, as Grandma would call him, a boy. A boy with no job, no home, and no plans. A boy who I inexplicably trusted. A boy who would certainly make a mess of things.

I feigned a dramatic yawn, rubbing my eyes with the heels of my hands before the tears could escape. "I'm so tired of sitting here. Where is this ferry already?"

He rolled the paper into a tight, thin tube and tucked it in the side pouch of my suitcase. We sat in silence, the air between us crackling and tense. I felt him looking at me, but I couldn't meet his gaze.

"Can't control the weather," he said finally before scanning the room for his next subject.

I closed my eyes, focused my breath, and asked myself, *What the hell am I doing?*

# chapter nine

There are no clocks on a casino floor. No windows, either. It's a strategic decision, designed to distract you. The idea is to get you to lose track of time, disconnect from reality. It's a labyrinth of sensory overload, with flashing lights and chiming bells, and a pervasive miasma of smoke and perfume. If you need a break from the bedlam or a breath of fresh air, you'll walk in circles trying to find an exit, weaving between tables, spinning into a trance while you watch the cards shuffle and flip. The dealers stand by, with cool yet benevolent smiles, existing only to dole out your fortune. Before you know it, you fall victim to the impossible fantasy. Your money's on the table, and then, in an instant, it's gone.

"Let's pop in for one second," Carson said, then led me by the hand toward the glass doors of Macau's oldest and most opulent casino, the Grand Amadora. Reluctant to follow him, I looked up at the towering structure stretching into the sky and fanning out like a showgirl's headdress. We'd walked for twenty minutes from the Outer Harbour Ferry Terminal to the edge of Nam Van Lake, where a strip of shiny buildings lined the waterfront. My legs were jelly and my stomach growled. All I wanted was to unload my luggage, kick up my feet, and grab some dinner. But with the sun already on its downward slope, I worried we might not find anywhere to stay and envisioned us roaming the streets with our bags in our hands all night.

"Only for one second," I said. "Then we really have to find a room somewhere before there are no vacancies left."

"There will be plenty of vacancies. I've been traveling like this for months, Sophie. Have a little faith in me."

Every sensible cell in my body was telling me this unplanned excursion to Macau was a risky endeavor. I'd only known Carson for a few days, and all I knew of him was what he chose to reveal. When I saw the fire burning in his eyes as we approached the casino, I wondered how much he'd kept hidden. What if he harbored a secret gambling addiction? His dead parents, his trust fund: It could all be a lie. He could be financing this trip with the proceeds from his winning wagers and making up for the losses by swindling foolish, sex-charmed women. The other day at the teahouse, he'd invented our engagement with such unflinching ease, spoon-feeding the older love-struck couple the story they wanted to hear. What if he was doing the same thing to me? And why hadn't this possibility occurred to me before?

"After you," he said, holding the door open and motioning for me to enter before him, ever the gentleman. There was no point in hesitating now; I was already there, having ignored the advice of my sensible cells all week. I summoned imaginary faith from deep within the pit of my stomach and crossed the threshold into the cold casino air.

I thought I knew what to expect. I'd been to other casinos, witnessed the raucous crowds surrounding the craps table, and heard the screams when the little silver ball found its landing spot on the roulette wheel. But inside the Grand Amadora, people spoke in hushed tones, barely audible over the piano music piped in on the loudspeaker. The entrance hall was freshly painted in shades of beige, accented with exotic flowers arranged in vases as big as tree stumps. Gilded chandeliers hung from coffered ceilings, and with each step, our shoes sank deeply into lush red carpet.

I'd started to think we mistakenly entered a museum, when I saw a cluster of tables ahead and to the right, cordoned off behind velvet ropes. Men sat around them, silently smoking, studying the cards as dealers passed them across the green felt.

"Why is it so quiet in here?" I whispered, afraid of making too much noise.

"Looks like the baccarat pit," he said. "Probably high rollers."

Thus far, my gambling experience had been limited to a few spins on the nickel slots at the Borgata the night Elena turned twenty-one. We'd driven down to Atlantic City and rented a room to celebrate her birthday—the last time we'd gone away together prior to Hong Kong. After losing twenty dollars before the cocktail waitress could return with my amaretto sour, I hustled us off the gaming floor and toward the thumping doors of the club Mixx, where we flirted our way into the VIP room and danced on a banquet until the wee hours of the morning. I knew nothing of baccarat, and certainly nothing of high rollers. Frankly, I wasn't interested. Placing a bet with unfavorable odds was as good as tossing money on a fire.

So my breath caught when I realized that Carson was heading toward the velvet ropes. I slowed my pace, hoping he would stop, turn around, tell me he was only joking. But he pressed forward with purpose, his eyes on the prowl. Immediately, I pictured our day ending with the empty, white pockets of his shorts hanging inside out while I slipped my credit card across the counter at the front desk of a dingy Macanese hostel. *Why have I been such a fool?*

"The other tables are over here," he said, and continued past the high rollers' pit with his arm outstretched, his finger pointing. I exhaled. At least he wasn't intent on losing it all in one sitting. Or did he not even have enough money to buy in?

Around the corner, there were no velvet ropes, only an endless corridor flanked by card tables. Baccarat. Blackjack. Different flavors of poker. More baccarat. No craps, no roulette. No jubilant screaming or victory high fives. Instead, players perched quietly on ivory leather chairs, hunched over their cards, their stern faces clouded in a haze of tobacco smoke. Apparently, gambling was serious business in Macau.

I waited for Carson to make a move, but he only looked around, slowing down at certain tables to investigate the play. Perhaps he was there to observe, I thought, taking snapshots in his mind that he'd later transfer to pencil and paper. My shoulders relaxed and I grabbed for his hand, following him as he wound his way around the floor. *He's not a shifty grifter; he's an artist with a trust fund.* I figured if I kept thinking this, I'd eventually believe it with certainty.

"I feel like we should play something," he said.

"There's plenty of time for that later." I instinctively clenched my fist around his hand, searching for an exit. By now I'd lost all sense of location and direction. "Why don't we go find a place to stay first?"

But Carson had his wallet in his hand before I could finish my sentence.

"Sic Bo," he said, reading the sign above our heads. "Wonder what this is about."

We examined the grid on the long table before us, dozens of squares to place bets on, each containing a different number or a picture of dice. There were no actual dice in sight, though. No spinning wheel, either. Not even a deck of cards at the ready in an automatic shuffler. Just a stone-faced dealer in a glossy vest and cuff links, his hands resting limply on the Plexiglas cover of the chip tray. He stared straight ahead, appearing wholly uninterested in offering gambling instructions to a couple of schlubby foreigners trailing suitcases.

"How do you play this?" I asked.

"I have no idea." Carson pulled out a red note from his billfold and placed it on the felt. Five hundred Hong Kong dollars, the casino's preferred currency over Macanese patacas. It amounted to sixty bucks back home, give or take. Not an extraordinary sum, but nothing to scoff at either, particularly for someone supposedly traveling on a limited budget. *Not your business. Not your money. Not your decision.* Still, I cringed when the dealer snatched up the bill and crammed it in the cash slot, replacing it with a short stack of pink chips. Carson scanned the table for inspiration, and I fought the urge to deliver a lecture on the importance of personal finance.

"What should I do?" he asked.

"This board makes no sense to me," I said. "What are you even betting on? From the pictures, I'm guessing dice, but where are they?"

"I don't know." He furrowed his brow and bit his bottom lip. We were the only players at the table; the dealer remained still, waiting for a wager. *Cash in your chips and walk away,* I thought, hoping Carson could hear me telepathically.

"Pick a number from one to six," he said.

"What?"

"Give me a number from one to six. Don't think about it, just say the first one that comes to mind."

"Two." Two of us traveling together. Two days left in my trip. Two more minutes of enduring this nonsense before I gave up and caught the next ferry back to Hong Kong.

He pushed his whole stack of chips across the felt, placing his bet on a picture of three dice, all faceup on the number two.

"Might as well go all in, right?" He was smiling but his voice quavered. I thought of all we'd done this week. I'd been basking in his unconventional lifestyle, enjoying his haphazard approach to travel, lost in a fog of sex and mystery. And here we stood, about to say good-bye to what could possibly be Carson's last sixty dollars. Regret washed over me when I imagined dipping into my savings account to pay for the next two nights' accommodations.

The dealer waved his hand over the table, the universal symbol for "no more bets," a pointless gesture considering we had nothing left to lose. He pressed a small black button to the right of the chip tray, next to which sat an inverted silver bowl with a handle on top, like the cloche cover on a room service platter, but in miniature. I hadn't noticed it there before, but no sooner had I spotted it than the dealer was lifting it up, revealing a glass globe underneath.

"I guess that's what we were betting on," Carson said. We leaned forward to see the contents. It matched the picture under the chips perfectly: three dice, faceup on the number two.

Was I dreaming?

"Oh my God," I said, two octaves higher than any other voice in the casino. "You hit it!"

Carson's mouth hung open while the dealer barked an unintelligible command summoning the pit boss to his side.

"How much did you win?" I asked.

"I don't know." His eyes were transfixed on the little red dice as if looking away might cause them to vanish. "Did I really just win this?"

"I'm pretty sure you did." I pointed at the pit boss, who was taking notes on a clipboard as the dealer counted out seven black chips, one green. He slid them across the table as a crowd slowly formed around us, people stopping by to scrutinize the winner, eager to piggyback off the freshly kindled luck. Carson snatched up his winnings and took inventory, thumbing through the chips three times to make sure he had counted correctly.

"Holy shit." He glanced over his shoulder and moved away from the group of budding Sic Bo enthusiasts. "Sophie, this is seventy-five grand."

"Holy shit!" I yelled, then quickly converted the currency in my head. "That's like nine thousand U.S. dollars!"

He shushed me and laughed, clinking the chips in the palms of his hands. Seconds ago, I'd convinced myself this man was an irresponsible liar, but now all I saw was a giddy, innocent child. Who was he really: a man or a boy? There was so much he told me, and so much I had yet to find out, but no way to distinguish the fact from the fiction. The sixty dollars he'd placed on the table could have been all he had left to his name, or it could have been chump change compared to his trust fund. He could be an orphan, haunted by his past, or a con artist with a talent for spinning sob stories. As he traveled around the world, there could be a different woman following him each week, or I could be the first to have shared in his adventures. The only certainty was the thrill racing through me; so far, blind surrender was paying off.

"I can't believe that happened," I said.

"Neither can I."

"Who wins a hundred-fifty to one odds on a game they've never played before?"

"The whole thing is insane."

"You are so lucky."

"It's all you," he said. "You're my good luck charm."

Carson pulled me close and I wrapped my arms around his neck, gazed into his blue eyes, tried to find the truth inside them. But then I thought, how much do we know about anyone, really? People are complex and full of surprises. The ones we trust to care for us can leave us high and dry. The ones we barely know can teach us invaluable lessons. We all have so many sides to us. Who we are on any given day depends on how the dice rolls.

"Let's cash these in," he said.

"You're done already?" I was disappointed, adrenaline clouding my judgment. Caught up in the excitement of the big win, I'd forgotten all about my aversion to gambling.

"I'm gonna quit while I'm ahead." He grabbed my hand and kissed the tips of my fingers. "Besides, we've gotta book a room. We're going to have a very comfortable stay in Macau."

## chapter ten

Our room at the Grand Amadora didn't have a number. It was identified only by name: the Chrysanthemum Suite. Carson told the concierge he wanted romance and a spectacular view; when asked for a price range, he spread out his chips on the marble countertop. I cringed at the sight and tugged lightly at the hem of his shirt.

"That's an awful lot of money to spend on a hotel room," I whispered in his ear, while the concierge tapped away at her keyboard.

"Okay." He wrapped his arm around my shoulders and pulled me in close. "I'm sure we can find a hostel around here with some vacancies. You know, someplace cheaper. With a shared bathroom. And bunk beds. And some snoring roommates."

I snickered and smacked him lightly on the stomach, then let my hand linger there for a moment, caressing his tight, firm abs through the thin cotton T-shirt. *We'll definitely need some privacy tonight.*

"Seriously," I said. "I'm sure we can find something private and quiet that doesn't cost thousands of dollars."

He pressed his lips to my temple and whispered against my skin, "Just let me do this for us. Please."

I buried my face in his chest, inhaling his musk, wishing I

could bottle it up and take it home with me. I realized it was pointless for me to argue with him. If I had won this money, I would've squirreled it away in a money market account for safe-keeping. But I didn't win this money; he did. That meant it was his decision to make. I already knew Carson's philosophy on saving: Why save when he may not have a future to save for?

But I also really liked that he was doing this for "us." The idea of an "us" made me tingle all over.

So I said no more and watched silently as the concierge slipped keycards into slender envelopes before a bellman whisked our bags away. We followed him to the elevator, where he pressed the button for the twenty-eighth floor and stared down at the linoleum. As we ascended, Carson held me in his arms and kissed me deeply, as if we were alone. We didn't realize the elevator arrived on our floor until the bellman loudly cleared his throat.

The foyer in the Chrysanthemum Suite was bigger and more tastefully appointed than my entire studio apartment back home. Porcelain vases on marble pedestals flanked the front door. Canned lights were scattered across the ceiling like stars, casting twilight across the marble floor. Against the wall, a great glass bowl overflowed with red chrysanthemums. Behind it hung a mirror like a full moon, in which I caught the reflection of my swollen pink lips pouting back at me.

Carson ushered the bellman down the hall and to the left, to deliver our bags to the bedroom. I walked straight ahead, across the deep pile carpet, past the cream-colored sectional with paisley pillows jutting out into the center of the living room.

Standing at the floor-to-ceiling windows at the far wall, I looked down at the scenery below, the city turning from daylight to dusk. Nam Van Lake stretched below us in a cornflower horseshoe, a million golden lights reflecting off the water. Macau Tower pierced the skyline, its pointed tip reaching up to the clouds, framed by the rolling mountains of mainland China beyond. I pressed my palm against the cool glass, as if to touch the whole city, absorb its energy from above.

The door clicked shut behind me. I spun around and saw Carson walking my way with an open bottle of champagne in one hand, two crystal flutes in the other.

"This was already chilling in the bedroom," he said. "Under the circumstances, I think a toast is in order."

He handed me a glass and poured the champagne quickly, froth foaming over the edges and dripping down onto our fingers.

"To good luck," he said.

"To Macau."

"To us."

We clinked our glasses and tilted our heads back, draining our drinks in a single gulp. Icy bubbles tickled my tongue and sent a chill through my chest as I swallowed. We set down our flutes on an end table and stared out the window, side by side.

"Another city filled with people," he said.

"The world really is a huge place."

Carson slid his arm around my waist. "And with all the billions of people living in this huge world, you and I somehow managed to find each other."

"Well, what was it you said?" I leaned into his embrace. "'The universe has its reasons for bringing people together,' right?"

His breath was so close, it tickled my ear. Then his lips touched my neck, cool and wet against my skin.

"I don't know what it is about you, Sophie," he said, "but you make me feel like I could do anything."

He worked his way toward my lips, and our mouths opened and melted into each other, tongues still tart from the lingering champagne. I pressed my pelvis against his and felt him respond. Our hands searched each other, first with caresses and then with urgent tugs. He pulled up my dress, and I lifted my arms over my head to let him slip it off. When he unhooked my bra, I watched his thick fingers guide the straps down the length of my arms until it dropped to the floor at my feet. I looked up to meet his cool, shimmering gaze and saw the twinkling lights of Macau reflected in the blue of his eyes. He tugged at the waistband of my panties, peeling them down over my hips and letting them slide down my legs until they pooled around my ankles. I stood before him naked, then leaned back against the window, exposed to the world below, feeling the chill from the glass seep beneath my bare skin.

Carson tore off his clothes and pulled a condom from his pocket before flinging his shorts aside, the tree emblazoned on his chest heaving with each breath. He stood still for a moment, his eyes combing the length of my body. Then he trailed kisses between my breasts and down my stomach until he was kneeling between my legs. The flick of his tongue numbed me; the heat of his breath brought me back to full sensation.

I closed my eyes and moaned, running my fingers through his thick, sandy hair.

As he rose to meet my face, his hands grasped my hips and hoisted me up, and I flung both my arms around his neck. Stretching my thighs back, he pressed me into the window with all his weight and entered me, grunting. As he swelled and pulsed inside me, I let him consume my senses: the scent radiating from his dewy skin; the salty flavor as I ran my tongue along his neck; his guttural groans reverberating throughout my trembling body. Angling my hips to meet his rhythm, we locked eyes, and a tidal wave of blue washed over me as we both came together, convulsing against the cool glass.

Panting, he gently lowered me to the ground and laid me down upon the plush, silky carpet. We stretched out on the floor next to each other and shared delicate, satisfied kisses. When we'd finally caught our breath, Carson propped himself up on one elbow and smiled down at me. "So, would that be considered, like, sex in public?"

"I don't think that really counts," I said with a giggle. "No one can see us all the way up here. Plus, the windows are mirrored on the outside. But if somebody did, then I hope they liked the show. We gave them a good one, I think."

Carson raised his eyebrows and widened his smile, revealing the dimple in his stubbled cheek. "You're wild, Sophie."

I snorted. "Wild? You're probably the only person in the whole world who would say that about me."

"Then maybe no one else knows the real you."

He planted a brisk wet kiss on my lips and hopped to his

feet, leaving me splayed out on the floor and stunned. *Was this the real me?*

"I'm gonna take a quick shower," he said. "Care to join me?"

"Not right now. I think I just wanna lie here another second."

"Tell you what, let's order room service." He patted a big black binder on the dining table. "Your choice. Pick something out while I shower, okay?"

He turned around and entered the bedroom, where I heard the bang of the bathroom door and the rush of water from the faucet. I stood up slowly and approached the dining table, where I thumbed mindlessly through the menus, all the while focused on the words Carson just spoke to me.

*You're wild, Sophie.*

*Disciplined. Practical. Sensible.* These were words that accurately described me. And, according to Elena, *controlling* and *passionless* also fit the bill. But wild? Not in a million years. Sure, I liked to travel a lot and try new things, and I partook in my fair share of casual sexual encounters. But I always made sure I did everything responsibly. I conducted thorough research; I made informed choices; I practiced safe sex. I was in no way wild. Was I?

*Maybe I really am wild. Maybe Carson sees the real me.*

Immediately, I rolled my eyes at how ludicrous the idea was. This couldn't be the real me, because this wasn't real life. This was vacation. Giving up my plans, taking blind chances, living in the moment: I indulged in these behaviors because I knew there was an end date, but I couldn't live like this forever. As soon as I boarded that flight back to New York, I'd go right back to disciplined, practical, sensible Sophie. Carson was seeing a very small sliver of my personality, and it wasn't representative of who I really was. There were many, many more sides to me, and not a single one of them was wild.

We'd shared some fun times and some intense orgasms, but other than that, what did Carson and I really mean to each other? In the grand scheme of things, not much. After all, if I hadn't swooped in and saved those sketches of our afternoon on the Peak, they'd be languishing in a trash heap somewhere. The memories of our conversation, the secrets we'd told each other, they'd all be thrown away and lost forever. *This is just a fling, nothing more.*

I took the big black binder in my hand and walked into the bedroom. Like the living room, it was spacious and opulent, with floor-to-ceiling windows in lieu of a back wall, inviting the city inside our private hideaway. The king-sized bed looked like a wedding cake frosted in buttercream, with its puffy down duvet and tufted velvet headboard. In the corner next to the walk-in closet, our luggage was piled on the floor. My tote bag was neatly stacked on top of my rolling suitcase, while Carson's backpack was torn open, the contents spilling out onto the rug. A sketchbook poked out from the puddle of crumpled T-shirts and boxer shorts. It was small with a faded gray cover.

Peeking over at the bathroom door to make sure it was still closed, I dropped the binder on the bed before tiptoeing over to his backpack, where I gently removed the unfamiliar sketchbook from the pile. *Let's see what kind of drawings are important enough for him to make room for.*

When I flipped the book open, my heart sped up at what I saw. It was me. Except it wasn't exactly me. It was a better version of me. My hair was tamer, my lips were fuller, my body was more voluptuous in all the right places. I kept turning pages and kept finding myself striking various poses captured in pencil. Staring off into the distance. Smiling dreamily. Sleeping peacefully. In all of them, I looked incredible. And, actually, kind of wild.

But this wasn't what I really looked like. Was it? With the book in my hand, I jumped to my feet, crossed the room, and stared at myself in the mirror. I glanced from the mirror to the book and back again, over and over, and I realized the face on the page was the same as the face in the mirror. *This is how Carson sees me, because this is who I am.*

"Going through my bag?"

At the sound of Carson's voice, I flinched, and his sketchbook tumbled to the ground at my feet. I whipped around to see him walking toward me with a towel wrapped around his waist, drops of water dripping down his bare chest.

"I'm sorry," I said. I couldn't even look him in the eye.

"It's okay." He scooped the book up from the floor and snapped it shut. "It's not like I have anything to hide."

"I just wanted to see what you were drawing."

"Well, now you know."

We stood in silence, and I stared at his feet, at a loss for words.

"Is it weird," he said, "that I'm drawing you like this?"

I took a deep breath and lifted my gaze to meet his. "No. It's really... It's nice."

"I've been doing them mostly in the mornings, before you get up."

"They're great," I said. "Just like everything you draw."

He set the book on the dresser and ran a hand through my curls. "This is one book I won't be abandoning in the sheets of some random hotel room."

My breath came fast and my tongue felt thick. I swallowed before I said, "Really?"

Carson cupped my cheek with his other hand. "Really. I need to hold on to this forever."

He wrapped his hand around the back of my neck and pulled my face in toward his. I hugged him tightly, feeling the warm damp skin of his back beneath my fingertips, and our mouths met with wild fervor. I knew how he felt about me now, that this wasn't just a fling to be forgotten. Knowing that truth, I fell deeper into his kiss, all of my questions and doubts and concerns disappearing into the ether.

I'd fallen for the impossible fantasy, and my money was already on the table. Was I just another gullible fool? Or was I about to hit the jackpot?

# chapter eleven

There's a famous landmark in Macau, the ruins of an old church, where tourists flock in droves. I'd read all about it in my guidebook; St. Paul's had been gutted by a fire in 1835, leaving behind wreckage that had since been turned into a museum. I figured it was the kind of thing Carson would want to avoid, considering his aversion to tourist traps. So when we woke up the next morning, I was surprised when he suggested we go there.

"I'd love to," I said. "You know it's going to be packed with people sightseeing, right?"

"Yeah, but I know you wanted to see it. Plus, it's supposed to be really beautiful and I can get some sketching done. We can find a quiet angle somewhere, I'm sure."

The Ruins of St. Paul's weren't far from the Grand Amadora, but we took a circuitous route to explore the city on foot. Macau was part China, part Portugal, part Caribbean island; each time we turned a corner, a different locality was revealed. A sea of mopeds lined the narrow cobblestone streets. Palm trees flanked pastel buildings with shellacked wooden shutters and wrought-iron gates. Laundry hung from balconies of run-down tenements, high above storefronts selling pastries and sheets of jerky. We ducked into shops, bought pork chop buns and egg tarts for an impromptu brunch.

The heat was palpable, a thick and sticky weight hanging heavy on my skin. I was glad I wore my sundress, the same lemon-yellow frock I wore that afternoon on the Peak. My hair was down, bouncing against my shoulders, a slave to the sultry air. Carson held my hand despite the slickness of our palms.

When we turned onto Rua de Sao Paolo, an imposing structure appeared at the top of a hill, looming high against the cloudless sky. At first glance, it seemed like any other church: a stone edifice embellished with lancet windows and religious effigies. Then I realized the blue sky was visible through the windows, and St. Paul's was merely a façade. A wall of weathered rock, with nothing behind it but steel buttresses to keep it from crumbling to the ground.

A carefully manicured garden edged the length of the stairs from the street to the base of the church. We sat on a bench at the bottom of the hill in the shade of a wide, leafy tree. Carson sketched with his book balanced on his knees while I savored my egg tart, the warm gooey custard melting on my tongue.

"You know," I said, "these egg tarts are the quintessential Macanese food."

"Is that so?" He traced the outline of the large second-story window, centered above what used to be the entrance to the church.

"Yup. You can buy them all over Macau, but the most famous ones come from a storefront in Coloane."

"They sell these little egg tarts everywhere in China, though,"

he said, his eyes still on the page. "They even had them in that little bakery in Hong Kong, where we got those pineapple buns."

"Ah, but this is not the same. This is the *Portuguese* egg tart."
I held up my half-eaten dessert and pointed to its features as I
spoke. "There are some subtle differences between this and the
varieties you'll see in China. Notice how the top of the custard is
slightly burnt, like a crème brûlée? That caramelization defines
the flavor in a different way from the more traditional Chinese
pastries."

He stopped sketching and looked up at me. From the way he
bit his bottom lip, I could tell he was holding back laughter.

"What?" I asked.

"You just seem to know an awful lot about these egg tarts,
that's all."

"I read about them in my guidebook." *When I still knew where
my guidebook was.*

"Well, you've got an incredible memory."

Shrugging, I popped the last bit of crust in my mouth. "I
just really like this kind of stuff. Travel facts, history, culture. It
sticks with me."

He pressed his pencil point back against the paper and began
shading the columns on the front of the façade. "You'd make a
great tour guide."

"That's my dream job," I said. "Ever since I was a kid, I've
been obsessed with travel planning."

"So why aren't you doing it? From that scowl you had on your
face the other day, it doesn't seem like you're too fond of your
current line of work."

"I'm not. But it pays really well. And I've got bills. Not to mention, a future to save for."

"A future in which you spend all your time scowling."

"That's not true," I said, trying really hard not to scowl. "Or fair. It's not like I have some terrible job. I get to travel the world. That's the best part about it."

"Yeah, but you don't get to travel on your own terms. You just go wherever they send you."

"Well, in real life, you have to make compromises."

"I don't think you should ever have to compromise your happiness." He said it so matter-of-factly, as if it was an obvious, undeniable truth.

I licked buttery crumbs off my bottom lip and looked off into the distance, toward the ruins. Behind the façade, there was a staircase leading to a scaffold, allowing tourists to climb up to the second-story windows and take in the views of the city. From our vantage point, the people looked like indistinguishable, faceless shadows, casting black silhouettes against the steel blue sky. But in Carson's rendering, the silhouettes didn't exist. He'd chosen to exclude them from the scene in his sketchbook, to make the picture more perfect than the reality. I thought of how flawless I seemed in those sketches he'd drawn of me, how I looked like a better version of myself.

"That's why you and I aren't compatible," I said.

Carson stopped sketching and cocked his head in my direction. "If we're not compatible, then what are we doing spending all this time together?"

"We're just having fun."

"Exactly. And we're having fun because we're compatible."

"No, we're having fun because this isn't real life."

"Of course this is real life." Carson's voice climbed an octave.

"No, it's not. Not for me anyway. It's vacation."

"Okay," he said, gesticulating with his pencil. "How are you different on vacation than you are in real life? Tell me. What are you hiding?"

"I'm not hiding anything."

"Then what is it?"

Suddenly I felt exposed, like my flimsy little sundress wasn't enough to keep me covered. Carson's eyes demanded answers. *Why can't I keep my big mouth shut?*

"It's just..." I stalled, grasping for words. "I usually don't do things like this."

"Things like what?"

"Like dropping all my plans to follow a guy around. I mean, I know it may be normal for you to pick up a different travel companion in every country you visit, but this is a totally new experience for me."

"Actually," he said, "I've never done this before."

"I don't believe you."

"Look, if you're asking me if I've hooked up with other girls on this trip, I'd be lying if I said I hadn't. But I usually say good-bye to them before the sun comes up."

I suppressed a grin. *Maybe we're more alike than I give us credit for.*

"Sorry," he said, mistaking my silence for discomfort. "I know that's TMI. I just want you to know, this isn't something I do all the time. So if that's why you think we're not compatible, you're wrong."

Not knowing what to say, I nodded, wishing I had another egg tart to shove in my mouth to avoid continuing this conversation. I silently folded the empty paper bag in half, then in quarters, folding and folding until it was a tiny little ball in the palm of my hand.

Carson cleared his throat. "So I'm having a hard time getting a read."

"What do you mean?"

"Your face," he said. "You know, I'm usually pretty good at reading faces to figure out what would go in the little thought bubble, if I were drawing your caricature. But right now, I'm stumped."

I inhaled sharply. "I think we have different philosophies on life, that's all."

"I don't disagree with you," he said. "But being different isn't necessarily a bad thing."

"I'm just saying, in real life, you and I wouldn't work. Like, for example, I'm way more conservative with money than you are."

"Okay. Don't all couples argue about money, though?"

"I suppose." I thought of how he dumped the entirety of his casino winnings into a fancy hotel suite. How he was blowing through his trust fund without keeping tabs on expenditures. In my mind, these offenses were more than subjects for mere arguments; in the context of a marriage, they would lead to all-out war. But it was a sore spot for Carson, living with the threat of sudden death, saving for a rainy day that may never come. So instead of bringing it up, I bit my lip.

"People don't have to be exactly the same to be compatible," he said.

"I think it helps."

Carson looked down at his sketchbook, ran his hand over the half-finished façade. "So you think you'd be happier with someone who had a real job? Not someone who spent all his time drawing pictures he never had any intention of selling?"

"That's not what I mean." I touched his forearm. "I love your art. I love that you're an artist. I've told you a hundred times, I think you're incredibly talented."

"Incredibly talented. But my head's in the clouds."

I winced. In avoiding one sore spot, I plunged right into another one, digging up the pain his aunt and uncle had planted inside him, the feeling of never being good enough. Why was I doing this? A gorgeous man was by my side, a man who defined romance for me, for the first time in my life, in ways I never could have imagined. Instead of losing myself in the fantasy, I kept fighting it, finding reasons to tell him no.

"You're a dreamer," I said. "The world needs dreamers. Dreamers innovate; they create; they make things beautiful. But it's not who I am."

"Who are you, then?"

"I'm a planner."

"Oh, right," he said. "Your five-year plan."

"Right."

"Maybe it's time to revise it. Or better yet, throw it away."

Fighting the urge to scowl again, I took a deep breath instead. "See? This is why I said we're not compatible."

"I'm not saying I wouldn't benefit from being a little more down to earth," he said, "but don't you think you'd benefit from being a little more spontaneous?"

"I am spontaneous! I came to Macau with you, didn't I?"

"You just told me that this isn't real life, though. What about when the vacation's over? Is it back to following your five-year plan, then? No more passion? No more fun when you go back home?"

Home. The haven I always returned to, my anchor in the choppy seas. In twenty-four hours, I'd be soaring somewhere high above the Pacific Ocean, headed back to my neat and tidy studio apartment. When the sun rose on Monday morning, I'd already be back at work, ready to tackle my next assignment, my sensible leather pumps planted firmly on the next rung of the corporate ladder. It was everything I'd ever planned for, everything I'd worked so hard to accomplish. So why did it suddenly sound so unappealing?

Carson studied my face, reading my expression, drawing the thought bubble over my head with his eyes.

"Don't go," he said.

"What?"

"Don't get on the plane tomorrow." His eyes flashed, feverish and feral. "Come travel with me."

"Carson—"

"You said you wanted to live abroad for a little while. Now's your chance. All the fun we've had this week, we could keep it going."

"But I—"

"I know you've got a bunch of excuses," he said, "but don't say no. Not yet. I want you to think about it."

"You're crazy."

"Let's just enjoy the rest of the day. You can sleep on it and tell me in the morning. Okay?"

The idea was preposterous. I had responsibilities and obligations at home, commitments Carson didn't understand. Bills to pay, work to do, plans to keep. I couldn't simply walk away from the life I'd built in New York. Could I?

"Okay."

He leaned forward and kissed me, his lips igniting a spark, setting my whole body on fire. I let the blaze consume me, falling deeper into the inferno, until all that remained was a pile of smoldering rubble.

# chapter twelve

Two hours later, we were back at the Grand Amadora, sprawled across a circular daybed at the edge of their tiled, turquoise pool. The air smelled of freesia and tanning lotion. Soft ripples danced along the surface of the clear water, and attendants brought us an endless supply of iced cocktails and frozen washcloths, protection against the oppressive afternoon heat. Carson rested his cheek on my shoulder, and the only sound I heard was the rhythmic whisper of his sleepy breathing.

To the outside observer, I was the picture of blissful calm. Oiled legs, floral bikini, sexy man beside me, just a carefree woman enjoying a romantic vacation at a luxury resort. But inside my head was a tempest of worry, a million questions ricocheting around my skull. Should I stay and travel with Carson, or should I say goodbye and go back home? I decided to do what I always did at work when I had to make a critical decision but the answer was not immediately clear: I weighed the pros and cons.

Pro: This was the most fun I'd had in my entire life.

Con: If I didn't show up to work on Monday, I'd probably be out of a job.

Pro: I'd prove Elena wrong about her whole "controlling and passionless" comment.

Con: I'd give up everything I had going on in my life in pursuit of a good-looking guy.

When I considered the implications of the cons, it was hard to justify choosing to stay. All the pros in the world couldn't outweigh the sacrifices I'd be making, all because Carson asked me to. For years, I'd been chasing down my goals, investing all my time and effort toward achieving them. I wasn't about to trade it all for the uncertainty and instability of a torrid affair, no matter how euphoric I felt in the moment. Who knew how long this could possibly last?

Carson inhaled deeply, rousing from his sunbaked snooze, and I felt his fingertips caress my thigh. Pressing his lips against my earlobe, he whispered, "Wanna go up to the room?"

Pro: The sex was incredible.

Just like that, the raging storm within me subsided, and I trailed him blindly into the elevator, up to our room, onto our king-sized bed, where we stayed until the sun disappeared behind the mountains.

* * *

In the evening, when Carson heard my stomach grumble, he asked, "Should we go out for dinner?"

I scoffed at the thought of putting on clothes, reached instead for the big black binder.

"Order something good," I said, and tossed the book at him before retreating to the bathroom to fill the tub with warm water and frothy bubbles. I left the door open, an invitation for him to join me, which he did, armed with two long-stemmed flutes and a half bottle of champagne he'd taken from the minibar.

"Food will be here in a half hour." He lowered himself into the Jacuzzi and handed me a drink before raising his glass in a toast. "To rolling the dice."

"To taking a chance."

"To us."

We clinked glasses and I took a long sip, feeling the frosty fizz slide down my throat. I thought back to our first champagne toast when we arrived in the room, the giddy high I'd been on in the wake of the big win. Before Carson had placed his bet, there were so many questions I'd had about his motivation, so many doubts I'd had about his character. Once the adrenaline kicked in, I'd forgotten all about them, but now they floated back up to the surface of my brain, begging to be answered.

"So do you go to casinos very often?" I was aiming for a casual and disinterested tone of voice.

"No," he said. "But after yesterday I'm beginning to think I should."

"Not much of a gambler, then?"

"No way. In fact, the Grand Amadora is the first casino I've ever been to."

"Really? How is that even possible?"

"I don't know. It's not like I ever had a lot of money to gamble with before I got this inheritance, so I was never really interested."

"But the first thing you wanted to do when we got off the ferry was go to a casino. You wouldn't even look for a hotel room until you'd seen the inside of one." My casual and disinterested tone of voice was fading; instead, I sounded like a detective coercing a suspect to confess his crime.

"Yeah, but gambling is what Macau is known for. Once we got here and I saw the big buildings and the flashing lights, I was kind of hypnotized. Don't you feel that way? Isn't it all kind of hypnotizing?"

"I guess." Carson had a point. I'd been in a bit of a trance since I got here. I wasn't sure if the bright lights of Macau were to blame, or if something else had cast a spell on me.

"I wasn't really thinking," he continued. "I wandered around the casino floor, and I saw that table, and the next thing I knew I was placing a bet."

"You seemed pretty nervous after you laid down your chips. For a second, I thought you were gambling away the last of your cash."

"I *was* nervous. I mean, it was only sixty bucks. Sixty bucks isn't going to make or break me. Not since I got my inheritance. But it still would've sucked to lose."

"I know what you mean," I said. "I hate that feeling of slipping a dollar into a slot machine, and then—poof!—it instantly disappears. It just seems like a huge waste. Like, why did I bother, when I know the odds are stacked against me?"

We raised our glasses to our lips and sat listening to the soapy bubbles crackle softly all around us.

"I think it would've sucked more to never know, though," Carson said. "To always wonder what might have happened if I'd been brave enough to take the chance."

His words shot through my chest like a lightning bolt, triggering the storm within me to rise up once more. The choice I made tomorrow could lead to a lifetime of regret. If I said goodbye to Carson, there was a high probability I'd never see him again. If I decided to stay with him, my career would come to a standstill. Surely, I could find another job to pay my bills, but I'd never be able to find another Carson.

Dinner arrived with a knock on the door, a three-course meal of traditional Macanese specialties: shellfish and rice tinged with tomato sauce; roasted chicken in a rich, spiced stew; and *minchi*, the national dish, consisting of minced beef stir-fried with potatoes and topped with a runny, golden egg. We ate wordlessly, wrapped in our bathrobes, the only sounds made by silver chopsticks tinkling against our porcelain plates.

After finishing the last of our champagne, we moved on to the *vinho verde* he'd ordered with dinner. By the time we discarded our robes and dove back under the sheets, both bottles had been drained, and my head was swimming. All night, I floated between the two worlds of possibility stretching out before me. One moment, I'd be convinced this was a fantasy, never meant to last. Then he'd kiss me, run his hands down the length of my body, and I'd think, *How could I ever let this go?*

When the first gray light of dawn glowed on the horizon, I realized I'd never slept. With my mind consumed by doubt and my body tied up by passion, sleeping seemed beside the point, a waste of precious, limited time. Soon I'd have to crawl out of bed, pack my bag, and figure out where I was going. To the airport or to the unknown?

The clock read 5:45. If I wanted to catch my flight, I'd need to be strapped into a seat on the ferry in an hour and fifteen minutes. But I found it impossible to move, to leave the comfort I had found beneath these sheets, knowing I may never return. Pressing myself into Carson's side, I ran my fingers along the tree trunk emblazoned on his chest, marveling again at the smoothness of his tattooed skin. The ink was visible but not tangible, like a mirage in the sweltering desert.

"What does it mean?" I asked.

"What does what mean?"

"Your tattoo. What does it mean?"

"Seize the day," he said. "We could die at any time. Gotta live while we're alive."

"I know what 'carpe diem' means. I meant the tree."

"Oh." He hesitated, raked his fingers through his tousled, sleepy hair. "Remember I told you about that house I grew up in with my mom and dad?"

"The one in San Diego?"

"Yeah. This is the tree that was in the backyard. At least, this is how I remember it. I was only three when I left."

"Wow." I was moved by the unexpected meaning behind the image.

He covered my hand with his palm, pressed it against his chest. "That house was the only place that ever felt like home. Now I carry it with me, over my heart. So home is wherever I happen to be."

In that instant, I realized exactly how different Carson and I really were. Sure, I loved to travel, but I also loved having a home to return to. A physical space, an anchor, a place to store my fireproof box of important papers. What's more, I always needed to know where I was headed. I needed the comfort and stability of a plan. Carson floated through the world, aimless, like a feather on the breeze. No goals. No plans. No home to return to. Carson was wild. But that wasn't me.

As I saw it, I didn't really have much of a choice.

"I can't," I said. "I'm sorry."

He closed his eyes, knowing what I meant. There was no need to elaborate, no more questions to be asked. Our vacation was over, and it was time for me to return to real life. Still, I couldn't bring myself to get out of bed. I needed one more taste of the fantasy before I let it go forever.

There were so many things I wanted him to know. How much fun I'd had. How much I would miss him. How much he meant to me. But my mouth had trouble forming the words. So instead I kissed his body, slowly, tenderly, covering his chest, his stomach, the thin line of hair trailing downward from his navel. I let my actions speak the truth of my emotions, the feelings I wouldn't allow myself to speak.

\* \* \*

We packed our bags without a sound, racing against the clock, the mood too thick for mindless banter or clever commentary. Carson hauled his backpack to the hallway, while I lingered behind to do my usual last-minute check for items we may have forgotten. The bathrooms, the closets, the cushions of the sofa.

Everything was empty. Finally, I pulled back the rumpled covers of the king-sized bed, expecting to find another sketchbook, but to my surprise, there was nothing.

*Maybe he really does plan to keep those sketches of me. Or maybe he'll meet a new woman and start a new sketchbook. Then my face will wind up abandoned in another set of sheets. He'll move on. He always does.*

I unzipped the front pocket of my suitcase and pulled out the sketchbook I'd plucked from the sheets in our Hong Kong hotel room. Flipping through the textured vellum, I relived the memories, the sights of the city drawn out in smudged graphite, our time together filtered through Carson's eyes. When I found the scene from Victoria Peak, the view of the harbor from high above the skyscrapers, I took a long last look.

*I don't have room for this.* I set the book down on the mattress, covered it with a sheet, and wheeled my suitcase out the door without turning back.

Not a word was uttered in the elevator, on the drive to the ferry terminal, or while waiting to board the tottering boat. Our usual repartee had vanished, as if a cord linking us together had unexpectedly snapped, breaking our connection, sending us soaring off in different directions.

As the ferry made its way across the water, I forced a conversation, afraid to spend our last moments together in silence.

"Where are you going next?" I asked.

"Not sure yet." He was turned toward the window, looking at the horizon through the filthy, foggy glass. "I might stay put in Hong Kong a little while. See if that hostel still has vacancies."

"Back to the snoring Aussies?"

"Maybe. Or maybe I'll spring for a private room this time."

"The Chrysanthemum Suite spoiled you."

"Yeah." He turned away from the window, searched my face. "I think I'm getting tired of all this running around. It might be nice to just sit still for a second."

A vision flashed before my eyes: me and Carson, sitting still on Victoria Peak, high above the city. Wind rustling through the trees, sun beaming down on my face, his hand on my lap and my head on his shoulder. *The universe has its reasons for bringing people together.* Blinking once, twice, I cleared the image away, saw only Carson looking at me with expectation. I swallowed hard, unable to find my voice.

"Or maybe I'll get restless and take off again tomorrow," he said, turning back to the window. "I guess I'll have to see how I feel when I wake up."

With nothing left to say, I rested my hand in his lap, and we sat quietly until the ferry docked in Hong Kong. When the doors opened, we were swept away in the crowd of people streaming off the ramp and into the bowels of the subway.

"You don't have to come all the way to the airport with me," I said, but Carson ignored me and tapped his Octopus card twice at the turnstile: once for me, once for himself. At Central Station, we transferred to the Airport Express and spent most of the half-hour journey in uncomfortable silence. He fixed his stare at the scenery rushing by beyond the window, his chin resting in his fist. The whole ride, I touched him, caressing his arm or gently squeezing his thigh. Any small gesture to maintain physical contact while I still had the chance.

At the airport, the check-in lines for Cathay Pacific snaked around the terminal. I headed for the self-serve kiosk, proud of my ability to fit a vacation's worth of clothing into a carry-on tote and a small rolling suitcase, eliminating the need to check a bag. The machine spit out my boarding pass in under a minute, leaving me free to go straight to security. Normally I'd have rejoiced at getting through the check-in process so quickly, but when I turned from the screen to face Carson, I wished I hadn't been in such a rush.

"This is it," he said. He scanned the security line off to the right before settling his eyes on mine. I saw what looked like panic flash across his face, the first trace of anxiety he'd displayed since that moment in Macau, just after the dealer waved his hands over the table, just before the dice revealed his fortune. A knot formed in my stomach and I could feel the bitter burn of my morning coffee crawling up my throat.

"You know," he said, "it's not too late to change your mind."

"Carson, I can't."

"Why not?"

The knot in my stomach grew tighter. I had an overwhelming urge to bum-rush the security guard, barrel through the metal detectors, and hurl myself onto the next departing plane.

"Because I have a job to get back to," I said.

"You don't even like your job."

"Yes, I do."

"You told me the only thing you like about it is that it lets you travel the world. You don't need your job for that. You can travel the world with me."

He reached for my hand, and I pulled away. "I can't just wander aimlessly around the world with you. I need to know where I'm going."

"It's fine to want to know where you're going. But wherever you're going, it should be a place that makes you happy. Are you happy?"

His eyes settled on me like two blue laser beams. The heat was so intense, I had to look away.

"Are you happy, Sophie?" he asked again.

"I'm fine."

"It doesn't sound like you're fine. It sounds like you're afraid."

Why did everyone think they knew me better than I knew myself? Elena, Grandma, and now Carson—a guy I'd met less than a week ago. I'd had enough of other people psychoanalyzing me, telling me how I was supposed to feel.

Tipping my suitcase onto its back wheels, I began to walk away. "I'm going to miss my flight."

"Sophie." Carson grasped my arm, his voice urgent.

"What?"

"How can I reach you?"

"I don't know," I said. "You don't check your e-mail. You refuse to own a cell phone. Maybe carrier pigeon?"

"I'm serious. What's your number? Or your address? This can't be the last time we ever see each other."

His gaze turned from steely to pleading. With a heavy sigh,

I reached into my carry-on bag and unearthed a blue and gold McKinley business card with "Sophie Bruno" printed on the front.

"This is where I work," I said, handing it to him. "My cell number's on there."

He held my card with two hands, staring at it for a long moment. "I'll be in touch."

I nodded impatiently. This good-bye was taking way longer than I'd hoped it would.

"I love you," he said.

"I love you, too." The words took me by surprise as soon as they escaped my lips. *Did I really just say that? Did I mean it? Does it even matter now?*

Carson pulled me close and kissed me. A deep, openmouthed, all-consuming kiss. I fell into his arms, surrendering to his touch. For a second, I forgot I was in the middle of a crowded international airport. Instead, I was in Wan Chai, standing in a secluded corner of the waterfront promenade, with the early morning bay breeze blowing through my hair and every skin cell tingling with desire. When he withdrew, I opened my eyes and a wave of disappointment crashed around me.

"Good-bye," he said.

"Bye." I turned and walked toward the security line with my head down, fumbling around in my purse for my passport, fighting off the stinging, swollen feeling behind my eyes. *Deep breaths. Don't make a scene.*

I managed to crack a smile when I reached the black barrier tape, the security agent at the end of the line scrutinizing my face against my photo ID. When she waved me on, I turned around, longing for one last glance of his blue eyes, his sandy hair. But all I saw was an unattended self-serve kiosk and a mob of weary travelers.

Carson was gone.

# chapter thirteen

I cried the whole flight home. I'm not a cry-in-public sort of person, but I couldn't control myself. As soon as the plane picked up speed on the runway, a lump formed in my throat, growing tighter the higher we climbed through the air, until finally it burst and broke me down. Desperate not to attract attention from fellow fliers, I choked back my tears, closed my eyes, and dabbed at them with tissues. When I felt a spate of sobs coming on, I escaped to the privacy of the bathroom to set them free. By the time the plane landed at JFK late on Saturday night, my eyes were bloodshot, but the tears had mercifully stopped. In the cab on the way to my apartment, I drifted off. Upon reaching home, I dropped my bags at the foot of the bed and fell asleep as soon as my head hit the pillow.

On Sunday morning, I lingered in the sheets, caressing the empty space beside me in my queen-sized bed. Before I met Carson, waking up alone had been the norm. In fact, it'd been what I preferred: the uncomplicated silence of solitude. Now the quiet felt endlessly gloomy, like a part of me had been left behind on the other end of the earth.

*Watch out. You're beginning to sound like Elena.*

I tossed back the sheets and hopped to my feet, determined to transition out of my dreamy vacation mind-set and back to the rigors of real life. I made my bed, put on a pot of coffee, and tied my frizzy nest of hair up in a bun. Then I took a deep breath and knelt on the floor next to my luggage. It was time to put this trip behind me.

Unzipping my suitcase, I thought of how many times I had unpacked this bag, only to pack it again hours later. Dozens. Maybe even over a hundred. This time would certainly be no different. Because, in all likelihood, I'd be back on another airplane by sundown the next day, headed toward whatever big project I was assigned to. My flight was probably already booked, and our corporate travel agent was likely waiting for me to confirm receipt of the itinerary.

A twinge of disappointment rippled through me when I realized I could no longer ignore my phone. I found it in my tote bag, buried underneath ticket stubs and used tissues. The charger was sitting on my nightstand, where I'd left it before I took off for Hong Kong. I plugged it in and powered it on, and while the silver start-up circle spun on the screen, I marveled at how great it had been to unchain myself from it, how restorative the break from work had been. Whatever consequence I had to face for skipping that meeting with Martin Chu, it almost certainly would have been worth it.

When the home screen loaded, a voice mail alert flashed red on the screen. Assuming it was the travel desk with the details of my next international assignment, I pressed the call button and pulled a pen from my purse, prepared to jot down my flight number.

"Sophie? Are you home yet?"

I dropped my pen and pressed my fingers to my temples. The message was not from McKinley's travel desk. It was from my grandmother.

"Call me when you get this. I thought you landed last night. Where are you? I'm very worried."

She hung up abruptly, most likely to continue pacing around her kitchen in a full-blown panic. Immediately, I dialed her number. It only rang once.

"Hello?"

"Hi, Gram."

"Oh thank God, you're home! When did you land?"

"I got in really late last night." In truth, I'd arrived right after sundown. I just hadn't been willing to face real life yet. And nothing was realer than Grandma's inquisitions. "I only woke up a few minutes ago."

"How was your flight?"

"It was fine. On time, no bumps." *Though there were a few tears.*

"I was so worried with you being alone that whole time, and so far away. I'm so glad you're safe. And home."

I cradled the phone in the crook of my neck and turned my attention to removing dirty clothes from the suitcase, methodically sorting the laundry into piles of light, dark, and dry-clean only. The orderly task gave me something to focus on aside from Grandma's worry.

"I'm fine, Gram."

"I saw your idiot friend yesterday," she said.

"Who?"

"Elena. She was over at her mother's house with that loser

boyfriend of hers, packing up a truck. Made a racket outside all morning. Is she moving in with that jerk?"

"That was the plan." *But I didn't think it was going to happen so fast.*

"Shacking up together, and they're not even married. It's disgraceful."

I balled up a pair of dirty jeans and flung them in the dark pile, suppressing a sigh of aggravation. My grandmother was the first person I called after arriving home from the most momentous, life-changing travel experience I'd ever had. And she'd yet to ask me how it went, what I did, if I had a good time. Instead, she decided to rag on Elena for her choices in life and disparage her boyfriend, whom she'd only met once.

"Well, she seems really happy with Roddy," I said. "They're definitely in love."

"Love," she snorted. "That's a laugh. Is love a good reason to have left you all alone?"

I plucked my lemon-yellow sundress from the suitcase, recalling the last time I wore it in Macau. Holding hands with Carson, following him through the sunny streets toward the beautiful ruins, where he asked me to stay with him. An invitation to travel indefinitely, with no boundaries and no rules. Just a chance to chase down happiness, and I didn't take it. I had a home; I had a job; I had other plans. Were these all good reasons for turning him down?

"I wasn't exactly alone," I said.

"What are you talking about?"

"I kind of met someone while I was there."

"What do you mean, 'you kind of met someone'?"

"I met a guy."

I didn't know why I was telling her this. She wouldn't be happy for me; she wouldn't understand. She would only be judgmental, and I would only be upset. But I couldn't stop. The words just flowed from my heart to my mouth, with no filter.

"Oh God." Her voice was morose and foreboding, as if I'd just announced a natural disaster instead of a romance. "So, what, are you moving to Hong Kong now?"

"No!" I said. "It wasn't anything serious. We were just having fun."

"Yeah, I know what 'fun' means, Sophie. I wasn't born yesterday. You better not wind up pregnant. You'll ruin your life."

I bit my tongue and counted silently to five. If I didn't, I'd say something I'd later regret. I knew exactly what my grandmother was implying. That my mother ruined her life by having me and ran off when she couldn't take the pressure. That if I wasn't careful, I'd end up exactly like her.

"So who was this that you met?" she asked.

"His name is Carson."

"Does he live in Hong Kong?"

"No, he was traveling. He's from San Francisco."

"What does he do for a living?"

To my grandmother, this was the most important question of all. The question by which she would determine Carson's worth as an individual. And I knew how she'd feel about the truth. *Better make up some lie. Like he's a doctor or an investment banker or something.*

"He's an artist." *Nice going.*

"Is he famous?"

"No."

"So he's broke." It was a statement, not a question. She'd already drawn her conclusions about him. I furrowed my brow and scolded myself for confiding in her. *Why can't I ever keep my big mouth shut?*

"No, actually," I said. "He's got plenty of money. He paid for a really beautiful suite for us in Macau."

"Macau? I thought you were in Hong Kong."

It was clear that my big mouth had a mind of its own. "We were only there for a couple of nights."

"Isn't that the city with all the casinos?"

"Yes, but there's more to it than—"

"So he's a gambler, too? Sounds like a dream."

"It *was* a dream." My voice boomed, unintentionally, and the sound made me flinch. No matter how annoyed or frustrated my grandmother made me, I never raised my voice to her. *Deep breaths. She only does this because she loves you.*

"I'm sorry," I continued. "I didn't mean to yell. It's just that first you were worried about me traveling through Hong Kong alone. But now I told you that I was actually with someone— someone who treated me wonderfully, by the way—and you have nothing but negative things to say."

"Because you should be with someone who deserves you, Sophie," she said. "Someone who's worth being with, someone with a bright future. Not some flighty artist with a gambling problem. Not some nobody."

"You don't know the first thing about him."

"Do you think you know him so well? When did you meet him, a week ago? Gallivanting around in a foreign country, playing blackjack and drinking and doing God knows what else? How do you know he was telling you the truth?"

"It was just . . . I had a feeling about him. I felt like he was being honest with me."

"Sophie, sweetie, please. You're too smart for this nonsense. You've come so far and accomplished so much in your life. Don't let some man make a mess of it."

"I would never do that," I said. When I looked around, though, I couldn't help but notice the mess I was currently in. Piles of laundry, an unmade bed, and a tote bag full of tissues I'd used to wipe away my tears on that long, weepy trip back home. *When men get too close, they make a mess of things.* It was a lesson Grandma taught me years ago, a mantra I'd repeated in my head over and over a thousand times. So when I met Carson, why had I chosen to ignore it?

"Don't let anyone distract you from your plans, Sophie."

"I know, Gram."

"Will I see you on Sunday?"

"If I'm in town. I'm not sure if I'll be traveling next weekend. I haven't checked my e-mail yet."

"Well, let me know. I love you."

"I love you, too."

I hung up the phone, dejected and feeling like a fool. Even though I was reluctant to admit it, Grandma was right. After spending only a week together, Carson and I didn't really know each other. He thought I was wild, after all, and nothing could be further from the truth. I was disciplined, sensible, and practical. And what did I know of him? Not all that much. He liked to draw. He had a trust fund. He refused to make plans for his future. Essentially, he was bobbing around the open seas without a compass or an anchor. I could never do that. I needed a state-of-the-art GPS. And I needed a destination.

Carson was a dreamer, and I was a planner. I had fun playing make-believe inside our little bubble of romance, when I had unplugged from the rest of the world and decided to live in the moment. Now the bubble had burst, because I'd plugged myself back in, and in real life, we would never work. For me, real life wasn't about living in the moment; it was about moving up, moving forward, moving on. And that's exactly what I had to do. Move on.

I peered at my phone and pulled up my e-mail. There were a little over a hundred new messages. Not too bad for a week away from the office. I scrolled through them, expecting to find some information about my next assignment. But there was no project plan, no schedule, no travel itinerary. Only a bunch of mass e-mails on which I'd been blind-copied and about two dozen increasingly urgent messages from Elizabeth. Her subject lines read things like, *Please provide status update,* and *Martin Chu has been waiting for you all morning,* and *Where are you?* The very latest one had a timestamp of six o'clock this morning. Elizabeth had been working way before I'd even opened my eyes.

To: Sophie Bruno
From: Elizabeth Fischman
Subject: Status

I thought you were returning from Hong Kong yesterday. I have not heard from you in six days. Please send me notice as soon as you read this.

Unsurprisingly, Elizabeth had been less than thrilled with my decision to unplug from work for the week. I tapped the REPLY button and jotted off a hasty response.

To: Elizabeth Fischman
From: Sophie Bruno
Subject: re: Status

I'm back. Sorry I've been out of contact; I had some technical difficulties with my phone. Do you know where my next assignment will be? I haven't heard from the travel desk yet.

I hit SEND and continued to scroll through my inbox, where I noticed a number of messages from Elena. Yet another person who was eager for me to get in touch with her as soon as I was back in town. After dealing with my grandmother and Elizabeth, though, I wasn't sure if I could handle another discussion in which I had to apologize for being out of reach or defend any of my choices. I knew I had to respond to Elena, but now was not the time.

Instead, I leaned over to empty out the last items from my suitcase. Underneath my black ballet flats, I noticed a tear in the polyester lining of my bag.

"Shit," I said, thinking there'd be no time to repair it before I had to pack again. Inspecting the ripped fabric, I briefly considered whipping out my travel sewing kit to perform a little impromptu surgery, when I saw something had fallen underneath it, trapped between the lining and the outer plastic case. I reached inside, pulled it out, and was surprised to find my long forgotten guidebook. The front cover was bent back and the spine was torn, a victim of my neglect. I flipped through it, looking at all the dog-eared pages, the sights I never saw, the itinerary I never followed. They were the best plans I ever abandoned.

Out of the corner of my eye, I spotted the blue light on my phone flashing. An e-mail had arrived. Looked like Elizabeth was still hard at work.

To: Sophie Bruno
From: Elizabeth Fischman
Subject: re: Status

Please be in my office at 8AM tomorrow. We have a lot to discuss.

# chapter fourteen

The next morning, before the sun rose, I walked from my apartment on 44th and 10th to McKinley headquarters on 42nd and 6th. At dawn, Broadway was shuttered and Times Square was eerily subdued. The empty streets were slick with the remnants of an overnight rainfall, and I stepped carefully to avoid puddles, the rubber soles of my sensible pumps thudding lightly against the damp pavement. Most of the city was just rolling out of bed, but I was wide awake and wired. Because after reading that e-mail from Elizabeth, I hadn't slept all night. All I did was toss and turn, scolding myself for my irresponsible behavior. When my phone died in Hong Kong, I should've run out to the nearest electronics store and bought a replacement charger. I should've stuck to my original plan of visiting Martin Chu. And I definitely should've kept in touch with Elizabeth the whole time. What did I do instead? I locked my phone away in the hotel room safe and jumped back into bed with Carson.

I'd always been proud of my ability to shut down the outside world and zero in on my work with single-minded vision, like I was looking through the crosshairs of a rifle. But in Hong Kong, I'd let my target get away from me, lost in a daydream, preoccupied with a silly fantasy. Really, that's all my relationship with

Carson was: a silly fantasy. It wasn't love. How could it have been? Like Grandma said, we barely knew each other. And what I knew of him was completely wrong for me.

So anytime my thoughts wandered thousands of miles away—anytime I found myself picturing Carson's eyes, his hair, the tattoo on his chest—I quickly swept them out of my mind. My job was at risk and my head was a mess, all because I'd allowed myself to fall for someone who I knew from the start would never work out. Someone who distracted me from my plans.

I pushed through the revolving glass doors at One Bryant Park and strode through the cavernous lobby toward the second row of elevator banks, where I swiped my badge at the turnstile and pressed the button for the thirty-fifth floor. McKinley occupied three entire floors of the building, and rumor had it they were in the process of acquiring a fourth. It was a period of explosive growth for the firm, having been ranked by Forbes as the nation's third most prestigious consulting group three years in a row. In certain circles, a business card with the McKinley logo was a status symbol. Even after three years on the job, I still felt a rush when I handed someone that little blue and gold rectangle.

There were no assigned cubicles in the office for traveling consultants, only a neat row of white desks with ergonomic black chairs, available for temporary visitors and transients waiting for their next assignments. At this hour of the morning, there were a few stray employees scattered around the workspace, none of whom I recognized. McKinley employed hundreds of people across the globe, all of them traveling from office to office, wherever their skill set was needed most. I'd often be partnered with someone on a project for weeks, sit next to them at conference room tables for fourteen hours a day, and then once our assignment came to an end, I'd never see them again. Such was the nature of the traveling consultant. Getting close and then saying good-bye.

Sitting at a desk next to a window overlooking the park, I popped my laptop out of my bag, plugged it in, and fired it up. There were no new messages in my work inbox. No itineraries from the travel desk, no schedules for the upcoming week. I should've already known the details of my next assignment by now. That I had no hint of where I'd be going was troublesome, to say the least.

I took a deep breath and skimmed the headlines of the *Wall Street Journal* and the *Financial Times*. Concentration was futile, though, because I kept thinking about the impending meeting with Elizabeth. In my head, I ran through all the excuses I could think of to justify why I'd spent the past week ignoring all her e-mails. *I didn't have my phone charger. I was on vacation. We all need some time to unplug and unwind, right?*

Finally, at ten to eight, I yanked the power cord from the side of my laptop, packed my bag, and gripped the handles tightly in one fist. With my chin in the air and my shoulders pushed back, I walked down the hall to Elizabeth's office, exuding all the false confidence I could muster. When I knocked on the door, her muffled voice beckoned me inside, and I ducked my head around the door frame to find her slouching behind her mahogany desk, scowling down at her computer screen while her fingers flew across the keyboard at full speed.

Without looking up, she snapped, "Why have you been out of contact for the last six days?"

*Good morning to you, too.*

I lowered myself into the leather guest chair, trying to recall all the lines I'd been inwardly rehearsing all morning. "I accidentally left my phone charger at home."

"You couldn't purchase a replacement charger in Hong Kong?"

"W-well," I stuttered, "you see, I wasn't exactly intending for Hong Kong to be a business trip. It was more of a pleasure trip."

The clacking of keys halted abruptly as she turned to face me. "A pleasure trip." She tested the words out on her tongue, like she was repeating a foreign phrase.

"Yes. A vacation."

When I saw Elizabeth's sour expression—the puckered lips and flared nostrils—I knew I had made a grave error in my choice of words.

"You are expected to remain accessible at all times. Furthermore, when I approved this time off, I made it clear you were to check in with Martin Chu in the Hong Kong office while you were overseas."

"I'm sorry," I said. "I didn't know he'd be waiting for me all morning. I didn't realize it was a required meeting. Since it was technically my 'time off.'"

By now, I was pretty sure I saw thin wisps of smoke escape from her ears. I knew damn well I was expected to work while I was in Hong Kong; I'd simply chosen not to. And Elizabeth was fully aware that my declaration of ignorance was a bold-faced lie.

"Do you know how lucky you are to have this job, Sophie? Do you know how many people would kill to be in your place?"

"I—"

"The correct answer is two thousand five hundred and sixty. That's how many applicants we had for a single open junior analyst position last month."

I gripped the armrests and kept my lips tightly sealed. Obviously, Elizabeth had no interest in what I had to say on the matter. This was a one-sided conversation, in which she lectured and I listened.

"You showed great promise when you were first hired, but frankly, I'm beginning to question your dedication to this organization. So if you don't want to work at McKinley, then there's a long line of bright, young, talented prospects just waiting to scoop up your position."

Suddenly, I envisioned myself being forced to surrender my smartphone and laptop at the front desk. Jeanette, our receptionist, would give me a pitying look, and security would escort me through the lobby of the building until I was safely out on the sidewalk. Word of my poor performance would spread rapidly throughout the industry, and as a result, I'd be blacklisted from ever attaining another job as an IT consultant. Without my generous salary, I would no longer be able to afford my fancy Manhattan digs, and thus I'd have no other choice but to pack up all my belongings and move to a run-down hovel in the farthest reaches of Queens—or heaven forbid, back to my old bedroom in New Jersey with Grandma, who would never let me forget about the miserable failure my life had become, all because I'd decided to screw around with some guy.

At times like these, there was nothing left to do but grovel. "I swear I won't disappoint you on my next assignment." I sat so far forward on the edge of my seat that I almost fell off. "Wherever you choose to send me next, I will give a hundred and ten percent of my efforts."

Elizabeth turned back to her computer. For the next few moments, she clicked her mouse, while we sat there in palpable silence. Her pale face glowed green in the light of her widescreen monitor. Finally, she said, "I think an in-house job might be best for you at the moment."

What should have been an overwhelming sense of relief at having preserved my employment was quickly eclipsed by a wave of distress. In-house jobs were arguably a fate worse than New Jersey. I knew I'd be assigned to a project with a partner who was either fresh out of college or completely incompetent, meaning I'd be bearing the brunt of the work. It was an open secret that in-house jobs were reserved for the lowest people on the totem pole, people who couldn't be trusted to work unsupervised. As expected, I had a lot of in-house jobs when I first started out at McKinley, but after six months of diligent service within the New York office, I learned the ropes pretty thoroughly and was finally given the green light to begin working all around the globe. Up until this point, I'd only ever returned to the New York office for two reasons: biannual performance reviews and McKinley's yearly over-the-top holiday party. So the fact that I was now assigned to an in-house project did not bode well for my status at the company.

Not to mention, for me, the sole redeeming quality of this increasingly miserable job was the perk of traveling the world. I wasn't sure if I could tolerate being stuck at home for weeks on end. Especially if I'd be spending lots of one-on-one time with Elizabeth, like this, sitting in a state of catlike readiness while she glowered at me from the other side of her desk.

"Are you sure you don't need me to join up with the team working on Crawford Capital over in London?" I suggested, desperation seeping from my pores. "Or maybe send me to Asia? I really enjoyed my time in Hong Kong. I'd love to go back, if I could be of any use on a project over there."

"Ha!" It was the first time I think I'd ever heard Elizabeth laugh. "After the way you blew off your meeting with Martin Chu, I don't think anyone in the entire Asia division is eager to work with you."

*Great. Looks like news of my bad reputation has already started to spread.*

"No," she said. "We have internal IT audits coming up in four weeks. So you'll be working on gathering the data necessary for our auditors to facilitate their expedient implementation. And you'll be partnered with Seth Ramsey."

I discreetly inspected the corners of the room for hidden cameras. At this point, I was convinced that Elizabeth must be playing some sort of cruel prank on me. But no, it turned out she was completely serious about assigning me to a shitty internal audit with the notoriously lazy and inept son of John Ramsey, one of the partners who'd founded McKinley thirty years prior. Seth was a few years older than me but graduated from college—without honors—eighteen months after I did. Once the job market chewed him up and spat him back out, he went running to Daddy for employment. So his father hired him on as a junior analyst—apparently, he didn't have to wait in line with the other two thousand five hundred and sixty candidates—but Seth quickly proved himself useless and was relegated to a position as a permanent in-house staffer. Oblivious to his own total lack of skill or smarts, he'd convinced himself he was the hottest guy to ever walk the halls of One Bryant Park.

I'd also made the terrible mistake of having sex with him.

Really, *really* bad sex.

It only happened once, at the last McKinley holiday party. I place the blame squarely on Jeanette, for mixing up such delicious eggnog that I couldn't stop refilling my cup. After my fourth—or possibly fifth—visit to the punch bowl, Seth's smarmy pickup lines started to seem less oily and more charming, and I followed him back to his office on the thirty-third floor for what I thought would be an exciting romp. Three minutes later, I was bent over the spare desk with my skirt hiked above my hips, and Seth was already collapsed in a postorgasmic heap. It was, quite possibly, the most disappointing sexual encounter I'd ever had.

Thinking back on it, I wasn't really attracted to *him*, per se. Sure, he was good-looking—if you're into run-of-the-mill ivory-skinned preppy boys—but what turned me on more than anything else was his invincibility. The idea that he could do whatever he wanted around this company and he'd never lose his job. He had what every other McKinley employee craved: power, influence, and the ability to get John Ramsey on the phone with a snap of his fingers.

Of course, after that unsatisfying quickie, the allure of his power promptly disappeared. I hadn't seen him since, and I assumed I could successfully avoid him for the remainder of my tenure at McKinley. I hadn't planned on ever sinking so low as to be assigned to another in-house project. Or being partnered with the firm's most unqualified staff member, the guy who put in zero effort but would never be fired, merely because of his last name.

If I'd had the slightest bit of courage or self-respect, I would have told Elizabeth to go to hell and quit on the spot. Instead, I whimpered a feeble, "Okay," and sat there while she dictated a three-page to-do list.

"That just about covers what we'll need completed by Friday," she said.

"*This* Friday?"

"We're on a very tight timeline, Sophie." She turned back to her computer. "You can get started right away. Seth's office is on the thirty-third floor. He's got an extra desk in there you can use."

*I'm familiar with that office. And that extra desk.*

I excused myself and made a beeline for the stairwell, where I could hyperventilate in private. Elizabeth said I'd started this job with such promise. But now it was clear my career was on a vertiginous nosedive, and I was having a hard time pinpointing exactly when things began to head south. It was easy to say Carson had distracted me from my plans, but truthfully, I'd started slacking off before I'd even packed my bags for Hong Kong. If my head had really been in the game, I never would've forgotten to put my phone charger in my suitcase. What's more, as soon as I discovered it was missing, I would've run out and bought a replacement. I wouldn't have slowly allowed the battery to drain as it sat untouched in the hotel room safe. The fact is, I wanted to forget about work, long before Carson ever entered the picture.

What I needed to do was recapture my sense of commitment. It had temporarily fallen by the wayside, but now that I'd returned from vacation, it was time to buckle down and show Elizabeth just how determined and competent I was. I'd blow her away with my professional attitude and my efficient, expert performance on these internal audits. When it was over, she'd be so impressed that she'd ask Martin Chu to reconsider my lifetime ban from the Asia division.

*Yes. I can do this.* With my breath steadied, I walked down to the thirty-third floor and emerged from the stairwell with a new sense of purpose. When I reached Seth's office, the lights were still out. Naturally, he hadn't arrived yet; it wasn't even nine o'clock, and he routinely rolled in after ten. So I took advantage of the quiet and began to set up my workspace on the empty spare desk. With my laptop, legal pad, and highlighter pens carefully arranged on the black leather desk blotter, it was starting to look less like the site of my last bad decision and more like the place where I'd rebuild my damaged reputation.

An hour and forty-five minutes later, I'd already checked off the first two items on Elizabeth's lengthy to-do list. I was confident. Undaunted. On top of the world.

And then Seth appeared.

"Well, well, well." He clucked his tongue and slithered into the office. "Look what the cat dragged in."

*Deep breaths. Remain professional.* "Hello, Seth."

He approached my desk and ran his finger along the oak laminate top. "I see you couldn't stay away."

I forced a tight smile. "I just go where Elizabeth tells me to."

"I have to say, I was pleasantly surprised when she told me we'd be working together."

"When did she tell you that?" I'd only found out about this two hours ago. The fact that Seth knew about this before I did was disconcerting.

"Sometime last week? I don't know. I hardly pay attention when she talks." He rapped his knuckles on my desk. "But when I heard your name, my ears definitely perked up."

"Well, I'm so glad you're looking forward to it." *At least one of us is.*

"Oh, yes." His mouth curved into a greasy smile and he ran his tongue across his upper lip. The sight of it made me queasy. "I'm definitely looking forward to a lot of late nights together in this office."

# chapter fifteen

By 5:45 on Friday afternoon, I only had three unchecked boxes left on my to-do list. Of course, this was not the original list Elizabeth had dictated to me in our tense Monday meeting. Since then, she'd issued four revisions. Each morning, I'd arrive before 8:00 a.m. to discover a freshly printed checklist waiting for me in the center of my desk blotter. And each morning, the number of unchecked boxes seemed to grow. Seth received his own separate lists, which he'd glance at indifferently before tossing them on top of his mountain of messy paperwork and heading to the kitchen for his first of many coffee breaks. I had no idea how much—or how little—progress he was making. Elizabeth had done a good job of assigning us discrete tasks, so my only concern was ensuring *my* half of the work was complete.

To that end, I implemented a filing system to keep myself organized and on track. Each piece of paper had a sticky flag attached to it. Red stickies were for flowcharts, green stickies were for financial statements, and blue stickies were for business requirements. The papers were then stacked in color-coordinated folders, which were placed neatly in a vertical incline file sorter on my desk. The orderly display brought a sense of calm to an otherwise tumultuous and hostile work environment.

Because, frankly, things with Seth weren't going so well. At least, not since sometime around Wednesday afternoon, when I'd turned down his sexual advances for about the twentieth time. After that, he accused me of being frigid and had barely said two words to me since. The only sounds filling the room on this early Friday evening were my fingers tapping on the keyboard, his intermittent guffaws at whatever viral video he was watching, and the incessant buzzing of my smartphone against my desk.

"Will you answer your goddamn phone already?" he said. "It's driving me nuts."

Without saying a word, I reached over and clicked it to silent mode. He sat up in his chair and peered at me over the chaos strewn about his desk.

"Who keeps calling you, anyway?"

"No one's calling," I said, my eyes still on the laptop screen. "They're texting."

He grunted. "Some poor man who hasn't yet realized you're completely asexual?"

I balled my hands into fists and dug my nails into my palms. *Deep breaths. Don't give him the satisfaction of letting him see you get angry.* "It's not a guy. It's a woman. My best friend."

"If it's your best friend, then why aren't you answering her?"

"I'm too busy." Which was the truth. I *was* really busy. And right now, I was also too worried about working myself back into Elizabeth's good graces to stress over whatever Elena wanted to talk about. Undoubtedly, she sought to bury the hatchet and move on from what happened in Hong Kong. I just didn't have the energy to listen to her sob, and I certainly had no desire to hear any more of her opinions on how controlling and miserable I was. I knew I'd have to pick up the phone and call her at some point. But I wasn't going to do it before I'd checked off the last of these three boxes. And certainly not with Seth in the room.

"I swear," I said, "this to-do list Elizabeth gave me has tripled in size since Monday morning."

"That bitch is so uptight."

Instantly, I felt protective of her. "She's under a lot of pressure. It's not easy being a partner at McKinley." *Especially when you don't have Daddy bailing you out all the time.*

"Whatever." He rolled his eyes. "She just needs to get laid."

Until this point, I'd actually been okay with letting Seth's comments roll off my back. After a few deep breaths, a clench of the fists, and an occasional bite of the tongue, my desire to chew him out would fade. But this was one misogynistic remark too many. Surely the fact that he was John Ramsey's son couldn't preclude him from following basic laws against sexual harassment in the workplace.

"You know, Seth," I said. "I think—"

My speech was interrupted by someone banging on the door, then flinging it open without waiting for an invitation.

"Sup, bro?" A lanky guy with a buzz cut and a pair of rimless eyeglasses burst into the room and smacked Seth's open, waiting palm. "You ready to bust outta here, or what?"

"Hell, yeah." Seth leapt to his feet and slapped his laptop closed.

"Did you finish everything on your to-do list?" I asked.

He snorted and rolled his eyes at the stranger in the room.

"Owen, have you had the pleasure of meeting Sophie? She's one of Elizabeth's lapdogs."

"Hardly," I said. "But she's gonna flip out if this stuff isn't done on time."

"Chill out," said Owen. "It's happy hour. Wanna grab a beer with us?"

"I have to get the rest of this done." I gestured to the folders spread out beside me. "Some of us actually do work around here."

Owen scowled. "For your information, I do plenty of work. In fact, I'll be back here tomorrow."

"Tomorrow's Saturday, man," said Seth.

"Yeah, but I'm on deadline. I may be hungover as fuck, but I'll be here. Gotta get my shit done, know what I mean?"

Seth shrugged. "Whatever. I'd never waste my Saturday at work. I'm gonna hit the can. I'll meet you at the elevator in five."

"Cool," Owen said. "I'll see if I can round up Claire and Jeanette."

Just like that, they disappeared into the hallway, without so much as a good-bye.

Not that I minded. I was happy to be rid of those fools. With a quiet office, I could finally concentrate. If I set my mind to it, I could bang out those last three tasks in an hour—two at the very most. Maybe I'd actually escape the office before the sun went down. If so, it'd be the first time I'd done it all week.

Too bad the only thing I could focus on was the fundamental unfairness of life. Seth had been born to an enterprising and resourceful father, and as a result, he'd been gifted opportunities that the rest of us had to beg and sweat for. While he was out getting loaded without a care in the world, I was stuck behind this desk, crunching numbers and ignoring messages from someone who I claimed was my best friend.

I picked up my phone and saw twelve new texts. The first eleven were from Elena. She asked if I was okay, if I was still mad at her, if I'd please meet her for dinner this weekend or at least let her buy me a drink. Reading them one after another made me feel very small. She'd made a mistake, and she apologized. Did I really need to make her grovel? How long was I going to hold this grudge?

Then I opened the twelfth and final text, from an unfamiliar fourteen-digit number.

did you get my package?

At first, I assumed it was meant for someone else, a wrong number. I hadn't received any packages at home this week, unless maybe it had arrived today, while I was at work. But just in case, I wandered over to the reception area, where Jeanette had already abandoned her post to go bar-hopping with Seth and Owen. After poking around in the incoming mail bin, I unearthed a legal padded envelope with my name scrawled in thick black marker, right above "c/o McKinley." There was no return address, but the postmark on the upper right-hand corner plainly read "Hong Kong."

For a second, I could've sworn my heart stopped. Then I felt it thumping madly against the inside of my rib cage, so hard I was afraid it might burst. I knew it was from Carson—

who else could it possibly be?—but I stared at that envelope, frozen and confused, as if it had been delivered from an alternate universe. As if hearing from him was beyond the realm of the possible.

I ripped it open right there, standing over the front desk. Inside was a spiral-bound book with a smooth brown cover. Flipping through it transported me back in time. The pages were filled with brilliant sketches of scenes from our trip throughout Hong Kong and Macau: a round table piled high with bamboo baskets of dim sum, the casino floor at the Grand Amadora, the two of us sitting side by side on a bench at the top of Victoria Peak. And then, at the very end, a sequence of images so graphic that I automatically snapped the book closed. Even though the reception area was completely deserted, it didn't seem appropriate to look at them in public.

With my cheeks burning, I hustled down the hall and back to my office, where I quickly shut the door behind me. I picked up my phone and read the message again; then I tapped the screen and frantically composed a reply. There were so many things I wanted to say to him, so many questions I wanted to ask. But the first thing that came to mind was:

when did you get a cell phone?

Carson had worn his technophobia like a badge of honor, decrying the impersonal nature of texting and the destructiveness of that big black hole known as the "Internet."

"Everyone's always got their noses buried in their phones," he'd said. "Reading other people's stories and snapping photos for the future instead of living in their own realities, in the here and now."

I'd nodded in agreement, deeply moved by the profundity of his words, momentarily convinced I'd leave my smartphone behind in the hotel safe rather than bring it back to New York with me. Back then, I'd been committed to living in the present moment and soaking up my immediate surroundings. But now I bathed in the glow of this slender handheld device, grateful for its ability to connect me to the other end of the world. Was Carson feeling the same way? Had he finally caved to the detachment and convenience of twenty-first-century technology? I pictured him jabbing clumsily at his new gadget with one thick index finger, drafting his reply. When it arrived, I read it while the phone was still buzzing in my hand.

> yesterday. figured it was time. maybe you rubbed off on me.
> :)

My heart was still throbbing, and the words on the screen began to blur and melt together. I couldn't shake this feeling of disbelief, like there was a phantom sending me these texts just to mess with my head. Fear paralyzed me, and as I struggled to think of what to say next, another message popped up on my phone.

> can you talk now?

Without thinking, my thumb slid to the CALL button, and I listened to the digital click of the ringtone while my leg bounced nervously under the table. Then, from across the miles of land and ocean between us, I heard his voice in my ear, deep and smooth like butter.

"That was fast," he said.

"So you gave in and got a phone."

"I wanted to check if my package arrived. I know you don't spend a lot of time in the New York office, but it was the only address I had for you. I figured they'd forward it on to you, wherever you were. Did you get it?"

I leaned back in my chair and swiveled around, biting my bottom lip. "Yes. I'm actually working out of the New York office right now. And your gift is lovely. I don't remember seeing that notebook when I was in Hong Kong, though."

"I bought it right after you left," he said. "Without you around, things became a little less interesting. So I started visiting all the places we went together, remembering everything we did, and recapturing all the memories in pencil and paper."

"I noticed you captured some rather...intimate memories as well."

His laugh was soft and wicked. "Did you like them?"

"I haven't looked at them carefully yet," I said. "I opened it when I was in the hallway, and I was afraid someone would see. Good thing for you no one was around."

"Is anyone around now?"

"Nope. I'm all alone in my office."

"Good. Turn to the last page." I did as he commanded and saw a sketch of our naked bodies tangled together, pressed up against a windowpane. His head was nuzzled in the crook of my neck; my mouth was open wide in ecstasy. The skyline of Macau was visible over my shoulder. "That's the scene I haven't been able to get out of my head all week."

My breath halted and I closed my eyes, trying my best to envision every curve and line of his face.

"Remember that first night at the Grand Amadora?" he asked.

"Yes." I tugged gently at the collar of my shirt.

"Remember when I had you up against the glass?"

At once, I felt the slick, cool pressure against my back, smelled the peppery scent of his aftershave. A chill quivered through me.

"Yes." It was the only word I could say.

"I wish we were doing that right now."

Muffled voices echoed in from the hallway, shattering my fantasy. I opened my eyes to find I wasn't in the Chrysanthemum Suite, limbs entwined with Carson. Instead, I was seated at my desk, the stack of color-coordinated folders beside me, my laptop open and glowing on top of the leather desk blotter. In one swift movement, I stuffed the sketchbook in my top drawer and slammed it shut. "This isn't the kind of conversation I should be having in the office."

"I thought you said you were alone."

I cleared my throat. "There are still some people walking around on my floor."

"What happened to the Sophie who liked to put on a show?"

"That was different. No one knew me in Macau. Here I could lose my job."

Carson heaved a sigh of defeat. "Okay. Well, next time we

talk on the phone, make sure you're at home. Because I was just getting started."

His words made me shiver. "It's so good to hear your voice," I purred.

"Now that you've got my number, you can call me whenever you want."

I glanced at the clock. Six-thirty. How had so much time passed by? I could easily spend all evening with my ear glued to the phone, losing myself in Carson's voice as it echoed through my head. But I needed to get back to work; those three unchecked boxes awaited.

"Can we do this again tomorrow?" I asked.

"Absolutely," he said. "I can't wait."

"Me neither."

"I love you, Sophie."

The last time I told him I loved him, it had been a gut re-action. An automatic response that came straight from my heart without thinking. This time, I didn't want to answer right away. Instead, I counted slowly to five in my head.

*One.*

If I was going to say it, I wanted to mean it.

*Two.*

I didn't want to give some knee-jerk answer, said merely because it seemed like something I was supposed to say in that moment.

*Three.*

I wanted to think it through. To give a rational, reasonable reply.

*Four.*

So if I stopped to consider how I felt about him, how he made me feel, the effect he'd had on me ever since I met him, the way I desperately didn't want to hang up the phone and say good-bye, was this really and truly love?

*Five.*

It must be. Because I couldn't think of any other word to describe it. I felt it in my bones.

"I love you, too."

"Talk to you tomorrow."

I heard a click on the line and the screen went black. With my skin still tingling, I covered my face with my hands and suppressed a squeal. Happiness oozed out of every pore.

My to-do list loomed before me, those three unchecked boxes taunting me with their emptiness. The sun was going down. In less than an hour, it'd officially be dusk. I had wanted to get out of this office while there was still a hint of daylight in the sky. Now it looked like that might not happen.

The unruly pile of papers on Seth's desk threatened to collapse onto the floor at any moment. How many boxes had he left unchecked before he sauntered out the door? He probably didn't even know. And if that jerk wasn't wasting his Friday evening worrying about his work, then why was I?

I slapped my laptop closed, packed up my briefcase, and headed for the door.

# chapter sixteen

I firmly believe the travel bug isn't something you catch but something you're born with. An inherent trait encoded in your genes, like the color of your eyes or your dominant hand. It's a craving I'd always needed to satisfy, even when I was a little kid living in the Jersey suburbs whose most exotic excursion had been a day trip to the shore. Without a passport or a plane ticket, I settled for seeing the world the only way I could: by cramming my shelves full of every guidebook, travelogue, and map I could find. I alphabetized my library from Australia to Zimbabwe and spent all my free time leafing through the pages, absorbing history and culture, compiling a list of sights I needed to see before I died.

When I graduated high school and moved into my cramped college dorm room, I left my collection behind at my grandmother's house. There wasn't much time to plan fantasy vacations while I was cramming for honors classes, trying to score straight As so I could land a respectable job. So I said good-bye to Rick Steves's *Scandinavia* and *Lonely Planet Thailand* and abandoned all those spiral-bound notebooks I'd filled with dream itineraries for trips I knew in my heart I'd never take. But there was one book I couldn't bear to part with, so I stuffed it in my suitcase and took it with me wherever I moved. *The Wild Wo-*

*man's Guide to Traveling the World* followed me from New Jersey to college, and then on to my tiny Manhattan apartment, where I tucked it away in the top drawer of my nightstand.

*The Wild Woman's Guide* was one twentysomething traveler's tale of her round-the-world solo adventures. She went everywhere—to the tourist traps and off the beaten path—for no other reason than to indulge her wanderlust, and she chronicled her exploits in two hundred fifty funny and frisky pages. I'd lost count of how many times I'd read it, but I remembered the moment I bought it very clearly. I was eleven years old, perusing the used books in my neighborhood thrift shop, when I spotted its cracked spine among the pile of dusty tomes. I slid it from the stack and was immediately captivated by its cover image: an illustration of a sassy girl with a mischievous smile and a head full of untamed curls. Curls just like mine. She waved from the window of an airplane as it traversed a map of the world. *One day,* I thought, *that'll be me.*

And now it *was* me. Finally, I was that woman with the curly hair, flitting across the ocean. I'd made it out of New Jersey. I was living the dream.

I was a wild woman.

At least, I certainly felt wild as I was flying through the revolving doors of One Bryant Park that Friday evening, after casting aside my unfinished task list. It was the first time I'd ever planned to deliver a project behind schedule. And the wildest thing of all? I didn't even care.

Instead, I walked home with a spring in my step and a smile on my face. As I strolled down 42nd Street, I pulled the clip from my hair, allowing my curls to tumble and bounce freely behind me in the city breeze. At home, I climbed the five flights of stairs to my apartment, where I dumped my briefcase in the foyer and promptly shrugged out of my confining suit. With the memories of Hong Kong still fresh in my mind, I ordered Chinese takeout, flopped down on the bed, and cracked open *The Wild Woman's Guide to Traveling the World.* By midnight, I'd devoured an entire container of noodles and reread it from cover to cover.

After I turned the final page, I briefly considered clicking off my bedside lamp and going directly to sleep. The three unchecked items on my task list were now officially past due, and I needed to wake up early the next morning to deal with them. But after reading all those tales of international adventure, my body vibrated with restless energy and repressed wanderlust. Salty soy sauce lingered on my tongue, leaving me parched, and I suddenly craved a Bitburger to quench my thirst. So I threw on a comfortable pair of jeans and went back down the five flights of stairs to Zum Bauer.

When I opened the front door, a tiny brass bell tinkled against the front door, announcing my arrival. Inside, the crowd was sparse, unsurprising given the time of night—the kitchen had been closed for two hours already, and soon they'd be announcing last call—but the atmosphere was lively nonetheless. Beside the window, a small group of businessmen with loosened ties hooted and bumped fists around a table cluttered with empty pitchers they'd no doubt been collecting since happy hour. Animated chatter and the occasional belly laugh echoed up from the far back corner of the room. I walked past the unmanned host stand, toward the long oak bar in the center of the restaurant, where the owner, Kat Bauer, stood in leather leggings and a Metallica tank top, wiping down goblets before sliding them into the hanging rack above her head.

"Hey," I said, hopping onto a sturdy wooden stool. "You still serving?"

She tossed the dishtowel over her shoulder and smiled at me with smoky eyes. "For you? Of course."

"Then I'll take a Bitburger, please."

Kat nodded and angled a glass beneath the tap, expertly filling it to the brim with minimal foamy head. I'd been a regular patron for at least three years, ever since I'd moved in upstairs, yet I'd never seen her pour anything less than a perfect pint. This was a woman who took her work very seriously.

"What brings you in at this hour?" she asked in her soft Bavarian accent before setting the drink on a cardboard coaster before me. "Did you just get home from another one of your trips?"

"Nope." I swallowed a mouthful of beer, feeling every bitter bubble burst against my tongue. "I've actually been in New York all week."

"That's strange for you to be in town for so long, no?" When I nodded, she offered a sympathetic frown. From our wardrobes to our schedules, Kat and I lived two very different lives, but we shared the controlled intimacy so typical of the bartender–customer relationship, illuminated by scant track lighting and

lubricated by lager. In general, our conversation topics remained light and breezy—the different varieties of German
beer, our experiences with bad first dates—but she knew how
much I loved to travel, how infrequently I spent more than one
or two consecutive nights at home, how restless I got when I
was forced to sit still for too long. "I'm surprised you haven't
stopped in sooner."

"I've been working really late," I said. "By the time I get
home, I'm so exhausted that all I wanna do is crawl into bed."

"You've told me before, but I forget now: As a consultant,
what *exactly* is it you do?"

I exhaled a disgusted breath. "It's too annoying to describe."

"Well, at least it pays well, right?" There was her sympathetic
frown again.

"I'll drink to that." I raised my glass in the air before taking
another hearty swig. If I kept guzzling beer at this alarming rate,
I'd assuredly be nursing a hangover at my desk the next morning. I didn't want to go home yet, though, to be alone in my
quiet apartment, curling up in my big, barren bed. I needed human interaction, the comfort of camaraderie. And there was no
better place to catch convivial vibes than Zum Bauer.

Far enough from Times Square to avoid significant tourist
foot traffic, Zum Bauer belonged to the locals: Midtown office
workers, Port Authority commuters, neighbors and residents of
the surrounding community. Always vibrant but never overcrowded, it was the perfect place to gather with others to catch
a soccer match, decry the abhorrent state of politics, or simply
shoot the breeze. Plus, it was one of the only places in New York

City that had Bitburger on tap. A taste of Germany in the middle of Tenth Avenue.

Wooden picnic tables and folding bistro chairs evoked the festive atmosphere of an outdoor beer garden. Hanging from the rafters were oversized flags bearing the bright blue diamonds of Bavaria and the fearsome, growling bear of Berlin. The posters tacked up along the exposed brick walls featured tourist destinations I remembered seeing on my abbreviated jaunt to Munich: the Marienplatz with its glockenspiel, the sky-high tower in Olympiapark, the roller coasters of Oktoberfest looping around Theresienwiese. Taped above the cash register was a photograph, curled at the edges, of a young Kat flanked by two doting parents.

"How old were you in that picture?" I asked, pointing to the brown-haired girl in the photo.

She glanced at it, running her fingertip over the faded surface. "Six or seven, I think. This was taken in Fürstenfeldbruck, a little town where we'd go every summer to pick strawberries. Those trips were some of the best memories of my childhood."

"Where are your parents now?"

"Still in Munich. I don't get to see them as often as I'd like. They used to come to New York quite a bit but now that they're getting older, the flight is hard on them. I try to visit them when I can."

"Do you think you'll ever move back to Germany?"

"No. I miss my family, but I could never leave all this behind." She held her arms out wide, gesturing to the kaleidoscopic tap handles, the chalkboard inscribed with daily specials, the antique tin signs advertising Spaten, Schlossbräu, and Karlsberg. "Owning my own business was a lifelong dream of mine. I'll be tending bar here until I'm old and gray."

I chuckled at the thought of an elderly Kat Bauer pouring pints, rocking a heavy metal T-shirt and tight pants. She was probably in her late thirties or early forties but seemed ageless, exuding a satisfied sparkle and a sense of inner contentment. Like there was nowhere she'd rather be than working the tap. "How did you do it, Kat?"

"Do what?"

"Make your dream happen."

She ran a hand through her hair, a mussed shag dyed the color of ripe plums. "Well, it was a long road. When I first came to New York from Germany, I was young and full of energy and ready to take whatever job I could find to make ends meet. After a few stints walking dogs and checking coats, I finally got a steady job waiting tables at an upscale restaurant in SoHo. The tips were fantastic, so I worked as many shifts as I possibly could. It wasn't really my scene, very pretentious, and the customers were so rude and demanding, they made my life miserable. But it's easy to overlook how unhappy you are when you're cashing a big paycheck at the end of each week. I think you know the feeling, yes?"

I smirked at her over the edge of my glass.

"Anyway," she continued, "I stayed there for years, climbing the ladder from server to shift leader and eventually to general manager. At that point, I was making good money and establishing a name for myself in the restaurant business. I was also working crazy hours, and after spending my days immersed in this flashy, flamboyant world, I found myself missing the humble comforts of my childhood home. The food, the friends, the fun. More than anything, I missed my youthful idealism, the dream that I could do anything or be anyone. That little girl in the picture, she didn't care about the big paycheck; she only cared about doing things she loved, chasing joy. So, after one particularly miserable workday, I looked at myself in the mirror and said, 'You have only one life, Katarina. Why are you wasting it?' Almost immediately, I quit my job and found a storefront for rent. Ten years later, here I am."

"That took an incredible amount of guts."

"It certainly wasn't easy, but I won't pretend I did it alone." She stroked the solid wood surface of the bar. "See this? My father crafted it by hand. He constructed all the picnic tables, too. And the menu? Curated by my mother, also known as the best cook in all of Bavaria. As soon as I told them about my desire to open an indoor beer garden in the heart of Manhattan, they hopped on the next plane to help support me."

"So Zum Bauer is a family affair."

"Oh yes. My mother and father, they've always believed in me, no matter how crazy my ideas have been. Parents love you like no one else in the world ever could. Know what I mean?"

"Totally." Of course, that was a lie. My parents were a gargantuan question mark in the story of my life. My mom never taught me secret recipes; my dad never built me custom furniture. There wasn't a single family photo of me and my smiling parents to tape on the wall. Maybe if there had been, my life would've gone in a very different direction.

I slugged the last of my beer and set the glass down on the table with a hollow *thunk*. Kat's eyebrows knit together in a question, but all she asked was, "Would you like another round?"

"That would be great."

Resentment crept into the corners of my consciousness, a bitter longing for the parents who never loved me. My grandparents had given me all they could, had cared for me deeply and provided me with a stable home. But I was still plagued by an internal void, an ever-present gap in my self-identity: If I didn't know my mother and father, would I ever really know myself?

As I watched Kat refill my beer, I forced myself to beat back these senseless thoughts. What would I gain by feeling angry or envious? What point was there in focusing on the immutable past? Instead, I pondered the future, the good things that filled me with gratitude. Like the empty pages in my passport, waiting to be stamped. Like Carson, in Hong Kong, waiting for my phone call.

Kat placed the beer before me, its flawless one-inch head gently undulating, skimming the rim of the glass.

"Your love for your job is evident in every perfect pint you pour," I said.

"When a job is a passion, it doesn't feel like a job." She slid a pilsner glass beneath the tap and pulled the handle. "Especially when you can drink a beer while you're on the clock." She raised her drink and looked me in the eye. *"Prost!"*

"*Prost!*" We clinked glasses, and I took a long sip. With my eyes closed, I thought of nothing else besides the cool sting of Bitburger sliding down my throat. As Carson would say, I was living in the moment. Savoring the present, instead of lamenting the past or overthinking the future.

"So," Kat said, "when are you heading out on your next big trip?"

Just like that, my meditation was broken. I opened my eyes and uttered the seven most depressing words in the English language: "No travel plans for the foreseeable future."

# chapter seventeen

Sunlight peeked through the cracks in my blinds, penetrating my closed eyelids. Rolling to my side, I pulled the covers up over my face in a vain attempt to recapture the slippery solace of sleep, but a vicious pounding tore through my head, and the bed began whirling in sickening circles. Suddenly, I was wide awake, consumed by nausea and filled with regret.

If I'd been behaving responsibly last night, I would've stopped drinking after that second pint of Bitburger. Instead, I chose to have a third, and a fourth, and then, after Zum Bauer closed its doors to the general public, I lingered at the handcrafted oak bar, chatting with Kat about dream fulfillment and travel destinations. While she closed out the cash register, her headwaiter, Wolf, swept the floors and emptied the trash, and when all tasks were complete, she procured a bottle of Jägermeister from the ice bin and asked, "Care for some parting shots?"

Jägermeister: always my downfall.

I hadn't experienced this level of hangover since the morning after my first encounter with Carson. Back then, I'd powered through the pain, motivated by the promise of a day spent exploring the Peak with a gorgeous companion. Now what was my motivation supposed to be? A Saturday in the office with my unfinished task list? That certainly wouldn't have been enough to motivate Seth. Didn't he say he'd never waste *his* Saturday at work? And he was much farther behind than I was.

Truthfully, hangover or not, I didn't want to put on my sensible leather pumps and strap that briefcase over my shoulder. I didn't even want to get out of bed. All I wanted to do was daydream about traveling, the way I used to do when I was a kid, when all I'd cared about was, as Kat put it, "chasing joy." So I chugged a glass of water, popped open my laptop, and planned a vacation.

Of course, it was a vacation I knew I'd never take. There was no way I could ever fit a twenty-one-day tour of Peru into my hectic, overworked schedule. But I took pleasure in the mere dream of hiking the Inca Trail, viewing Machu Picchu at sunrise and floating down the Amazon on a riverboat. Designing an imaginary itinerary was a far more amusing way to spend a Saturday than sitting cooped up in my office checking boxes.

By the time the sun went down, I'd planned three different dream vacations on three different continents, without ever leaving the comfort of my bed. When Carson called me that night, he listened to me blather on about camping in Australia for fifteen minutes before either of us even mentioned phone sex. When we finally got down to business, our fantasy involved being naked together under the stars in the middle of the Outback.

After I hung up the phone, I fell right to sleep. All night, I dreamed of adventure.

On Sunday morning, reality slowly reared its ugly head. Because I'd made plans I definitely couldn't cancel. Grandma would be expecting me for breakfast, and she most certainly didn't want to hear about the make-believe journey I'd just taken around the world and back. So I threw on my clothes and caught the 8:07 train out of Penn Station straight to Woodbridge, the town I'd grown up in and my grandmother still called home. Her house on Garden Avenue was seven blocks away from the train station: Go straight until you hit the flower shop, then make a left, a right, and another left. I could've followed that path with my eyes closed. I'd walked it countless times in high school, when the tranquility of the suburbs felt like a prison with well-manicured lawns. Every weekend, I used to arm myself with New York City guidebooks and take the train to a place I'd yet to discover. Times Square, the Cloisters, the Guggenheim Museum. With each train ride, I designed a new itinerary and kept a log of my adventures in my spiral-bound notebooks. I knew the city like the back of my hand before I'd ever officially lived there. Those weekends were my first taste of real-world traveling and exploration outside the confines of my childhood bedroom.

Of course, my one-woman excursions always made Grandma a little nervous.

"Don't make eye contact with anyone on the subway," she'd say, "and if someone tries to mug you, throw your wallet in the opposite direction and run!"

No one ever tried to mug me, and I'd made eye contact with more than a couple of cute guys on the subway, too. But I smiled and said okay, assuring her I'd be home before midnight. And I always was.

Soon it came time to apply to college, and I searched far and wide for schools offering degrees in travel and tourism. When the brochures started appearing in the mailbox, Gram sat me down at the kitchen table and peered at me over a steaming cup of tea. "What's your plan?"

"What do you mean?"

"I mean, what are you gonna do with a degree in tourism?"

"I'm not sure yet," I said. "I could work as a travel agent. Or maybe as a tour director."

"You think you're gonna make back enough money with those kinds of jobs to pay for the student loan debt you'd rack up?"

Turns out I hadn't given that much thought. "Maybe I'll get a scholarship," I offered. "My grades are really good."

"Sweetie, please." She spoke slowly, her patience wearing thin. "Don't waste those good grades on something so frivolous. Get a real job and make real money. Go to a real college."

With that, she dumped my brochures in the trash, and I set about trying to find a college that Gram would consider to be "real." One weekend, on a trip to the city, I found an ivy-covered oasis in the midst of skyscrapers smothered in soot. Grandma nodded in approval when I showed her the pamphlet. Several months later, I received my acceptance letter, and I was delighted to discover that not only was my tuition taken care of, but so was my room and board. Grandma, however, was less than pleased.

"Why can't you live at home and commute to school, like Elena's doing?" she asked.

"Elena's school is only twenty minutes away," I said. "And she has a car. I'd have to commute for an hour and a half in each direction."

"So? You take the same train ride every weekend and I never hear you complain."

"It's different if I'm going to school there every day, Gram. I'm going to have classes really early in the morning and really late at night. Plus, there are going to be extracurriculars, internships, clubs. I can stay way more focused if I'm living in the dorms."

While, technically, everything I told her was true, for me, the most important reason to board at school was to get the hell out of Woodbridge, and more specifically, to get away from Grandma's constant supervision. On the surface, I humored her anxious meddling, her persistent barrage of questions and comments and unsolicited advice. But deep down, it was eating away at me. She'd always been overprotective and opinionated, and after my grandfather died, I became the singular focus of all her earthly fears. The only person left in this world whom she loved. The pressure was too much to bear, and I found myself becoming resentful. I needed to get out before things got worse.

So I moved to the other side of the Hudson River, but I don't think Grandma ever got over it. Case in point: My old bedroom remained preserved in the same condition in which I'd left it seven years earlier. The same striped bedspread with matching valance and dust ruffle. The same posters hanging on the walls, depicting rock bands who'd long since broken up. The same stack of dusty guidebooks on the shelf. I kept urging her to redecorate the room, turn it into something useful, like a comfortable space to read or sew.

"I want to keep it the way it is," she'd say. "Just in case you ever decide to move back home."

I didn't have the heart to tell her that would never happen. But I did try to visit her whenever I could. In between business trips, if I could spare a few hours, I'd hop on the train and do the familiar commute in reverse.

When I arrived on Grandma's stoop that cloudy Sunday morning, she greeted me with a lingering hug and a tear in her eye.

"I missed you so much," she said, then ushered me into the front hallway. "Are you hungry? I've got eggs. Do you want some eggs?"

"That's okay. I ate a bagel on the train."

"How about some coffee?"

"Sure."

We sat around the dining table and she served me coffee in my very own mug, the one I'd had since high school with the purple cartoon cats on the front and the brown ring around the inner lip. After all these years, she still remembered exactly how I liked it: extra light, one sugar. I sipped it and felt gratitude begin to warm me from the inside out. Sure, she was a handful, but she'd also given me so much love. Love my own mother had never expressed.

In order to keep my visits with Grandma as pleasant as possible, there were certain topics of conversation I needed to avoid. Guys. Travel. Any experience I'd recently had that might be construed as questionably unsafe. They'd only lead to arguments, in which she would insist I took too many risks, and I would grit my teeth, trying desperately to find a way to change the subject. Usually I'd start off by asking about things that were going on in her life and steer clear of discussing my own.

"What's going on at the senior center this week?" I asked.

In general, this was a safe question. It guaranteed fifteen minutes of uninterrupted gossip, in which she criticized everything from the quality of available lunch selections to the shoes Sadie Sherman wore to Bingo, which, in Grandma's opinion, were "tacky and over the top." She took great pleasure in delivering her diatribes, while I sat wordlessly and offered the occasional sympathetic grumble.

"We had a good-bye party for Sadie," she said.

"Where's she going?"

"She's moving down to Florida with her sister. The two of them bought a condo in Miami. Have you ever heard of anything so ridiculous?"

"A lot of people retire to Florida. What's so ridiculous about that?"

"You retire someplace calm and quiet, like Fort Myers or Boca Raton. Not Miami! It's such a crazy city. So crowded and crime-ridden."

"I'm sure they'll be living in a nice part of town, Gram."

"They're moving into one of these luxury apartment buildings for the fifty-five-plus crowd." She dragged out the word *luxury* with a roll of her eyes, as if the notion was frivolous and not to be believed. "They kept telling me I should come visit them after they're settled in. They're out of their minds."

"You should go!" I smiled. "It could be a lot of fun. Who knows, maybe you'll decide to move down there yourself."

"Fun?" Her nostrils flared. "Of course *you'd* say something like that, with the way you like to gallivant. You don't know how to stay in one place."

"I just like to travel." I shrank and fell backward in time. Being here always made me feel like I was eleven again, eager for Grandma's approval, afraid to say anything that might stir up controversy. "Most of my traveling is mandatory for my job. I don't get to pick where I'm assigned."

"Well, I'm glad you're back home now, where you should be."

She patted my wrist, and her hand felt like a vise, fixing me in place, pinning me down to the kitchen table. The same table that had been here for as long as I could remember, its varnish now cracked and peeling away. How long had she had it? Twenty years? Thirty? My eyes scanned the room, taking note of how little had changed since my childhood. The same floral wallpaper, the same handmade café curtains, the same photos of me in the same frames, lined up along the top of the same credenza. Everything covered in a thin sheen of dust, everything yellow around the edges. A shrine to the past, a manifestation of all her fears: the fear of loss, the fear of change, the fear of the unknown.

When the doorbell rang, I jumped.

"Who the hell is that?" she said.

"I'll get it." I walked toward the hallway, and through the sidelights, I spotted a colorful bouquet of flowers in the grip of a pale, bony hand.

*Elena.*

# chapter eighteen

She didn't wait for me to say hello. As soon as I opened the door, Elena started laying into me.

"You haven't been answering my texts. Or returning my voice mails." Her pleading eyes betrayed the chilly tone of her voice. "So I figured I'd come see you in person. You can't avoid me if I'm staring you in the face, right?"

I puffed my cheeks and blew out a long breath. "I'm sorry."

Elena blinked, suddenly speechless. Maybe she'd expected me to put up more of a fight.

"I've been so busy with work," I continued, my voice dangerously unsteady. "Things are kind of a mess." I had to force myself to stop talking before I said too much. My grandmother's stoop was not the proper venue for an emotional confession about my long-distance love affair, or my miserable job, which I despised more and more with each passing minute. Did I really want the neighbors to hear the details of my quarter-life crisis?

"It's all right," she said. "I'd probably be ignoring me, too, if I were you. I just wanna make sure... I mean, are we okay?"

"Yes." I nodded. "We're fine. It's water under the bridge. Let's just move on. How did you know I'd be here today?"

"Your grandmother said you were coming over."

"Wait, you've been talking to my grandmother?"

"No. I think she's still mad at me for leaving you alone in Hong Kong. But my mom ran into her at the supermarket on Thursday, and she told her you were in town and would be coming over for breakfast today. So I was just sitting at home, and when I saw you walking down the street, I decided to come over."

"What do you mean you were at home? I thought you moved to Hoboken with Roddy."

She cleared her throat and stared down at her shoes, the corners of her mouth fighting against gravity. "We're taking a little break."

They hadn't even lasted a full week of living together. Was that why she'd been texting me nonstop? Was she only seeking to mend fences so that I could be a shoulder for her to cry on about this breakup—their fourth? It took every ounce of self-control within me not to roll my eyes and shout, *"I told you so!"* Instead, I stepped aside and invited her into the foyer. "Come in."

Elena shuffled into the kitchen, where she thrust the bouquet in my grandmother's face. "Hi, Mrs. Bruno. I brought you some flowers."

Grandma pursed her lips, as if the asters and Stargazer lilies gave off a foul odor. Elena turned on her Little Miss Innocent look, the one I knew so well, where she raised her eyebrows ever so slightly and thrust out her lower lip in a plea for compassion.

"Mrs. Bruno, I am really, really sorry for leaving Sophie alone in Hong Kong."

*Oh God.* "Elena, you don't have to—"

"I know how much I made you worry," she continued, like I hadn't even spoken, "and for that I truly apologize. From the bottom of my heart. You know how much I love Sophie, and I wouldn't have left her if I didn't think she was totally fine on her own. I mean, you know how tough she is."

Grandma flicked her gaze from Elena to me and quickly back again. Her eyes were slits, her mouth still puckered.

"I was really unhappy there," Elena said. "She was actually better off without me dragging her down all week. So I hope you'll be able to forgive me."

She stood batting her eyelashes and pouting, while the room filled with an uncomfortable and humiliating silence. I wanted to scream, to tell them both that this was ludicrous. That I was an adult woman who didn't need her grandmother's permission to hop the globe and that this drawn-out, sappy apology demeaned us all. Instead I bit my tongue. *No sense in starting a fight.*

Finally, Grandma snatched the flowers out of her hand. "Get me a vase. They're in the cabinet over the sink."

She leapt to Grandma's command and dug through the cupboard. "Do you want the cut glass or the ivory porcelain?"

"Glass," Grandma said. "And put some sugar in the water. It makes them last longer."

As Elena busied herself trimming stems under the running faucet, I sat back down, eager to shift the conversation back to safer, more pedestrian topics. But Elena started asking me questions before I'd even parted my lips.

"So, Sophie, how was the rest of your vacation?"

I could tell by the way Grandma's nostrils were flaring that my solo trip to Hong Kong was neither a safe nor a pedestrian topic.

"It was fine," I said hurriedly, eager to keep things as vague as possible. "Saw a lot of sights, ate a lot of food. But now it's over. Time to get back to the grind."

"Have you been at home in New York all week?"

"Yup."

"That's weird." Elena placed the flowers in the center of the dining table and sat down across from me. "You almost never stick around the city for more than a couple days at a time."

"I'm on an in-house project right now. In the Bryant Park office."

"Doing what?" she asked.

I sipped my coffee. "Do you really want to know? I mean, it's not like it's that interesting to talk about."

"Stop that," Grandma said. "Your job is very interesting. And very important. You work for one of the most prestigious consulting firms in the world. You know how many people would kill to be in your position?"

Had I not heard that exact phrase only a few days ago? I began to suspect my grandmother was having covert conversations with Elizabeth, in which they both decried my lack of gratitude and enthusiasm.

"I know," I muttered. "I'm lucky to have this job."

"It's not luck," she said. "You *earned* it. You worked hard and stuck to your plans, and now you're shooting straight to the top. You're gonna run that company one day. Just watch."

She patted my hand and beamed with pride. In that instant,

I realized there was no way Grandma had been talking to Elizabeth behind my back, because Elizabeth would've set the record straight about my status at McKinley. Which, at the moment, wasn't exactly on a meteoric rise.

"You know who's lucky?" I said. "Seth Ramsey. He's my partner on this project, and he's done absolutely nothing to contribute. But his dad is a founding partner, so no matter how little he works, he'll never get fired. Even if he did, what would it matter? His family's got plenty of money to sustain him for the rest of his life. He'll never need to worry about a paycheck."

Elena straightened up in her chair. "Is he single?"

"I think so," I said. "But trust me, he's the furthest thing from a great catch."

"What are you asking about single men for anyway?" Gram chimed in. "I thought you were shacking up with that boyfriend of yours."

"I wasn't asking for myself. I was asking for Sophie." Elena's lower lip began to quiver, and this time, I couldn't stop myself from rolling my eyes. "Roddy and I... we're on a little break," she whimpered.

"Good," Grandma barked.

Elena was so taken aback by the terse reply, her tears dried up before they spilled. "What do you mean, 'Good'?"

"You're better off without him. What does that kid have going for him? Nothing!"

"Roddy has a good job at the gym."

Grandma snickered. "Isn't he interested in getting an education?"

"He already has a degree. In kinesiology."

"What the hell's kinesiology?"

"The study of body movement," Elena said.

"But he couldn't ever get a *real* job with that kind of degree."

"Gram," I interjected, speaking slowly and cautiously, like I was talking to a five-year-old, "Roddy *has* a real job."

"Yeah," Elena added. "Not everyone's cut out for the corporate world, Mrs. Bruno. Besides, he makes more money than I do. Sometimes I wonder why I even bothered to get a degree. Three years after graduation, and I'm still stuck at a receptionist's desk, with no clue of what to do next."

"Maybe if you'd spent less time chasing after that gym rat, you would've had more time to devote to advancing your career." Grandma shook her head, sneering down into her coffee cup. "I don't know what it is with you girls."

Normally, I would've ignored a comment like this. Or maybe I would've nodded in agreement before swiftly changing the subject. Either way, I would have let it float away with little acknowledgment, in the interest of keeping the peace. But this time, I couldn't tune it out. This time the comment lingered in the air, hovering above my head, taunting me, imploring me to respond.

"What's that supposed to mean?" I said.

Grandma widened her eyes at me. "Is it so hard to find a man who does something respectable?"

"Being a personal trainer is a decent, respectable profession," I said.

"And that artist of yours, I suppose he's decent and respectable, too?"

"Yes. As a matter of fact, he is."

In the edge of my vision, I saw Elena cock her head to the side. As far as she knew, I'd never been involved with an artist. Or anyone at all, for that matter. At least, not for more than an evening. I'd have some explaining to do, but now wasn't the time. Not when Grandma was on one of her tirades against blue-collar work and relationships.

"Don't be so naïve," Grandma said. "You two associate with these boys who are so obviously beneath you. Do you honestly think either of them can give you a good future?"

"Why does a good future have to be about having a prestigious job?" I said. "What about happiness? Doesn't love count for anything?"

"Love?" she snorted. "Give me a break. Love causes nothing but problems."

"So you think I should be alone forever?"

"It's better to be alone than with some loser, Sophie. I'm telling you, all it takes is one man. One man can screw it all up for you."

I knew what she was really talking about. One man had screwed it up for my mother. He got her pregnant, and he disappeared. Then she disappeared.

But I wasn't my mother, and I never would be. What more did I have to do to show my grandmother that I was a completely different person from the woman who'd given birth to me?

"You know," I said, "for years, I've done nothing but try to prove to you how responsible I am. I don't understand why you still don't trust me not to mess up my own life."

She grabbed my hand and leaned forward in her chair. "Sophie, all I've ever wanted to do is keep you safe. I don't want you to make some terrible, irreversible mistake that you'll regret for the rest of your life."

"I'm not going to."

"I know you don't *think* you're going to. But it can happen in the blink of an eye. It can happen without you even knowing it's happening." Her eyes glistened in the sunlight streaming in through the kitchen window. "Forget about these boys. Concentrate on yourself. On your plans for the future. On becoming a success. Because when it comes down to it, *you're* the only person you'll ever be able to rely on."

I glanced over at Elena, who was chewing on her lower lip and staring sadly into the bouquet of flowers, as if they held the answers to all her desperate questions. Was this what became of women who trusted men? They abandoned their best friends overseas—or their baby daughters, still in diapers. They became unreliable and unambitious. They made messes of their lives.

Maybe Grandma was right.

"I should probably get going." I stood up and finished the last of my coffee.

"But you just got here," said Grandma.

I rinsed my empty mug in the sink and turned around to face her. "I've gotta get back to work."

After exchanging hasty good-byes with my grandmother, Elena followed me to the front door. As soon as the lock clicked behind us, she pounced. "Who is he?"

"Who's who?"

"Don't play dumb. The 'artist' your grandmother was talking about. Are you dating someone?" Her eyes were alight with expectation and excitement, and beneath it all, a spark of solidarity. Like she was thinking, *Now you know what it feels like.*

The words came in a rush. "No, of course not. You know how she is, she exaggerates everything."

"Well, she seemed awfully huffy about it."

"It's a long, stupid story, but honestly, it meant nothing." I winced, feeling unexpectedly sucker punched by the gravity of what I'd just said. *Carson and I meant nothing.*

Elena gently squeezed my arm. "Hey, listen. When I first got here, you said things were a mess...Do you want to talk about it?"

Sniffing back my sorrow, I straightened up and shook my head. "Not right now. I've really gotta get to the office. I'm so behind in my work. Let me call you later."

Before she could press any further, I spun around and headed for the train station. Though I could feel her eyes on me, I refused to turn back, too afraid that my crestfallen face would betray my thoughts. There was no way I wanted to commiserate with Elena about lost loves or romantic woes. Over the years, she'd allowed her relationship to consume her whole life, while her career and her independence paid the price. That could never be me. I wouldn't allow it.

After the train pulled into Penn Station, I power walked uptown to my apartment, where I quickly changed into professional attire and grabbed my briefcase from the foyer before heading back out to One Bryant Park. There were approximately six hours of daylight left, and I intended to finish up those last three items on my task list before sundown. I was a woman who stuck to my plans, who never allowed myself to get distracted by frivolities. A tour of Peru? A camping trip through Australia? Those were silly daydreams. They weren't real life.

So I buckled down, focused on my work, and didn't look up from my desk until after five o'clock. When I did, I had a crick in my neck, and my stomach was growling, but all the boxes on my task list were finally checked. Plus, there was still at least an hour left before the sun began to set. It was funny, though, because after I finished up, I didn't feel some great sense of accomplishment. All I felt was trepidation, knowing there'd be yet another task list waiting on my desk blotter before I showed up to the office the next morning.

As I waited for my laptop to power down, I fished my smartphone out of my bag. I'd heard it buzz a few times while I was working, but I'd ignored it, too afraid to break my fragile concentration. Now I scrolled through my texts to find a series of messages from Carson.

hey babe, got a sec to chat?

where are you?

call me when you can.

The last message had been received forty-five minutes earlier. In Hong Kong, it was the wee small hours of the morning. Either Carson was really drunk or battling insomnia. I slid my thumb to the CALL button and listened to it ring.

"Hey there." His voice was low and smooth. He didn't sound especially drunk or tired.

"Hi," I said. "What's up?"

"What's the matter?"

"Nothing, why?"

"You sound like something's wrong."

I was fully aware of how frosty I sounded, but for some reason I couldn't make it stop. "I'm just working."

"Oh. That explains it. You're scowling."

I pressed my fingers to the space between my eyebrows and confirmed he was right. I *was* scowling.

"Is everything okay?" I asked, massaging my temples. "Why are you up at this hour?"

"I'm at the airport. I've got an early flight."

"Flight?" My heart began to thump.

"Yup. I'm done with Hong Kong."

"Really?" The thought of him leaving the country made me inexplicably nervous. Why did I care so much if he left? "Where are you headed?"

"Sydney."

"Australia?" My heart began a free fall to my stomach.

"Yeah. Last night, our little chat got me thinking. It sounds like a pretty incredible country. Wanna come meet me? We can explore it together. Maybe make that fantasy of camping in the Outback into a reality."

At this point, I was pretty sure my heart stopped beating. There was nothing I'd rather do than hop a plane and meet Carson in the arrivals section of Sydney Airport, or lie naked with him beneath the Southern Cross. But that would never fly in real life. "You know I can't do that," I said.

"I know. But I figured I had to ask." The muffled echo of a voice on a loudspeaker rang through the earpiece of my phone. "My flight's boarding. I've gotta go. So, listen, I'll call you as soon as I can. I'm not sure how this international cell phone thing works, though. I'll go talk to someone at a store when I get to Sydney, but I don't know if, like, I'll have the same phone number or—"

"That's okay, Carson. You don't have to."

"I don't have to what? Go to a store? You mean, it'll just automatically work when I land in Australia?"

"No. Well, actually, I'm not totally sure about that. What I mean is, you don't have to call."

Heavy silence filled the thousands of miles between us. Finally, he said, "I don't understand."

"I mean, what's the point?"

"What's the point of what?"

"Of us. I'm here; you're there. This isn't going anywhere. It can't."

"Why does it have to *go* anywhere? Why can't we just enjoy what we have, where we are, in the moment?"

"You know the answer to that already."

I heard him swallow and release a long breath. "You need to know where you're going. At all times."

"Right," I said, trying hard to steady my voice. "But I hope you have a great time. And see a lot of amazing things. And create a lot of beautiful sketches."

The announcement in the background grew louder, more urgent. "So, this is it?" he said. "This is the last time we ever speak?"

Was this really what I wanted? To say good-bye right now and never hear his voice again?

I loved him. But love caused nothing but problems. I didn't want to be Elena. I didn't want to be my mom.

"It's better this way," I said.

"Fine."

A click, and then silence.

No good-bye.

I glanced down at my completed task list. All the checked boxes looked fuzzy through my tears.

My life wasn't exciting. It certainly wasn't wild. And, if I was being totally honest, it didn't make me particularly happy, either.

But at least it wasn't a mess.

# chapter nineteen

Unsurprisingly, there was a new task list awaiting my arrival at the office the next morning. Two double-sided pages, still warm from the printer. I counted the number of checkboxes. Eighty-seven.

I laughed out loud.

When I turned on my laptop, I found half a dozen messages from Elizabeth, in which she picked apart all the work I'd done, criticizing my approach and lack of attention to detail. She even asked me to revisit a few of the items I'd already completed last week. The crazy thing was, I'd followed her instructions to a T. It was almost as if she was changing the rules of the game after it was already over. And not once did she say thank you.

She did, however, complain about how long I took to finish the job.

To: Sophie Bruno

From: Elizabeth Fischman

Subject: Due Dates

These tasks were expected to be delivered by COB Friday. Instead, they were handed over last night (Sunday). Please keep in mind the importance of due dates for future project work.

Again, I laughed out loud. Because, really, in the grand scheme of things, what difference did it make? I'd compiled the data exactly as she'd requested it and presented it to her in a perfect package, ready for her to review first thing Monday morning. She didn't *have* to work over the weekend; that was her choice. The auditors didn't need this information for at least another three weeks. As long as they had everything by their deadline, the interim due dates were irrelevant. She was only being such a stickler because she was on a perpetual power trip.

I couldn't help but wonder if she was giving Seth this much grief over his missed targets. From the disorder on his deserted desk, I had serious doubts that he'd made any sort of progress since we'd parted ways on Friday. Between his late arrivals, long lunches, and early departures, last week he'd hardly been in the office more than six hours a day, and most of those six hours were spent fielding personal calls or surfing the Web. There could be no way his task list was already finished.

Then again, Elizabeth probably didn't want to run afoul of John Ramsey's son. Unlike Seth, she had to tread carefully if she wanted to rise through the ranks at McKinley. Which meant she needed to keep the founding partners—and their family members—happy. I just wished I wasn't the one who had to suffer the blowback.

There was nothing else to do but settle in and work. What choice did I have in the matter? So I started checking boxes. By the time Seth strolled in at 10:15, without a word of greeting, I'd already finished two tasks. After another wordless hour and a half, he left for lunch with Owen, and I'd checked off two more.

At 1:45, the cramps in my stomach demanded I take a quick break. All day, I'd consumed nothing but coffee and a buttered roll, but at least I had six check marks to show for it.

I decided to work through lunch, so I ran down to the deli on the first floor and returned at once with a prepackaged salad. If I was going to spend so many sedentary hours at my desk, I figured I should at least make up for it with a healthy meal. When I snapped the cover off the plastic bowl, I winced at the rancid odor it produced. Had the sprouts gone bad? Or maybe the tomatoes were moldy. Whatever it was, the salad was inedible. I set down my fork, feeling defeated. The worst part was, for a split second, I actually considered eating it anyway.

As I sat there, surrounded in festering funk from this putrid, pathetic excuse for a lunch, I had a realization. This was my rock bottom. I mean, it couldn't possibly get any worse than this, right? From here, I had nowhere to go but up. Up the ladder, to bigger and better things. I made a vow that my next project would be on the road. I'd just have to start kissing up to Elizabeth so I could rebuild my reputation with these boring audits. Then, when they were finished and I'd proved my value to this organization, I'd get back to doing the thing I loved most: traveling.

I looked at the clock in the lower right corner of my computer screen: 2:10. Which meant, on the east coast of Australia, it was a little after four in the morning. My thoughts strayed to Carson, wondering where he was sleeping right now. From the research I'd done, there were tons of great hostels in Sydney. Cheap, centrally located accommodations. Maybe he was in one of them. Or maybe he'd sprung for a private hotel room on Bondi Beach.

Before I knew what I was doing, I had opened a browser window and loaded an interactive map of downtown Sydney. I traced an impromptu walking tour starting at Hyde Park, trailing through the Royal Botanic Gardens, and ending at Circular Quay. Did Carson know you could climb to the top of the Sydney Harbor Bridge? They even offered a special night climb, with headlamps. *I'll bet the Opera House looks otherworldly from up there, glowing on the cove. Like the convention center at Victoria Harbour.*

*I miss him.*

The office door swung open and in walked Seth and Owen, midconversation.

"She wants it, you can tell," said Seth.

"You think?" Owen leaned against the wall and slipped his hands in the pockets of his khakis.

"Abso-fucking-lutely, dude." Seth plopped down in his chair and spun around, knocking a pile of papers from the top of his ever-growing mountain onto the floor. He didn't bother to pick them up. "Did you see the way she licked her lips when she dropped off the check? I say you bust out of here at four forty-five, head back to Friday's, and grab her number. And maybe grab a quickie in the bathroom stall while you're at it."

Seth winked in my direction and a pain shot through my empty stomach. He wrinkled his nose and asked, "What's that stench?"

"Oh." I grabbed for the cover of my salad bowl, quickly popping it back on. "It's this salad. There's something rotten in it."

"Nasty," said Owen. "The whole room reeks now."

"Well, fortunately, you have your own office to return to," I said. Owen stood there, blinking blankly. Clearly he couldn't take a hint. "Don't you have to get back to work? Like, now?"

He sucked his teeth and tilted his chin in Seth's direction. "Later, bro."

Seth didn't acknowledge his exit. He was already lounging back in his desk chair, surfing the Web, staring slack-jawed at his screen with cold, dead eyes. Low bass thumped from his speakers; it was a tune I'd gotten used to over the past week. He liked to watch these blooper reels of skateboarders suffering disfiguring injuries, set to techno music. Before this, I hadn't realized how many of these videos existed. Apparently, there were enough to keep Seth distracted from his work for hours on end. Even days.

"Don't you ever get tired of sitting around in this office?" I asked.

"What are you talking about?" he muttered, his eyes still fixed to his screen.

"I mean, don't you have any desire to branch out? Maybe get a gig as a traveling consultant or something?"

He flashed me the same look of disgust he'd displayed when he first got a whiff of my salad. "Why would I want to travel?"

"Why *wouldn't* you?"

"Because it sucks. Lumpy hotel mattresses. Shitty continental breakfasts. Jet lag. It's all such a pain in the ass. I'd rather stay put in my full-service condo, with my ninety-inch TV and my thousand-thread-count sheets."

Of course. Why wouldn't it have occurred to me that Poor Little Rich Boy had his very own luxury condo? Probably paid for outright by his doting dad. No wonder he didn't want to travel anywhere. He already had the world in the palm of his hand.

The door swung open again. This time, it was Elizabeth. *Doesn't anybody ever knock?*

She scrunched up her face in revulsion. Which, frankly, didn't look much different from her usual expression. "What is that smell?" she asked.

"Sophie's rotten salad," Seth said without missing a beat.

"Well, for God's sake, throw it away."

I picked up my untouched, twelve-dollar takeout lunch and dumped it in the wastebasket beside my desk. The scent still lingered in the air.

"I come bearing bad news." Elizabeth placed freshly printed task lists on our desks, mine in the center of a pristine blotter, Seth's on top of a heap of junk. "The auditors are seeking a more aggressive timeline for our deliverables."

"How aggressive?" I asked, perusing the list. It was twice as long as the one she'd given me just hours before. Suddenly, the six check marks I'd managed to make so far today didn't seem like such a triumph.

"They want all the data delivered by this Friday."

My jaw fell open. I looked over at Seth, who was clearly zoned out, most likely watching blooper videos on mute.

I laughed. "That's impossible."

"Well, you don't have much of a choice," she said. "Start with this list, and I'll review to see if I've left anything out." Elizabeth turned on the ball of her foot and strode out the door, leaving me stunned.

"Do you believe this?" I said, knowing full well Seth didn't grasp the severity of this situation. Odds were, he wasn't even paying attention, but I couldn't stop myself from vocalizing my outrage.

He snickered. "Man, I know. Elizabeth's so uptight. She needs to get laid, like, yesterday."

"Are you serious?"

"What?" Seth finally took his eyes off the screen and peered at me over his pile of papers.

"Have you ever heard of sexual harassment laws, Seth?"

"Calm down." He leaned forward and leered at me. "Or are you looking to get laid, too? Tell me, was I the last one you had?"

"Shut up, Seth."

"'Cause I could give it to you again. Real good. Right on that desk you're sitting at. Just like last time."

"Fuck you."

"Gladly." His smirk made me feel dirty, in the worst possible way. I wanted nothing more than to bust out of that office and never look back. But this task list loomed before me like an unspoken threat. If I didn't finish it, I'd probably be out of a job. Or, at the very least, I'd never get out of this godforsaken New York office. I'd be doomed to spend the rest of my career working alongside McKinley's most worthless employee, picking up his slack and enduring his verbal vomit. Forget about finding a job elsewhere; without a ringing endorsement from my direct supervisor, I'd never get hired at another consulting firm.

What would Grandma tell me to do?

*Think of the big picture. Stick to my plan. Keep chasing success.*

She would definitely not tell me to reopen that browser window and start researching the history of the Sydney Opera House. But that's precisely what I did. Three hours later, I'd produced a five-day itinerary hitting all the hot spots in New South Wales: two days exploring Sydney on foot, followed by a hike in the Blue Mountains, a wine tour of the Hunter Valley, and wrapping up with a day of relaxation on Manly Beach.

I'd been so engrossed in my vacation planning, I didn't notice Seth had left the office. The clock on my computer screen read 5:40, which meant he'd absconded at least forty-five minutes ago. Probably longer. He hadn't touched his task list since Elizabeth set it down on his pile of papers.

Then again, neither had I.

*How much could a plane ticket to Sydney possibly cost?*

I navigated to the Qantas website and searched for flights out of JFK. The shortest flight time was twenty-three hours. The earliest I could get there was two days from now. And to buy it, I'd have to pay the equivalent of one month's rent. *Damn Elena for wasting all my frequent-flyer miles.*

It was a stupid thought anyway. What was I going to do? Quit my job to hop on a plane and surprise Carson? I didn't even know where he was. Or if he'd already found a new partner to travel with.

With slumped shoulders, I shut down my laptop and stuffed

it into my briefcase. I figured I should bring my work home with me to make up for all the time I'd wasted in the office. I still had to get all this done. Somehow.

I walked down the hall like I was being led to the guillotine. But as I pressed the button for the elevator, I felt stupid for feeling so glum. Really, my life wasn't that bad. Wasn't I lucky to have this job? Wouldn't hundreds—no, thousands—of people kill to be in my position? That's what everyone kept telling me. So why was I so miserable?

As I descended to the lobby with a crowd of other white-collar workers, I stared down at my sensible pumps. *Maybe I should've said yes when Carson asked me to meet him in Sydney. Maybe I should've said yes when he asked me to stay in Hong Kong. It would've been messy, but it would've been worth it.*

In the lobby, the revolving door felt heavier than usual, and outside, the setting sun momentarily blinded me. When I regained my vision, I stood there, unable to move, my soles glued to the pavement.

Sitting at the curb, leaning against a worn canvas backpack, was a sandy-haired man with a sketchbook in his lap. His pencil danced across the page. When he smiled up at me, I had to grasp the side of the building to prevent myself from falling to the ground.

He was here, in real life.

Carson.

# chapter twenty

Is it really you?"

My tongue felt thick in my mouth. I was dumb-founded. How could Carson be standing right here, on 42nd Street? Was this merely an apparition, the ghostly manifestation of my fantasies? Slowly, I reached out to touch him, half expecting my hand to pass right through his body. Instead, I felt the warmth of his chest, sturdy and solid, and I couldn't help but trace my fingers up his shoulder, down his bicep, along his waist. Feeling every inch of him, every curve, to make sure he was real.

"In the flesh," he said.

I stepped closer, my heart pounding as he cupped my face in his hand. He stroked my cheek with his thumb and I leaned into his caress, breathing in his scent, at once foreign and familiar.

"What are you doing here?" I asked.

"I needed to see you."

"What about Australia?"

"Australia's not going anywhere." He stroked his thumb over my lips. "I'll get there eventually. Right now, being here with you is more important."

"I can't believe it."

He smiled, revealing that deep dimple in his stubbled cheek.

"You'd better believe it, because I just traveled for almost twenty-four hours. The only ticket I could get at the last minute had a crazy short layover in Tokyo, where I actually had to change airports. I made it to the boarding gate at Narita just before they closed the doors."

"When did you get here?"

"About an hour ago. I've been sitting here, sketching. The people-watching in this city is phenomenal. I could fill a whole book with the scenery from this block alone."

I looked up at the fifty-five-story skyscraper towering high in the sky, then around at the busy street, where a sea of white headlights sailed by in the encroaching dusk. Suddenly, I remembered that Carson had never been to New York before.

"How did you know where to find me?"

"I had your work address, remember? The business card? With all the time you spend at your desk, I figured you'd be in the office at least until sundown. And, of course, I was right."

I shook my head in disbelief. "You're unreal."

"Maybe," he said. "Maybe this is only a dream. Maybe I'm a figment of your imagination."

He drew me closer, fixing his blue eyes on my parted lips, and when he pressed his hips to mine, I felt his gentle, rigid pressure rise against me. There was no denying that he was real, that I was wide awake, that everything was actually happening. So I opened my mouth, and I let him in, and we kissed like we weren't standing in the middle of a crowded New York sidewalk, like there weren't a dozen tourists watching us with jealous, wide-eyed stares. In that moment, we were all that existed and all that mattered, and I needed him more than I'd ever needed anything in my whole life.

"Let's go to my place," I muttered.

"Where do you live?"

"A few blocks away." I was already at the curb, hailing a taxi. I didn't have the patience for a twenty-minute walk through the chaos of urban bustle. I wanted Carson all to myself, to stare at him, to talk to him in the privacy of a chauffeured car. I wanted to get him home as quickly as possible, behind closed doors.

But it turned out I didn't have the restraint to keep my hands off his body. After we piled into the backseat and slammed the door, my fingers were sliding beneath the hem of his T-shirt and working their way up his hard stomach, grasping at his chest. He grabbed the back of my neck and pulled me toward him, enveloping my mouth in his. Our kisses were savage and powerful. I could taste nothing but his tongue, smell nothing but his musk, feel nothing but his smooth skin beneath the palms of my hands.

When the cab screeched to a halt on Tenth Avenue, right outside Zum Bauer, I swiped my credit card in the kiosk as Carson retrieved his backpack from the trunk. I thanked the driver, but he remained silent, avoiding my gaze in the rearview mirror. Perhaps we'd made too much of a scene.

I didn't remember unlocking the door or climbing the five flights of stairs. I didn't remember how my clothes wound up strewn across my apartment. Because the next thing I knew, I was on my back on my bed with my hair splayed across the pillow and Carson hovering above me. My fingernails clawed at his shoulder blades as I told him to go harder, go deeper, to give me everything he had. I was frenzied, unbridled, releasing more and more stress with each of his powerful thrusts, until the burden was gone and I felt so light I could float up to the clouds.

When he slumped forward to bury his face in my hair, I could feel his heart beating through his chest. The heat of his breath, the weight of his body, the rhythm of his pulse. We were a sweating, panting mess of flesh and heat. Nothing had ever felt so right.

"Shit," he said, still gasping for air. "That was intense."

He rolled onto his back and I turned to nestle my face in the crook of his arm, slinging a leg across his slack body.

"All that phone sex really built up the tension," I said, my voice raspy.

He kissed me tenderly on the lips. "Nothing compares to the real thing."

"I'm so glad you're here."

"Me too."

We lay together in my bed, listening to the sounds of our own breathing. I ran my fingers along the lines of his tattoo, stroking each tree branch from base to tip. I thought of its meaning, how it was the home Carson carried with him wherever he roamed.

"So how long are you here for?" I asked.

"Not sure yet. I bought a one-way ticket. Why, are you ready to get rid of me already?"

"Of course not." I kissed his chest. It was so hard to keep my lips off of him. "I just want to know how many condoms to buy. If you're gonna be here for a while, we should probably buy them in bulk."

My head bounced against him as he laughed. "I don't think it'd take us very long to go through one of those big boxes. But that was my last one. Do you have any? If not, I think I'll have to make a run out to the corner store and buy a little pack to get us through the rest of the night."

"I'm not sure. Check my nightstand."

Carson rolled over and opened the drawer. "I don't see any." He rummaged around for a moment, before unearthing my copy of *The Wild Woman's Guide to Traveling the World.* "What's this?"

I snatched it from his hand. The string of obscenities I'd uttered while we were in the throes of sexual ecstasy didn't embarrass me as much as his discovery of my oldest book. "It's nothing."

He smiled and raised his eyebrows. "If it were nothing, I don't think you'd react like that."

Clutching the book to my chest, I bit my lower lip. "It's my favorite book. I've had it ever since I was a kid."

"That's cool. Can I see it?"

Reluctantly, I handed it over. He flipped through the yellowing pages and took a long look at the cover image. "This girl looks just like you."

"I know." I propped myself up on one elbow and turned to face him. "I've always dreamed about being her."

"And now you are."

"No, I'm not."

"Yeah, you are." He leaned forward to kiss my shoulder. "A wild woman traveling the world."

"I'm not exactly wild. And I'm not traveling on my own terms. Remember? You're the one who said that."

"I only said that because I didn't want you to leave me in Hong Kong. Look, I know how important your career is to you, how important it is for you to be financially stable. Your job may not be perfect, but at least it lets you see the world. Although, I was thinking, what are you still doing in New York right now?"

My eyes welled with tears. I flopped back down on the pillow and pressed the heels of my hands against my face to keep him from seeing me cry, but it was too late.

"What's wrong?" he asked.

"Things aren't going so great at work." My voice was unsteady. I wiped my eyes and swallowed against the lump in my throat. "When I came back from Hong Kong, I got assigned to this shitty in-house job, so I can't travel. And now my boss is nitpicking everything I do."

"Shit. What do you think is going on?"

"I don't know." I stared at the cracks in my ceiling. "Actually, that's not true. I do know. It's because I've been really distracted lately. I can't focus. I can't bring myself to stay late when I know I should. And I hate my partner more than anything."

Carson played with my curls, twirling them gently around his thick fingers. "Do you think it's just a temporary thing? Like, post-vacation blues or something?"

I considered this for a moment. Could I simply be in a funk? One I would snap out of as soon as I'd readjusted to real life again? I turned my head to look at him and saw his eyes scanning my face with admiration and concern. With Carson here, in my bed, the lines between real life and vacation were all blurred. I realized there was no going back to what I knew before I met him.

"My heart's not in it anymore." Saying the words out loud made me feel lighter, free. But I wondered, had my heart *ever* been in it to begin with?

"Well, you shouldn't be doing anything when your heart's not in it."

Of course that's what he'd say. His entire life was lived in pursuit of his heart's desires. "What made you realize art was your passion?"

"Hmm." He scratched his head, as if he'd never before pondered the answer to this question. "I'm not sure. There was no aha moment, if that's what you mean. It was just something I'd always felt, even when I was a little kid."

I knew exactly what he meant. His affinity for art was inborn, like my travel bug had been. "Lots of crayon drawings on construction paper in your childhood?"

"Yup. But it didn't take me long to move on to pencils and sketchbooks. Then I spent my teen years doodling my way through math and science, counting the seconds until art class started." He bit back a smile, his cheeks flushing the palest shade of pink. "Not many people know this, but I was the president of my high school's art club."

"Get out." An image flashed in my mind: Carson, in the prime of his adolescence—skin a little spotty, hair a little shaggy, but still the kind of dreamy, artsy guy that all the girls were crushing on. "I don't even think my school had an art club."

"Our art department was great. There was a studio with easels and drafting tables, a darkroom, even a ceramics workshop. You should see how talented I am with a pottery wheel and a slab of clay." He inched closer and slid his hand around my waist, nuzzling my ear with the tip of his nose. And as tempted as I was to shut up and surrender to his touch, I was dying to know more.

"Then what happened?"

"What do you mean?"

"Well, it sounds like the art department was a very formative experience for you. So why didn't you continue your studies? Go to college and get a BFA or something?"

He snickered and pulled away from me slightly. "Been there, done that. Wasn't for me."

"You went to college?"

"Only for one semester. I consider it a failed experiment."

"Why?"

With pinched brows, he scrubbed a hand through his hair for a moment, before answering, "It was hard."

"College is supposed to be hard."

"Yeah, but art school isn't just about hard work. It's about talent, too. Once I got there, I realized I wasn't as talented as I always thought I was. In high school, I was a big fish in a small pond; it wasn't hard to be the best artist in a group of a few hundred kids. But when I got to college...man, everyone was more talented than me. *Way* more talented. My freshman roommate, Johnny, specialized in sculpture and got his own pop-up gallery show three weeks after orientation. Meanwhile, I was struggling just to keep up with all my classwork."

"Well, some of that boils down to luck. Maybe Johnny just had the right idea at the right time, you know?"

"No. He was gifted in a way I never would be. All those kids were. I just didn't belong there. After I got my first shitty grade report, my aunt and uncle said, 'I told you so,' and I couldn't argue. It seemed all my professors agreed with them about how talentless I was. So I quit. That's when I moved out on my own and started working all those odd jobs."

I simmered with anger on Carson's behalf. Of course he didn't have the self-esteem to navigate the challenges of art school. With his aunt and uncle constantly criticizing him, they taught him to give up before he ever had a chance to find success. What could he have accomplished if only they'd believed in him?

"But it worked out for the best," he said. From the scowl on his face, I wasn't completely convinced he believed his own words. "I wasn't really interested in paying a bunch of people to tell me how to be an artist. I'm a lot happier doing my own thing."

There was nothing I could say to change his mind. How many times had I already tried to convince him that his work was remarkable, that he was brimming with talent and capable of anything? Instead, I pulled him closer to me, dancing my fingertips along his bicep, eager to lighten the mood. "That makes sense. You are a dreamer, after all."

Immediately, his brow relaxed. "Well, there's something to be said for being a planner, too."

"Right, because my five-year plan is working out so well for me."

His mouth twitched. "You know, I actually put together a five-year plan of my own."

I rolled my eyes. "Yeah, I'm sure Mr. Seize the Day has developed a detailed five-year plan of all the goals he wishes to achieve."

Without a word, he hopped off the bed and strode toward his backpack, which sat in the entryway beside his discarded T-shirt. As he knelt down to unzip the side pouch, I watched his muscles flexing beneath his smooth, tanned skin and marveled once again at how gorgeous he was, how lucky I was to have met him. When he returned, he sat on the edge of the mattress, holding a folded piece of paper in his hands.

"Here," he said, handing it to me. "Take a look."

I sat up and took it from him. It was a thick piece of white vellum, the shredded edges still hanging from the side where he tore it from one of his spiral sketchbooks. I opened it carefully and read the words written in smudged pencil:

### FIVE-YEAR PLAN

*1. Find a way to be with Sophie.*

The sight of my name in his handwriting made me tremble. Only twenty-four hours ago, I thought there wasn't a point in continuing our relationship, that we weren't going anywhere and never would. Now I realized we had already arrived.

When I finally peeled my eyes away from the page, Carson was aiming his blue spotlights on me, warming me with his gaze.

"This is all I need," he said. "I can sketch in Hong Kong, in Australia, in New York. I can find an adventure wherever I am. The only constant I need in my life is you. So wherever you go, I'll follow."

"But what about San Francisco? What about all the things you had going on there before you left?"

He shook his head. "There's nothing there for me except a half-empty storage unit, filled with stuff I don't need anymore." His voice was deep, rough, tinged with sadness and a shade of regret. He cupped my chin, ran the tip of his thumb against my bottom lip. "I told you, San Francisco never felt like home to me. You're the closest thing I've felt to home in a long, long time."

"Really?"

"Really. I already let you get away once, Sophie. I'm not making that mistake again."

I folded his five-year plan and placed it on my nightstand, then straddled his hips and gently raked my fingers up the sides of his scalp. With my hands full of his soft, dense hair, I leaned forward and kissed his lips, wrapping my legs around his body and pressing myself against him. As his fingertips traveled up the small of my back and over my stomach, I thought, *This is too good to be true.*

# chapter twenty-one

At 6:30 the next morning, the alarm on my phone emitted its shrill, continuous beep right on cue. Some people preferred to wake up to a gentle, melodious tune. A sound resembling the chirping of crickets or the strumming of an acoustic guitar. Something so soothing would never get me out of bed on a workday anymore, though. I needed to be jolted into action, provoked into opening my eyes.

I snatched the phone from my bedside table and automatically pressed the snooze button. The thought of heading into the office for another miserable day was too much to bear at the moment. *Didn't I only just close my eyes and go to sleep?*

"Just five more minutes," I muttered in my hazy half-asleep state.

"Don't get up on my account. I've got a perfect view right here."

Carson. How could I have forgotten he was right next to me? When I cracked my eyes and saw him sitting there, naked, his sketchbook open on the disheveled sheets, I remembered why I felt so fatigued. We didn't really sleep much last night. My grimace turned into a smile. "Hi."

"Don't move. I just need to finish this one little detail on your collarbone."

I obeyed his command. With his gaze transfixed on my naked body, I felt like the Venus to his Botticelli, the Mona Lisa to his da Vinci. His eyes explored every last detail of my body, and his fingers immortalized them in the pages of his notebook. A notebook I knew he would keep forever.

And while I reveled in being the sole object of his adulation, I also felt a vague sense of foreboding. It was one thing to be Carson's source of creative inspiration, a muse for his artwork, but it was quite another to be the only line item on his five-year plan. How could he have no other aspirations in life aside from tagging along behind me? Despite all the discouragement he'd encountered over the years, I knew the old Carson—the ambitious teenager, the president of his high school art club— must still be trapped somewhere inside of him, yearning to be set free.

He snapped his book shut. "Okay, you can move now."

Stretching my arms above my head, I shook the worry out of my brain and slinked closer to him, feeling the warmth of his bare hip against my own. "What are you doing up so early?"

"Jet lag," he said. "I think this is the first time I've ever seen you awake before eleven, though."

"I have to be at work in an hour." I leaned over, brushed my lips against his neck. *Goddamn, he smells good.*

He tossed his notebook on the floor and pressed up next to me. "Then you've got plenty of time before you've gotta get out of bed."

I knew I should be marching into the bathroom and turning on the faucet, letting the shower heat up while I put on a pot of coffee. And of course, I needed to figure out an outfit to wear. I hadn't had a chance to iron my clothes last night as I'd planned, with everything else going on. If I didn't get my act together right away, I was going to show up at the office looking like a rumpled mess.

"I can't be late." I threw back the duvet and leapt to my feet.

In the bathroom, I yanked open the shower curtain and reached for the faucet, only to be pulled backward before I could turn on the water. Carson's strong arm encircled my waist, his palm sliding across my stomach. "Why don't you call in sick today?" he whispered into my curls.

"I can't."

"Why not? Say it's a fever. You're burning up. You can barely get out of bed." The tip of his tongue trailed along the edge of my earlobe and my knees turned to jelly.

Every sensible cell in my body told me to get in the shower. *Go to work,* they said. *You've got a task list a mile long waiting for you on your desk.* Yet somehow, I ignored them and let Carson prop me up on the bathroom sink. My head fell back against the medicine chest, and a groan of ecstasy escaped from deep within my chest.

At 7:42, I typed a hasty e-mail to Elizabeth telling her I'd been up all night, I wasn't feeling like myself, I couldn't possibly come into the office today. I mean, it wasn't exactly a lie, was it? Maybe it'd make me come off as indifferent about my work, an unenthusiastic contributor. But frankly, with the way things were going—Elizabeth's unrealistic expectations, Seth's nasty attitude—I didn't care what they thought about me anymore. All I cared about was having a good time. Seizing the day. Being happy.

By ten o'clock, we finally made it into the shower without getting distracted.

"Show me New York today," Carson said as he soaped up my chest.

"Gladly." Though his slippery fingers sliding all over my body threatened to distract me all over again. "What do you want to see?"

"What's good?"

"It's New York. Everything's good." I squirted a dollop of raspberry-scented shampoo in my hand and worked my hair into a lather. "But you know, it's been a long time since I've been a tourist in my own town. It could be fun to play one."

"I don't want to be a tourist. I want to know what the real New York is like."

"Oh, come on," I said. "Indulge me for a day. Let's take one of those red double-decker tour buses. There's one that takes off from Times Square every hour."

"That sounds so cheesy."

"Look, think of it as a way to orient yourself in Manhattan. You'll get a quick bird's-eye view of the whole island."

"Of all the tourist traps, you mean."

"Yes, all the overpriced, overcrowded tourist traps that you hate." Suds dripped down my back and I ran my soapy hands over his chest. "Please. Do it for me."

He squeezed my shoulders and planted a wet kiss on my lips. "Okay. But only because I love you."

I suppressed a squee over his profession of love. Instead, I played it cool, tipped my head back into the shower spray, and rinsed the shampoo out of my hair. "You won't regret it."

* * *

An hour later, I was eating my words. By the look on Carson's face, he was very much regretting it. Not that I could blame him. The bus tour was turning out to be a bit of a dud.

And that was putting it mildly.

When we first boarded, things seemed promising. The afternoon was bright and clear, and the bus was half empty, which was actually pretty surprising, since New York is one of those rare tourist destinations that never experiences a slow season. This meant there were plenty of free spaces on the second story, so we were able to enjoy our tour from on high, basking in the sunshine of the open top. The guide sat on the first floor, in a bucket seat next to the driver, talking into a microphone that piped into speakers beside each of our seats. As we passed by historic landmarks and buildings, he described each one and discussed its history.

At least, that's what we assumed he was talking about. Really, we couldn't understand a single word the guy said. He spoke in an uninspired monotone, and his voice came through muffled and fuzzy, like the wires in the sound system had been chewed through by city rats. Even though the content of his speech was completely indiscernible, no one bothered to report the problem. Not a single person went downstairs to complain. Nobody even silently huffed in annoyance. They just sat there, staring at all these amazing New York attractions passing us by, without the slightest bit of context or background to go with it. Did those retirees in the corner even know they were looking at the flagship Macy's department store? Did the family of six over there realize that under Madison Square Garden lurked a train station that served over half a million passengers per day? I'd dragged Carson aboard this big red hunk of metal under the guise of giving him an overview of the city, and now this useless excuse for a tour guide was ruining it.

After we'd passed by the heart of Broadway without a coherent narration, Carson's eyes were glazing over. I'd had enough.

"See up there? Straight ahead?" I said to Carson. "That's Columbus Circle."

"What's Columbus Circle, and why should I care?"

"Well, Smartypants, aside from it being home to the iconic Time Warner Center, there is a statue in the middle of the roundabout that was built in 1892, commemorating the four hundredth anniversary of Columbus's arrival in America. And, you'll be interested to know, that statue is the point from which all official distances to New York City from around the world are measured."

"Really?"

"Really. So, when we say Hong Kong is 8,048 miles away from New York City, we really mean it's 8,048 miles away from that statue, right there."

"Wow."

Carson raised his eyebrows and nodded. I'd taught him something new and interesting. Perhaps I could salvage this failure of a bus tour after all.

I stood up, leaning against the bench in front of us for balance as the bus swerved and sped through city traffic. Affecting my best tour guide stance and smile, I pointed over the side of the bus. "We're now heading northwest on Broadway, where up ahead and to the left you'll see the famous Lincoln Center."

"And what, pray tell, makes Lincoln Center so famous?" Carson smiled. At this point, he was just trying to bust my chops.

"I'm glad you asked, sir. Lincoln Center is a sixteen-acre complex of buildings, including thirty indoor and outdoor performance facilities. Most notably, it houses the Metropolitan Opera, the New York City Ballet, and the Juilliard School."

"That's where Juilliard is?" A redheaded teenage girl in the back of the bus piped up. "Mom, look!"

My cheeks burned. I hadn't realized anyone else was listening to me. But when I looked at the dozen or so passengers scattered throughout the second floor of the bus, I noticed they were all staring at me with rapt attention, waiting for my next juicy bit of tourist information. Lucky for them, I had a lot of that to go around.

"As you can see," I said, projecting my voice, "we've now turned right and are heading straight toward Central Park, an oasis of green in the middle of the concrete jungle. Can anyone guess how many acres Central Park sits on?"

"Two hundred," yelled out one man.

"Higher," I said.

"A thousand," yelled a little boy.

"Lower." This game was fun.

"Eight hundred," said Carson.

"Very close, sir! The correct answer is eight hundred forty-three acres. It's home to a lake, a pond, and a reservoir, as well as a zoo, an ice-skating rink, and even a small castle."

"There's a castle in there?" The little boy was really into my spiel.

"Yes, Belvedere Castle. But no one's ever lived there. It was constructed primarily for decoration, but it also hosts weddings and houses the official weather station of Central Park."

I continued my performance as we passed by Strawberry Fields, the Museum of Natural History, and the Cathedral of St. John the Divine. People asked me questions, and I knew every answer, or at least knew enough to keep the crowd entertained and informed. Two hours flew by in a flash, and when we pulled back into our final stop at Times Square, the second floor gave me a standing ovation. Even Carson was on his feet, clapping his hands. My heart swelled. I felt like I'd accomplished more in that one little tour of Manhattan than I had in four years of undergraduate work and three years of hard white-collar labor.

The other passengers picked up their belongings and began to file out. I sat down in my seat, catching my breath. "What did I just do?"

"You put on an amazing show," he said, sitting back down. "I never thought I'd enjoy a sightseeing tour on a double-decker bus, but you had me captivated."

"Excuse me, miss?" The retired couple stood above me, the woman placing a gentle, wrinkled hand on my shoulder. "We've been saving our money for a trip to New York for close to fifteen years, and we finally made it here last night. I have to say, you've made our introduction to the city very memorable."

"Thanks," I said. "That's so nice of you to say."

"Well, it's true." The man held out a folded up ten-dollar bill. "For your hard work."

"Oh, I couldn't accept that."

"Take it." He pressed the money into my palm. "You're good at your job and you deserve some tips."

"Keep at it," she said. "You're gonna run this tour company one day."

They disappeared down the stairs and left me sitting there with my mouth hanging open and the money dangling between my fingers.

"Can you believe that?" I laughed.

"Yes." Carson stood and took my hand. "You've really got a natural talent for this tour guide thing. How many New York City guidebooks have you read?"

"Not sure. Maybe about a dozen? When I was a teenager in New Jersey, I used to come into New York all the time and go sightseeing. Even though I couldn't really travel anywhere, I still liked to play tourist. I collected guidebooks the way other little girls collected Barbie dolls."

"Sounds like you were born to do this."

"I know."

"So do it."

"What, be a tour guide?" I snorted. "I already told you. They make, like, nothing. I can't do that."

Carson shrugged. "If it's something you're really passionate about, you'll find a way to make it work."

He moved toward the stairs and I trailed behind him. Carson didn't get it. Maybe he'd been okay with scraping by and couch-surfing before that trust fund fell in his lap, but I wanted a home to call my own. And there was no way I could make that happen in New York City on the salary of a double-decker-bus tour guide.

But this was the man who had hit the jackpot on a casino game he didn't even understand how to play. A man who got on an airplane and came to see me on a whim—me, a woman he'd known for barely two weeks—just because he missed me. He followed his gut, even when all signs pointed in the opposite direction. Somehow it worked out for him. Life fell into place because he had the courage to keep taking risks.

I stepped down from the bus and set foot on the cracked city pavement. Carson laced his fingers through mine, and as we walked down the street, his words echoed in my head.

*Find a way to make it work.*

# chapter twenty-two

Playing tour guide had given me a buzz. When it was all over, I was jonesing for more. So I grabbed Carson's hand and led him south on Eighth Avenue, determined to maintain my high.

"Broadway theaters are right around the corner here," I said. "Let me show you a couple of my favorites."

"That sounds awesome," he said. "I definitely want to see them. But it's almost two and I'm starving. Can we stop off for lunch first?"

"Sure. Why don't we go to Sardi's?"

"What's Sardi's?"

"A restaurant that's been around since the early 1920s. Broadway stars and executives used to hang out there. Now it's more of a tourist trap—as you would put it—than celebrity hangout. But it's a vital part of New York City history. And you'll dig this: The walls are lined with celebrity caricatures."

"What do they have on the menu?"

"Oh, you know, typical restaurant fare. Steaks, sandwiches, salads. That kind of thing." I squeezed his hand and sped down the street. "It's just a couple blocks ahead and to the left. On the way we'll have to pass by the St. James Theatre, which, incidentally, is where Sardi's was originally located."

"I hope they've got burgers."

Sardi's did have burgers. Unfortunately, they had no open tables. In my hasty, impulsive decision to go there for lunch, I hadn't even considered the fact that a popular tourist attraction would require reservations made a week in advance, even at two o'clock.

"Not to fear." I was so hopped up on the idea of finding a hot spot for lunch that my voice was jittery. "Carmine's is right around here. That was built in—"

"Sophie?"

"Yes?"

Carson took both my hands in his and looked me in the eye. "I love you."

"I love you, too." I smiled.

"But I can't handle another historical fact until I have food in my stomach."

Without a word, I hustled us over to Famous Original Ray's Pizza, where Carson gobbled up two slices of pepperoni and a sausage calzone, while I savored a steaming rice ball parmigiana. When we finished, my belly was full and I was feeling sluggish. The post-tour high had crashed down around me.

"Where to now?" he asked, tossing a wadded up napkin onto his empty paper plate. "What other hidden New York City landmarks are you going to uncover for me?"

"Honestly," I said, "I kind of want to relax and get a beer."

"Is there a particular place you have in mind? Perhaps an Irish pub with some deep historical significance?"

"There's an Irish pub next door. It's not particularly significant, but they do have Guinness on tap."

"I'm sold."

We meandered over to the Playwright Tavern, where we sat next to each other in a vinyl booth and knocked back a couple of porters. The thick, brown beer went straight to my head, leaving me pleasantly dizzy and suddenly inspired.

"Let's do a pub crawl," I said.

"You're certainly being spontaneous," he said. "Who are you, and what have you done with Sophie?"

My lips grazed his ear. "She's gone," I whispered. "I scared her away. I think she thought I was a little too wild."

The tip of my tongue dragged lightly along the tender skin of Carson's neck. From the look on his face, I thought he might press me back against that tattered seat and ravage me right there in the middle of the bar. Instead, he said, "Let's go, before we do something crazy and they wind up kicking us out."

So began our spur-of-the-moment bar-hopping adventure. The rest of the day was spent sampling drinks at Midtown watering holes: Smithwick's at The Perfect Pint, Hurricanes at Jimmy's Corner, and Moscow Mules at Cock & Bull, where Carson finally got that burger he'd been craving. By the time we emerged from the underbelly of Cellar Bar, the sun had long ago disappeared and I was feeling good.

We walked along 42nd Street, arm in arm. "This is Bryant Park," I said, gesturing to my right. "It's where Fashion Week used to be held."

"Isn't that your office building?" I followed the direction of Carson's outstretched arm and saw One Bryant Park towering above us. Its brightly lit spire seemed to reach endlessly into the pitch-black sky.

"Yup. That's it. McKinley Worldwide Headquarters."

"Wanna take me inside and show me around?"

"No way. I called in sick this morning, remember? I can't take the chance of running into someone now."

He glanced down at his watch. "It's ten-thirty at night. No-body's gonna be there."

For the most part, Carson was probably right. Sure, there were a few dedicated souls who religiously burned the midnight oil. Like Elizabeth. I'd have bet five hundred Hong Kong dollars she was still up there, hunched over her keyboard with that ever-present scowl on her face. But her office was on the thirty-fifth floor, two flights above where Seth and I shared our little space. And there was no way Seth was still around. He'd assuredly left at five on the dot, bolting from the building so fast he likely left behind a cloud of smoke.

"What floor do you work on?" Carson asked.

"Thirty-three."

I tilted my head back and counted the skyscraper's stories, trying to figure out which row of windows housed McKinley's suite on the thirty-third floor, but I lost track at number eleven. There were still so many lights burning inside the building. *Do I really want to risk it?*

"I'll bet you've got a great view from up there," he said.

"I do."

"I'd love to see it." He slid his hand around my hips and tucked his fingertips beneath the waistband of my jeans. "It looks like those windows are all mirrored on the outside."

"Just like the Grand Amadora."

"Yup." His fingertips inched lower, brushing the lace trim of my panties. Then they were sliding beneath the lace, running gently down the curve of my hip.

In that moment, I wanted his body more than anything else in the world. More than a roof over my head, more than a blue and gold business card. The only goal I cared about attaining was a climax.

"Let's go," I said.

The security guard in the lobby didn't look up from his newspaper when we passed through the turnstiles and into the elevator. On the thirty-third floor, half the overhead lights were turned off. As we wandered toward my office, I scanned the floor for stragglers but found no other signs of life. Once inside, I shut the door and flipped the lock for good measure.

Carson looked from Seth's desk to mine. "Lemme guess: Your desk is the one without the pile of trash on it."

"You're correct." I grabbed Carson's hand and pulled him toward me, wrapping my arms around his midsection and peppering light kisses along his neck.

"Wait a minute." He pulled back, a mischievous grin playing at the corners of his mouth. "I don't think we should be partaking in this kind of behavior in the office."

Standing on my tiptoes, I nibbled at the edge of his chin. "It's okay. We're definitely alone now."

"Oh. Well, that's a different story." With one swift movement, he lifted me up onto my black leather desk blotter. My breath was ragged, and when our lips met, I released an unwitting moan. His hands went to the front of my shirt, unfastening buttons with grace and speed as his tongue teased and tickled my skin. My breasts spilled from my bra, and he trailed kisses down my chest. I leaned back with my eyes open, watching him treat my body with unmatched tenderness. My gaze floated across the room, to the tornado of papers littering Seth's desktop, and I briefly remembered the last time I'd had sex in this office. How awful it had been. Seth hadn't even bothered to unbutton my blouse.

Meanwhile, Carson was heading farther south, unzipping my jeans and slipping them down over my hips. When he caught sight of my panties, he groaned. "Red lace," he said, peeling my pants down over my ankles and slinging them over the back of my chair. "These look so hot on you."

In an instant, he was on his knees, moving my red lace panties to the side and stroking me with the tips of his fingers before following up with his tongue. I fell backward, no longer in control of my own movements. My arms jutted out, grabbing the desktop, sending my organized piles of manila folders crashing to the floor.

"Come for me," he said, his baritone voice sending vibrations through my core. "Come for me, Sophie."

And I obeyed. I came so hard that I crushed the corner of my expensive leather desk blotter in the palm of my spasming fist. When I relaxed my hand and opened my eyes, Carson was stepping out of his shorts and tearing a condom packet open with his teeth. "How do you want it?" he asked.

I answered by slithering to my feet and turning around to face the window. With my legs spread, I leaned forward onto my elbows. Bent over my desk, with Carson behind me.

It didn't escape me that Seth and I had sex in this same exact position. On this same exact desk. But I was no longer sure that what Seth and I had done could technically be categorized as sex. Not after feeling what Carson was doing to my body. He entered me slowly, his fingertips creeping around my body to touch me in just the right way, in exactly the right places. As I came, he ran his tongue up my spine. I couldn't remember if I wailed. All I recalled was looking at the window and seeing our faint reflection superimposed against the backdrop of the city, Carson standing behind me with his face twisted in pleasure.

No. Before Carson, I'd never known what sex was supposed to feel like. Nothing could ever compare to this sensation.

By the time we caught our breath, it was after eleven. We picked our clothes up off the floor, hid the condom in a ball of crumpled printer paper, and got dressed. The smell of sex in the air was pungent; I could only hope it would dissipate by sunrise.

"Where do these go?" Carson was crouching over the mess of folders I'd sent toppling to the ground in the throes of passion. Paperwork was the last thing I felt like dealing with.

"I don't know." I bent over and picked it up in one jumbled pile. "I'll figure it out tomorrow."

He righted a tipped-over pencil cup, the one that held the highlighters. "This is a really nice office you work in."

*Was* it a nice office? Right about then, all I could see were two disorganized desks, a chair with a squeaky wheel, and a whiteboard covered in smudged red ink, detailing a project plan I couldn't care less about. *I'd rather be working on a tour bus, hourly salary and all.*

"It's all right, I guess." An overwhelming urge came over me. The urge to flee from this building as fast as I could. I turned the lock and opened the door, but as I stepped into the hallway, a shriek escaped my lips.

There was Owen. Leaning against the opposite wall with his arms folded across his chest. Staring me right in the face.

"Hey, Sophie."

"Owen." *Deep breaths. Don't panic.* "What are you doing here?"

"Working late. I'm on deadline. I went to the kitchen for some coffee and heard some strange noises coming from down the corridor." He glanced from me to Carson and back again. "But it was just you two."

*Shit.*

"Okay." What else could I say? I was already moving toward the front door, my eyes on the stained Berber carpet beneath my feet. "See you tomorrow, then."

"Glad you're feeling better," he called out.

I couldn't look back. Hopefully Carson was still trailing behind me.

In the elevator bank, I jabbed the DOWN button, tapping it continuously until I heard the bell ring. Carson waited until the doors closed behind us to ask, "That wasn't, like, your boss, was it?"

"No." I stared at the red LED screen and counted the floor numbers as we went down: *28, 27, 26.* "It's just some random dude that works with me."

"He seemed like a weirdo. Do you think he was standing outside the door listening to us the whole time?"

*14, 13, 12 . . .*

I could feel Carson studying me. "Did you ever . . . you know . . ."

"Sleep with that guy?"

"Yeah."

"No." The thought made me shudder. "God, no. Gross."

Carson pulled me next to him, a movement that would normally make me melt. But my limbs felt stiff, my mouth dry. Because I was screwed.

There was no way Owen wasn't going to tell Seth about this. And there was a really good chance that Seth would then tell Elizabeth. He knew I was already skating on thin ice with her, and he had no reason to cover for me. Elizabeth would definitely give me the ax if she found out I'd skipped work to fool around.

After hours.

On my desk.

While drunk.

I needed a job. And not a job on a tour bus. I needed *this* job. My rent could not be paid on minimum wage. My primary goal in life could not be an orgasm. This day had been fun, but not fun enough to justify throwing away my entire existence. If I'd messed it all up on account of my hormones, I'd never be able to forgive myself.

# chapter twenty-three

When the alarm went off at 6:30, Carson didn't wake up. In fact, he slept through my entire morning routine. Even the coffee grinder didn't stir him from his sound slumber. At one point, I leaned over to make sure he was still breathing. He was. So I went back to blow-drying my hair, while frowning in his direction.

Carson couldn't grasp the gravity of my predicament. He was used to giving up when he encountered a problem: dropping out of school when he got some bad grades, flitting off to another destination when the going got tough. He had never held down a real job before, didn't understand the pressures of the professional rat race. He didn't get that climbing the corporate ladder wasn't a team-building exercise or even a good-natured competition, but rather a gladiator game full of carnage and spite, and if you took your hand off the rung for even a split second, someone would grab the opportunity to send you plunging to your death.

What the hell was I thinking? In the three years I'd been employed at McKinley, I'd never once called in sick. I worked through migraines, tonsillitis, even the flu. Once, I'd flown across the country with stomach cramps so debilitating, they had me lurching for the airplane bathroom every fifteen minutes; halfway to our destination, I'm sure the flight attendants were cross-checking my name against the no-fly list. But I'd been dedicated. Determined. Disciplined. Nothing could keep me from working toward those goals I had listed on my five-year plan. Yet here I was, messing up my hard-earned reputation with a guy who'd never had a plan in his life.

After leaving a spare key in plain sight on the kitchen counter, I stormed out the door, slamming it behind me. Maybe that would wake Carson up.

When I got to work, the only thing waiting for me in the office was the chaos I'd created on my desk the night before. I set down my briefcase and got to work reassembling my once-perfectly organized filing system.

"Hello."

At the sound of Seth's voice, I shrieked and dropped a stack of sequence diagrams to the floor around my feet. He stood in the doorway, one hand in his pocket, the other gripping the handle of a coffee mug.

"What are you doing here so early?" I said, scooping the papers up off my sensible leather pumps.

"Well, the project's behind schedule." He sauntered into the room and perched on his desk, his mannerisms conveying anything but urgency. "Someone's gotta get here early to take care of things. Especially since we were one man down yesterday."

"I'm sorry I was out. I wasn't feeling well."

He nodded, looking somewhat amused. "Feeling better now?"

"Mostly." I started riffling through my documents. Unable to focus my vision enough to comprehend the words printed on the papers, I just matched the sticky flags to their corresponding colored folders.

"Owen said he ran into you last night."

*Blue sticky. That means flowcharts, right?*

"He said you had a visitor."

*No, wait. Blue means financial statements.*

"Was it the guy in this book?"

My hands trembled at the sight of Carson's sketchbook in Seth's hands. I'd completely forgotten it was in my desk drawer. He flipped through it like he was perusing a magazine at the doctor's office.

"I know I saw a picture of him in here somewhere," he said.

I snatched it from him and shoved it in my briefcase. I knew precisely which sketch he was looking for. "That's private," I said. "Why were you going through my desk?"

"Well, when I got here this morning, the place was a mess. Your chair was on the other side of the room; your folders were scattered all around. I knew you'd never leave things in such a state of disorder, so I thought maybe we'd been robbed. I was just checking your drawers to, you know, see if it looked like anything had been stolen. But then Owen came by and told me about your little run-in last night. Then it all made sense."

I wanted to smack that shit-eating grin right off his face. "What do you want from me?"

"Whoa, hold on a minute." He put his hands up, like a white-collar criminal. "Who says I want anything from you?"

"It's written all over your face. Now just tell me what it is you need me to do so that you'll keep your mouth shut about this."

Seth looked out the window and stroked his chin, undoubtedly concocting a dozen different ways to blackmail me. What a
fool I'd been. A weak, irresponsible fool.

"You know what?" Seth slapped his thighs and stood up. "I
think I'm gonna take the morning off to ponder your question
some more. If Elizabeth comes by, just tell her I'm . . . conducting
research."

"Okay." This seemed too easy. He must've been expecting
more than just an alibi for his game of hooky. As it was, he barely
showed his face in the office. I braced myself against the desk,
waiting for the next blow.

"So, while I'm gone, I think you should take care of . . . this."
He heaved a pile of crinkled papers from his mountain of junk
and hurled it onto my desk. I turned and rummaged through
them. Right on the top was every to-do list Elizabeth had sent
since the project had started last week. Not one of the boxes had
been ticked off.

"Are you serious?" I asked. "You've really accomplished none
of these tasks?"

"I've been busy."

"Seth, I have my own to-do lists to take care of."

"Hmm. That's too bad." He pressed the back of his hand
against his forehead, feeling for fever. "'Cause I think I might be
coming down with something. It could keep me out of the office
for the rest of the week."

"You know, this is blackmail. And harassment. You could get
fired."

"What're you gonna do about it?" Seth leaned toward me,

so close I could smell the mixture of coffee and Altoids on his breath. "Run down to HR and tell them all about how John Ramsey's son is making you sad?" He mimicked a sob.

"Maybe I am."

He straightened up, sneering. "No one's gonna believe you, sweetie. And even if they do—which they won't, but let's pretend for a second that they'll buy your crazy story—what are you gonna tell them? That you lied about being sick? That you skipped out on work, then fucked some stranger on your desk after hours? You'll get fired, too. Frankly, I don't care if I get fired. I don't need this job. Certainly not as much as you do. So if I were you, I'd think long and hard before opening that pretty little mouth of yours."

Seth hovered over me, gliding the tip of his finger across my bottom lip. I stood as still as a statue, staring over his shoulder and out the window, trying hard not to breathe. Finally, after what seemed like hours, he stepped away and shuffled into the hall. I slammed the door shut behind him and gasped for air.

*Deep breaths. Do not cry. You don't deserve to break down in tears right now.*

And I didn't. Everything happening was my own stupid fault. I made this mess, and now I had to clean it up. Only I wasn't sure if that was even possible. I was already drowning in my own task list. Now I was supposed to pick up Seth's slack, too? For ten days, he'd done nothing. I could work around the clock and still not have this project done by Monday morning.

The only thing I could do was the only thing I'd ever done: sit down at the desk and approach it methodically. One task at a time. First, I had to get all these papers in order. I spread them out on the blotter and sorted them into piles. Flowcharts here, financial statements there. Then out came the sticky flags and the color-coordinated folders. By lunchtime, my desk had been tidied up, but I still hadn't checked a single box on my to-do list.

*Looks like I'll be eating another smelly, healthy salad over my computer keyboard.* As I stood up to head for the door, my desk phone rang. It was Jeanette.

"Ms. Bruno, Carson Greene is waiting for you at the front desk."

Wonderful. Just when I'd gotten my blood pressure back down to a manageable rate, Carson showed up unannounced.

"Send him to my office, please."

When he knocked on my door, I pulled him in by the arm and shut it immediately. "What are you doing here?"

"I know you tend to work through your meals, so I figured I'd come say hi and force you to take a little break." He hoisted a paper bag in front of my face. "I brought you some lunch. You know, there's a great little Cantonese hole-in-the-wall around the corner."

The office suddenly smelled of spring onion and ginger, sparking a memory of Hong Kong: standing with Carson in the sweltering streets, scarfing down *dai pai dong*, kissing soy sauce off each other's lips.

I shook the sentimentality from my brain and grabbed the bag from his hand. "You shouldn't be here."

"I was expecting a 'thank you,' but okay."

"Seriously, Carson." I set the bag down on my desk, ignoring the way my mouth had begun to water. "This is a bad idea. People are already talking. I could get in a lot of trouble."

"That creepy guy spilled the beans, huh?"

I nodded. "You should go."

"I'm sorry. I'll get out of here. I've got a little gift to give you first. Something to keep by your side while you work. Hopefully it'll make you smile."

He reached into his messenger bag and pulled out a sheet of paper. Another caricature. This time, a curly-haired woman stood on top of a double-decker bus with a microphone in her hand and a smile on her face. Behind her, the Statue of Liberty towered in the distance. The words inside the thought bubble read, *Sophie's Spontaneous Tours.*

"Catchy name, right?"

"What is this?"

"Think of it as a little inspiration."

It was really good, just like all his drawings. Clever, cute, flawlessly executed. But for some reason, the sight of it made my stomach turn. How exactly was this inspirational? It was a reminder of a life I didn't have and never would. Unlike Carson, I wasn't motivated by pipe dreams. I was motivated by plans. Like that task list sitting on my desk. The one that seemed totally insurmountable. Especially now that Seth had quadrupled the number of unchecked boxes I had to tick off.

I suddenly felt very dizzy.

When Seth flung the door open, I could have sworn the room shook. Perhaps it was the foreshocks of a devastating earthquake.

"Oh, hey," he said, his eyes fixed on Carson. "It's you."

Carson looked at me, then back at Seth. "Do I know you?"

"You're the guy from the pictures."

Carson furrowed his brow, and I tugged at his shirt. "Come on," I said.

"What pictures? What is he talking about, Soph?"

"Ignore him. He's an asshole."

"Now I'm an asshole?" Seth laughed. That cocky, arrogant, my-daddy's-a-millionaire cackle. "You weren't saying that when I had you bent over the desk."

I was pretty sure, at that very second, I saw the walls of the office begin to decompose. In a matter of minutes, I'd be up to my elbows in crumbling drywall.

"Listen, buddy," Carson said. "I don't know who you are, but—"

"Who I am," Seth said, puffing his chest, moving closer to Carson, "is the guy whose sloppy seconds you're sucking up. You didn't think you were the first person to fuck her in this very room, did you? She'll spread those legs for anyone."

The next sound I heard was the sickening crunch of bone against bone, as Carson's fist collided with Seth's shit-eating grin.

# chapter twenty-four

Blood spattered my leather desk blotter. That thing had certainly taken a beating in the last twelve hours. Not as bad a beating as Seth was enduring, though. He made an awful gagging sound, like he was swallowing his own tongue, and his arms flew up to shield his face from another blow. When I saw Carson jerk his arm back to hit him again, I grabbed his bicep and tugged with all my strength.

"Stop it right now!" I hissed. "This is a place of business!"

He bared his teeth but didn't throw the punch. Instead, he shook out his hand, wiggled his fingers, inspected the angry red splotches that marked his knuckles. A growl rumbled low in his throat, veins popping in his neck. For some strange reason, I thought about kissing him. Then I got mad at myself for even entertaining the notion. Because he'd just beaten up my coworker. A coworker who was a total asshole, and completely deserved it, but who could also make my life a living hell.

I stood between them, one arm extended in each direction like I was stopping traffic. Slowly, Seth lowered his arms, peering cautiously at his attacker. "Are you okay?" I asked him.

Seth touched two fingers to the bridge of his nose and winced. It was bright pink and swelling rapidly. Not knowing what else to do, I offered him a box of tissues from my desk. He snatched them and blotted the bloody mess dripping from his nostrils. Glaring at Carson, he said, "Leave. Now. Before I call the cops."

Without a sound, I trailed Carson out the door and down the hall. My shoulders slumped, my feet dragging along the carpet. I pressed the button for the elevator, then raised my trembling fingers to my lips. The descent to the lobby was painfully silent. I didn't look up from the ground until we made it through the revolving doors and out onto the pavement. Then I stared Carson right in the eyes.

"What is wrong with you?" I asked.

"You heard what he said. He deserved it."

"I don't care if he deserved it. You don't react to an insult by busting someone's face open. I think you broke his nose."

"Never mind his nose. I could've broken my hand." He massaged his fingers. "My *drawing* hand, by the way."

"That's what you're concerned with right now? Your *drawing* hand? You punched my fucking coworker *in my office*. How do you think this makes me look?"

Carson cocked his head to the side. "From the sound of things, he's not just a coworker. Apparently, you're having sex with him, too."

"I *had* sex with him. *Once*. Months ago. I barely even talk to him now. What difference does that make, anyway? What difference would it make if I'd slept with every guy in my company?"

"Well, if you're not talking to him anymore, what was he doing with my sketchbook?"

"He was snooping through my desk."

"Why was it in your desk? Why wasn't it at home, for safe-keeping?"

"Because you mailed it to my fucking office!" At this point, I was shouting and flailing my arms. Commuters on 42nd Street whizzed by without so much as a second glance. New Yorkers weren't fazed by anything. Not even the huge scene I was making. "Why the hell would you send something like that to the place I work?"

"You didn't give me your home address! When we said good-bye at the airport, you just shoved your business card in my face, like I was some client you'd had a sales lunch with. Were you just assuming we'd never see each other again?"

"Yes, actually. I was."

He flinched, like I hit him, and his voice got very quiet. "So I was just some random guy. Another one of your meaningless conquests. Is that why you told me not to call you anymore? Were you hoping I'd quietly go away?"

"It wasn't like that," I said. "What we had was special, but it was always meant to be temporary. You were going off to travel the world. I had a job to get back to. We both had other plans. Or so I thought. How was I supposed to know you'd show up here by surprise and put my whole career at risk by beating up my colleague?"

"He deserved it. No one insults you like that."

"I don't need a hero, Carson."

"What?"

"I don't need someone to swoop in out of the blue and save

me. My life is just fine. I'm getting along quite well on my own."

"Are you, really? Because I don't see someone who's getting along just fine. I see someone who's miserable."

A crowded city street, a heated screaming match, and a loved one telling me how miserable I was? It was Temple Street Night Market all over again.

"What I see," Carson continued, "is someone who's so obsessed with status and planning and obligations that she only allows herself joy in tiny morsels. As soon as she gets a little nibble, a taste of what happiness feels like, she willfully throws it away and chalks it up to a fleeting fantasy."

He paused, waiting for my reaction. But my vocal cords felt paralyzed.

"Contrary to what you may think, Sophie, what you and I had in Hong Kong was real life. What you and I have right now is real. What happened on that tour bus yesterday? Real. Don't deny it. Don't deny the person you really are. Stop being so damn afraid to be happy."

If only I could have snapped my fingers and made my fears magically vanish into thin air. How easy life would've been for me. I'd have been a fearless girl of action, a slave to my whims, the wild woman I'd always dreamed of being. But Carson didn't understand where I was coming from. Sometimes it felt like my life was going full speed ahead, passing me by, and I didn't have a say in where it went.

"Not all of us have a trust fund," I said. "Some of us have to actually work for a living. To earn money to pay bills. So we can have a roof over our heads. Instead of wandering the world like a drifter with no place to call home."

His jaw flexed and released. "At least I'm happy with the life I've chosen for myself. Every day, I get to follow my passion."

"You're not following your passion. You're not following anything at all! You're just floating around, completely aimless. The only goal on your five-year plan is me. Well, guess what? I'm a person, not a goal. What else are you working toward? Nothing! You draw and you draw. You create all these gorgeous, beautiful works of art. And then you let them go. You abandon them in a hotel room, or you throw them away, and you never think twice. And you do it because you're too afraid of failure to even try to chase success."

I stood there, panting, anticipating Carson's impassioned rebuttal. All he did was throw his hands up in surrender and say, "I guess you and I have very different ideas about what it means to succeed."

We stared at each other for a moment, both of us silent, until he said, "I'm gonna go back to your place and collect my things. I think it's probably best if I leave."

At first, he made no gesture to walk away. I think he was waiting for me to tell him no. Instead, I nodded in silent agreement.

He turned, and a violent tremor seized my whole body as I watched him disappear down 42nd Street. *Deep breaths. Keep it together.* But it was no use. Nothing I told myself could stop the tears from streaming down my cheeks.

* * *

Going back inside the building right away didn't seem like a reasonable option, so I decided to take a stroll to clear my head and dry my eyes. After containing my sobs, I crossed the street and climbed the seven steps to enter Bryant Park, where I was greeted by the burbling noise of a pink granite fountain. Which wasn't just any fountain; it was actually the first monument in New York City ever to be dedicated to a woman—Josephine Shaw Lowell, a businesswoman and progressive reformer. Somehow, I doubted Ms. Lowell ever had to break up a scuffle between two lovers in her office.

Heading east, I snaked through a maze of scattered folding chairs and bistro tables and popped back out on the sidewalk, where I walked past the entrance to the New York Public Library. Two marble lions flanked the wide staircase. Not many people knew those lions had names; during the Great Depression, Mayor Fiorello La Guardia dubbed them "Patience" and "Fortitude," the qualities he felt people needed to get through those troubling times.

I continued on toward Pershing Square and turned left to enter the lobby of Grand Central Station. Nothing quite defined this city for me like standing in the middle of the bustling terminal and soaking in its frenetic energy. Sunlight streamed in through the massive windows, while passengers rushed back and forth between ticket booths and tunnels, eager to catch their trains before they took off for their final destinations. So many people, so many places to go. All of them with different dreams to chase.

The four-faced clock on top of the information booth read 1:45. It was probably time to head back to work to confront whatever unpleasantness awaited me there. I returned to One Bryant Park, and when I arrived on the thirty-third floor, everything seemed like business as usual. Everyone sat with their heads down, busy typing or talking on the phone. Seth was nowhere to be seen. In my office, the bag of Cantonese food still rested on the edge of my desk. I opened it up, releasing an aroma that made me salivate. Without sitting down, I pulled out a plastic container of roast pork noodle soup and a plastic spoon, slurping it with gusto. Even lukewarm, it was delicious. The spice on my tongue stirred up memories. Warm embraces, carefree laughter, unexpected luck.

Happiness.

My desk phone rang, melting the memories away. When I picked up, it was Elizabeth. "I'd like to see you in my office immediately."

The soup churned in my stomach. I took slow, measured steps toward the staircase, feeling like I was dragging a thousand-pound weight up to the thirty-fifth floor. When I knocked, she told me to enter. Two pairs of eyes greeted me as I poked my head through the half-open door. One pair was severely bloodshot and swollen.

"Have a seat." She gestured to the empty leather guest chair beside Seth.

Elizabeth clasped her hands together and leaned forward on her mahogany desk. "Sophie," she began, "as you know, McKinley is the third most prestigious consulting firm in the world.

We pride ourselves on behaving responsibly and ethically and by serving our customers with the utmost dedication. As such, we can't stand for anything less than one hundred percent professionalism, at all times."

I nodded, hoping they couldn't smell the fear sweat pooling under my arms.

"Seth has told me some disconcerting things," she continued. "I'd like to make sure I hear your side of the story before we take any further action."

*Further action?* I looked over at Seth. His once-perfect nose looked slightly askew, and his eyes were puffing up as we spoke. Why wasn't he at the doctor? Was it more important for him to make sure I got reprimanded than it was to seek medical attention for his wounds?

I cleared my throat. "Well, I had a guest in our office for lunch, and—"

"She was in there having sex on her desk, in the middle of the workday," Seth interjected.

"No, I wasn't!"

"I have another witness who'll back my claim. Owen Rappaport was—"

"He's lying!"

"Okay," Elizabeth said. "Let's just calm down. One person at a time. Seth, I already heard your side, so let's—"

"Get my father on the phone," he demanded.

"Seth, I'm not sure that's necessary," she said.

"Yes, it is." He glared at me with his beady eyes, a spoiled little boy who wasn't getting his way. This whole ordeal felt like something out of middle school. An expulsion hearing where El-izabeth was the teacher, and I was the bully who'd beaten up the principal's son. It was a fight I would never win.

Despite the hesitant look on her face, Elizabeth turned on the speakerphone and dialed up John Ramsey. His secretary, Claire, said he was in a meeting.

"I'll take a message," she said.

"Claire?" Seth chimed in, leaning toward the desk with a greasy smile on his face.

"Oh, hi, Seth," she cooed. "Everything okay?"

"Not really, sweetie. I'm in a bit of a bind right now. I was hoping to speak to my father right away."

"Sure thing," she said. "I'll put you through immediately."

When Seth smirked at me, I was half expecting him to stick out his tongue and blow a raspberry, like a sixth grader. The three of us sat there, listening to hold music, a Tom Jones song in the silliest instrumental arrangement I'd ever heard. I think I detected a slide whistle. Even though the whole situation was objectively ridiculous, my heart was racing. This was it. I was about to be fired by a founding partner of McKinley Consultants Worldwide.

But, if I was being honest with myself, didn't I deserve it? Lately, I hadn't been giving this job one hundred percent of my ef-fort. At most, I was giving an unenthusiastic fifty percent. Because I didn't care. I hated everything about it. Sure, before I started mentally checking out, I was *good* at it, setting goals, crunching numbers, sticking to a plan: These were my inherent strengths. But they weren't my passions. They didn't bring me joy.

The hold music cut off abruptly. "What is it?" John barked. I'd always wanted to speak with John Ramsey. Perhaps not under these specific circumstances, though.

"Hi, Dad," Seth said.

"I'm busy. This better be good."

"Well, Dad, there's been . . . an incident."

"What kind of incident?" He sounded exasperated.

Seth's face went grave. "I've been assaulted."

"By who?"

"An unauthorized guest of Sophie Bruno."

"Who the hell's Sophie Bruno?"

I wasn't sure whether to be relieved or troubled that John Ramsey was completely unaware of my existence. Seth crinkled his eyebrows. He definitely seemed troubled. "She's a junior analyst here in the New York office," he said.

"You didn't call the cops, did you?"

"No."

"Well, what the hell do you want me to do about it?" John's voice blasted from the speakerphone and echoed off the walls. Elizabeth pursed her lips and stared at her twiddling thumbs. Clearly, she had no intention of contributing to this train wreck of a conversation.

"Well"—Seth was sputtering at this point—"I think that, you know, this kind of behavior cannot be tolerated at McKinley, and, so, some serious action needs to be taken to—"

"Seth, cut the shit." The gruff voice blared through the speaker. "I know what you do around here. I didn't work my ass off to build this company so that you can run around sticking your dick in everything that moves. You can't carry on like this and then act surprised when it comes back to bite you in the ass."

The color drained from his face. Even the swollen bruise between his eyes was now pale. Beads of sweat formed along his hairline. I bit my lip to keep from laughing.

"Dad, this isn't—"

"I know exactly what's going on here and I want no part of it."

Seth's expression changed from stricken to indignant. "Well, maybe I *will* call the cops, then."

"If you bring any negative press to this company, so help me God, Seth, I will disown you. Every day, you make me more and more sorry that I gave you this job."

*Click.*

A dial tone pierced the air and Elizabeth pressed the OFF button, plunging us into a desperately uncomfortable silence. She licked her lips and shuffled some papers on her desk. "Now that that's behind us, let's move forward." Her face was all business, as if we didn't just endure a heated conversation with the head of McKinley regarding allegations of assault and sexual misconduct. "We have the pressing matter of these audits being woefully behind schedule, and we still need to deliver the data to our auditors by close of business on Friday."

This time, I didn't bother to bite my lip. Instead, I let out a big, boisterous laugh. Elizabeth was not only persistent, but she was also completely out of touch with reality. "That's not going to happen," I said.

She didn't look nearly as amused as I was. "It has to."

"Well, I can't work with this injury." Seth leapt to his feet, his condition suddenly becoming a medical crisis. "I need to get to the hospital right away." He ran from the room with his hand concealing his mangled face.

When the door closed behind him, Elizabeth turned her stony brown eyes on me. "Well, Sophie, it looks like this will fall to you."

"I can't do this by myself in four days," I protested. "Not even if I work around the clock."

"As I see it, you don't have much of a choice."

I didn't know how to respond. I was helpless and screwed. I sat there with my mouth agape, my gaze traveling around the sterile office. Elizabeth's MBA diploma hung on the wall, framed in a tasteful brushed nickel picture frame. The shelves held thick books with titles like *Effective Project Management* and *The Functions of the Executive*. There were no photos on her desk, not a single sign of a life that existed outside this room— no smiling loved ones, no solo poses in front of tourist destinations. Just a black leather blotter and some color-coordinated folders.

In that moment, I realized I *did* have a choice. My life wasn't something that happened without my input. I guided my life where I wanted it to go. There were two paths stretched out in front of me: the safe, sensible, no-nonsense plan and the wild, risky, uncharted territory. I only knew where one of those paths ended up, and it definitely wasn't in a place that would make me happy.

I stood up, looked into Elizabeth's wretched eyes, and said, "I quit. Effective immediately."

Her jaw fell open, and I bounced out of the room, feeling a thousand pounds lighter.

# chapter twenty-five

The next few minutes were blacked out from my memory, like my sudden burst of courage had knocked me unconscious. When I finally came to, I found myself hovering over my desk on the thirty-third floor, trying to figure out what to take with me and what to leave behind. So much of what I'd surrounded myself with, day after day—those color-coded folders, that state-of-the-art laptop, that smartphone—wasn't even mine. It was all property of McKinley Consultants Worldwide. Only two things belonged to me and me alone: that bag of cold Cantonese food and that caricature Carson had hand-delivered alongside it. I grabbed them both, one in each hand, slung my half-empty briefcase over my shoulder, and bolted from the room with my heart beating against my rib cage.

On wobbly knees, I walked through the hallway, past people in suits who were no longer my colleagues. When I reached the reception area, Jeanette gave me an easy, friendly wave, like nothing had changed. When I realized it was the last time I'd ever see her sitting behind that front desk, the last time I'd ever stand in that elevator bank and press that DOWN button, I smiled. A goofy, gleeful grin, stretching from ear to ear. Because I'd done it. I'd made the risky choice. I'd decided not to compromise my happiness.

I floated through the lobby and sailed through the revolving glass doors. Outside, the city surged with excitement. People hustling back and forth along the pavement, cars weaving in and out of traffic. The energy pulsed through me. I could go anywhere. I could do anything. I was no longer bound by schedules or obligations. My life was my own.

*I can't wait to tell Carson.*

Except I couldn't tell Carson. I didn't know where he was, or if his cell phone was still working. For all I knew, he could already be at the airport, booking a ticket to Australia. Or back to Hong Kong. Or wherever he felt like going. And from the way we'd left things not even an hour ago, I wasn't sure if he'd ever want to speak to me again.

That's when the enormity of what I'd done struck me like a supersonic jet. I hadn't just burned a bridge at McKinley; I'd blown it up with a nuclear bomb. My career was poisoned. Any chance of ever getting a positive job reference had been completely obliterated. I would never work at another consulting firm, never get into a reputable MBA program. Not to mention, I now had no income, no way to pay my rent at the end of the month, no way to keep building a savings account. *I don't even have a goddamn phone.*

My adrenaline rush was officially over. Now I was in full-on panic mode.

*What the hell am I going to do?*

I stood on the corner of Sixth Avenue, clutching my bag of food in one hand and my drawing in the other, trying hard not to hyperventilate. Unsure of where to go next, I looked around, desperate for an answer. To my left, a hot dog vendor served a line of hungry customers. To my right, the Empire State Building shot high into the sky. Straight ahead, a red double-decker tour bus lumbered along the asphalt. As it passed me by, I could hear the muffled drone of a disinterested, incoherent voice buzzing through the speakers. I glanced up above the second-story railings, at those poor, cheated tourists who paid forty-nine dollars each for a half-assed drive around Midtown with a tour guide who neither knew nor cared about this incredible city.

*I could do a much better job than the guy behind the microphone.*

My gaze fell to the paper clutched tightly in my hand, and my own cartoonish face smiled back at me. At that moment, I realized it wasn't just a drawing, but a guiding light. The Sophie in the caricature was doing what she loved most in the world. She'd found a way to make it work. Come to think of it, she also looked a hell of a lot like the adventurous girl on the cover of *The Wild Woman's Guide to Traveling the World.*

Without a second thought, I dashed down the sidewalk, toward the corner of 46th and 7th, where the CityLights Sightseeing Bus Tours sold their tickets from a storefront the size of a toilet stall—and, frankly, not much cleaner than one. An unsmiling clerk sat behind the sales booth, leafing through one of those free daily newspapers they gave out at the entrance to subway stations. She didn't look up when I approached. Or when I cleared my throat to get her attention. Finally, I said, "Excuse me?"

She shot me a slit-eyed look and pointed to the wooden box

bolted to the wall beside the kiosk. "Complaints can be filed over there."

For a second, I considered registering a grievance about our shoddy tour from the day before. But I shook my head to clear the thought and pressed on with my original goal.

"I would like to apply for a job," I said.

The clerk stared at me but didn't move. I wasn't sure if she was being dismissive, or if she was merely contemplating whether to take me seriously. Admittedly, I'm sure I looked somewhat insane. My Brooks Brothers suit was rumpled, and my hair was coming loose from my once-tightly cinched bun. A leather briefcase hung from my shoulder, and I was carting around a smelly old bag of food. I was half businesswoman, half fruit loop. But there was no backing out now.

"May I speak to the manager, please?" I asked, my voice sweet as candy.

The clerk rolled her eyes and spun around on her stool, before hoisting herself to her feet and disappearing behind a back door. In her absence, I took a second to arrange myself into something resembling a stable, employable human being. I set the bag of food and briefcase down at my feet, placed the caricature on the counter in front of me, and removed the clip from my hair. With a quick glance in the plate glass windows of the storefront, I fluffed out my curls and tried on a sensible, professional smile. *Deep breaths. You can do this.*

"Can I help you?"

I turned around to see a balding gentleman emerging from the back room, the clerk trailing behind him with her arms crossed over her chest. He looked friendly—friendlier than the clerk, at least—but I could tell he was looking over my shoulder and out onto 46th Street, trying to locate the closest squad car should my presence require police intervention.

"Hello," I said, making sure to smile. "My name is Sophie Bruno, and I'm interested in applying for a position as a tour guide with your company."

He answered without skipping a beat. "We're not hiring."

"Uh...okay." I hadn't prepared myself for this scenario. In fact, I hadn't prepared myself for anything at all. The last job interview I'd had was three years ago, for McKinley, and to get ready for that, I'd researched and rehearsed for days. Now I was out of practice and flying blind. "Well, maybe you could find some room for me somewhere. Or let me substitute on days when guides call in sick."

"We're already fully staffed and have an adequate coverage policy in place."

He already had one hand on the knob of the back door. I couldn't let him get away so easily. "I really think you'd be impressed with my vast knowledge of the city." I spoke in a breathless rush. "At least let me audition. I can give you an impromptu performance, right here."

The clerk snorted, and the manager smiled through his fading patience. I could feel my cheeks burn.

"Listen," he said, "why don't you leave your résumé, and we'll call you if we have any openings."

Résumé. There was another thing I'd conveniently overlooked in my impulsive decision to switch careers. My current résumé was woefully outdated, and perhaps worse, contained nothing related to the travel and tourism industry. I started to think about ways I could spin my current job functions to be relevant to giving bus tours. *Excels at production of color-coded spreadsheets. Powers through checklists despite rapidly changing priorities and a hateful Big Brother of a boss.*

My hands tightened around the paper I'd placed on the counter. I held it up for them to see, as if a sketch of me conducting a tour of New York City qualified me for the job. "This is what I specialize in," I said, fully realizing how crazy I was beginning to sound. "I'm excellent at crafting itineraries and providing spontaneous narration based on the needs and whims of the customers."

The clerk was in a full-on cackle, and the manager's lips twitched as if he was suppressing his own fit of giggles. "We have the itineraries all planned out here at CityLights. Our tour guides just need to read from a script. So why don't you come back after you've put together a proper résumé and drop it off with Alicia here?" He patted the clerk on the shoulder before retreating to the back room and slamming the door behind him.

Without a word, I picked up my briefcase and walked out the front door. I left behind the bag of food, a parting gift to thank Alicia for her hospitable reception. Out on the sidewalk, I stood with my shoulders slumped and my head swimming with regret.

*What did I just do to my life?*

*What the hell is wrong with me?*

Just then, I was distracted from my own self-loathing by two men engaged in a heated conversation that was becoming louder and more aggressive by the second. One of them sported a red jacket with the CityLights logo emblazoned on the breast. The other man wore a fanny pack and clutched a brochure in his clenched fist.

"It was supposed to be here twenty minutes ago," Mr. Fanny Pack said.

The CityLights employee murmured unintelligibly into a walkie-talkie before turning to the tourist and saying, "The bus is caught in traffic."

"Well, how much longer before it arrives?"

"Sir, I can't tell you that now. There's police activity at Penn Station and all vehicles have been pulled over for inspection."

A collective groan sounded from the crowd of patrons standing at the curb, about a dozen tourists waiting for their indefinitely delayed tour bus.

"That's ridiculous."

"I have tickets to a show in three hours!"

"Can we get a refund?" asked Mr. Fanny Pack.

"No refunds," said the man in the red jacket, before turning away and lifting the walkie-talkie to his mouth again.

I empathized with these sightseers. All they wanted to do was explore the big city and enjoy their vacations, and now their plans were falling apart. Of course, the police activity at Penn Station was out of everyone's control, but couldn't the tour company have handled this situation in a more pleasant manner? Allowed refunds, or rescheduled their tours, or at the very least offered them an apology and a smile? *Maybe it's for the best that they didn't want to hire me. They're the perfect example of how not to run a business.*

And then I wondered how I'd do things differently if I ran my own tour company. For one thing, I wouldn't set my schedule based on an idealized vision of New York City traffic patterns. Every day, there was some reason for unforeseen gridlock: a visiting dignitary, a criminal act, a special performance. New York required you to stay on your toes, to keep things spontaneous.

I looked down at the paper in my hands. At the woman with the smile and the unruly head of curls. At the thought bubble floating above her head: *Sophie's Spontaneous Tours.*

*Find a way to make it work.*

"Excuse me," I found myself saying, loudly so the whole crowd could hear. "Is anyone interested in participating in a walking tour?"

The people exchanged quizzical looks, doubtful of this stranger in the wrinkled business suit. I quickly realized I needed to do a better job of selling myself to these tourists than I'd done to the manager of CityLights. So I took a deep breath, and I stopped overthinking it. I just let the words flow straight from my heart to my mouth, with no filter, no script, and no plan.

"My name is Sophie, and I'm a real New Yorker. Over the course of my life, I've spent thousands of hours pounding the pavement, searching for the most fascinating sights, the most intriguing stories, and the most surprising facts about this city. I know these streets like the back of my hand, and now I'd like to share them with you."

The crowd was silent, blinking at me. Even the guy in the red jacket had lowered his walkie-talkie to listen to my speech. I continued while I still had their attention.

"On my walking tour, you'll get to follow in the footsteps of a local. We'll go off the beaten path, exploring hidden gems most other big-box tour companies won't show you. As an added bonus, you'll have personalized attention. Any questions about things we see? I can answer them. Any requests to turn down a side street to investigate? I'll honor them."

I held the caricature high and smiled widely, trying to match the enthusiasm of the woman in the picture. "I'm Sophie, and this is my spontaneous tour."

Mr. Fanny Pack rested his hands on his hips. "I just paid this tour bus forty-nine bucks and they won't refund me. I'm not shelling out any more cash."

The rest of the group nodded in agreement.

"Well," I said, making it up as I went along, "I normally charge thirty-nine dollars for a two-hour tour. But under these exceptional circumstances, seeing as your bus is MIA and all, I'd be happy to honor your bus passes in lieu of cash payment."

"You can't do that," said the guy in the red jacket.

"Why not?" I said. "It's perfectly legal."

Mr. Fanny Pack turned to his travel companion and then back to me. "Okay, we'll do it."

"Great!" I squealed, collecting the tickets in my eager hand. Even though I was being paid for this gig in nonrefundable vouchers for the worst bus tour in the city, my enthusiasm was hard to contain. This was my dream job. And I was doing it.

Even though I didn't really know what I was doing. "Is anyone else interested?"

Four foreign teenagers huddled beneath the blue scaffolding that lined the sidewalk, speaking to each other in hushed German, discussing what I assumed to be the pros and cons of cashing in their bus passes to wander around the city with this random American. Out of the corner of my eye, I noticed the man in the red jacket duck into the CityLights storefront. I had to get this tour on the road before he alerted the manager to the fact that I was stealing away all their clients.

"Last call," I said. "Anyone else?"

"We'd like to join your tour," said one of the German boys, before handing over four red ticket stubs, which I promptly stuffed in the pocket of my blazer.

"Great!" I advanced toward 7th Avenue, letting a mob of passing New Yorkers obscure our departure. "Now if you'll follow me closely, our first stop is just around the corner."

At this time of day, the pedestrian plaza between 7th and Broadway was teeming with people, the postlunch crowd was out in full force, taking photos in front of the wild, blinking lights of Times Square. I ushered my small group to the center of the strip and came to a stop south of the long, winding TKTS line, then launched into a spur-of-the-moment speech.

"Take a look around." I gestured to the massive billboards and flashing neon signs that towered above us, in every direction. "This is Times Square. The beating heart of New York City. Each day, over three hundred thousand pedestrians pass through this intersection. On the busiest days, that number soars to almost five hundred thousand. And, of course, during New Year's Eve celebrations, close to a million people gather here to watch the famous ball drop from the top of One Times Square."

I pointed to the building behind me and smiled as I watched my tour group—*my* tour group!—survey their surroundings.

"Times Square came of age in the Roaring Twenties, when the area was a cultural hub full of theaters, cabarets, and upscale restaurants and hotels. Then, with the dawn of the Great Depression, the atmosphere shifted to one of danger and disrepute. Some of you may recall Times Square being referred to as a den of sin, brimming with drug dealers, prostitutes, sex shops, and peep shows."

The German boys exchanged low titters and I raised my eyebrows at them. "Fortunately, the neighborhood underwent a great transformation in the 1990s, when X-rated movie theaters were replaced with family-style restaurants, and drug dealers were replaced with people in Disney character costumes."

"Where's the Naked Cowboy?" asked Mr. Fanny Pack, looking around.

"He generally appears on Forty-Fifth and Broadway just before noon. I'm afraid we're a few hours too late." *Not that I've ever spent my lunch hour ogling him or anything.*

I pointed out the television studios overlooking the square, as well as the exact spot in which Chris Evans stood when filming the first *Captain America* movie. Then I stood silently, allowing everyone adequate time to drink in the environment, to smell the exhaust from the crush of passing taxis, to hear the dissonant babble of a thousand voices mixing with music and car horns and screeching brakes, to be adequately awed by the colorful spectacle soaring above our heads and all around us.

From there, I led everyone on a slow stroll through the theater district, recounting all the tales of Broadway history I'd picked up over the years. Everyone seemed attentive and happy, even the German kids, who I could tell only understood every third word I spoke. And Mr. Fanny Pack, who by now I'd learned was actually named Bill, was full of enthusiastic questions. Like which theater was the original production of *Cats* featured in, and how long did it run for?

And, yes, I knew the answers: the Winter Garden Theatre, and almost eighteen years.

We wound up meandering through my neighborhood, Hell's Kitchen, where I gave a brief overview of the now-gentrified community's crime-ridden, mob-run history and pointed out the buildings that functioned as speakeasies during Prohibition. Then we pressed on toward the Hudson River Greenway, where we stood in the shadow of the *Intrepid* aircraft carrier and a docked Carnival cruise ship. By then, I had no idea what time it was—and without my smartphone, I had no way of checking—but when Bill announced we'd been walking for two and a half hours, I pressed my fingertips to my lips. Wandering around the city, with no plan and no direction, had made the afternoon go by in a flash.

"I'm so sorry," I said. "I went a half hour over our schedule."

"Don't apologize," he said. "This has been fantastic."

"It has," said his companion, Theo, "but I'm starving. Where's a good place to grab something to eat around here?"

Looking up and down the street, I tried to think of the best place for a group of seven hungry people at the beginning of the city's dinner rush. We'd have to avoid the touristy destinations or anywhere that required a reservation. Then it hit me.

"I know just the spot. Two blocks from here, there's a fantastic little German restaurant that's popular with the locals." The teens regarded me skeptically and I held out my hands in defense. "Trust me, it's one hundred percent *authentisch*. They've got Bitburger. And schnitzel platters."

They conferred in their native language before shrugging in resignation and followed me east along 45th Street. When we entered Zum Bauer, I approached the host stand, where Wolf flashed a smile at me.

"Hello, Sophie," he said, his accent a strange mixture of Bavarian and Brooklynese. "How are you this evening?"

"Great." I craned my neck, looking around the room. "Is Kat here?"

"She took the night off. But don't worry, Henry's working the bar right now and he'll get you whatever you like."

"Actually, I'm gonna need a table. See, I've got this tour group with me, and—"

"You're a tour guide?" Wolf's eyes lit up. "How cool! I didn't know that about you."

"Yeah." I paused to revel in the moment. *I'm a tour guide. How cool.* "Anyway, we've just finished an exhausting walk around Midtown, so I was hoping we could get a big table in the back. Someplace sort of semiprivate, where we can all talk, maybe?"

He nodded and peeled seven menus from the side of the podium. "Absolutely. Right this way."

The German kids followed closely behind Wolf, chatting him up in their mother tongue. Bill and Theo went after them, commenting on the billowing flags and the posters adorning the walls. I brought up the rear, with my hand in the pocket of my blazer, my fingers tracing the edges of the six red bus tickets I'd collected. The payment I'd received for providing a service I loved so much, I'd do it for free.

But maybe next time I could actually earn some cold hard cash.

# chapter twenty-six

First things first: I needed a plan.

Yes, even though I was calling them "Sophie's *Spontaneous* Tours," I still had to figure out how to spin this awesome idea into a lucrative business. I couldn't very well give the same bumbling speech day in and day out and expect to turn a profit. People wanted variety in their sightseeing tours; they wanted choices. Plus, I had to prepare for contingencies: What if it rained? What if a suspicious package closed down everything north of Union Square? These things happened in the city, all the time. I wanted to show I could handle any unforeseen circumstances and still give my clients what they paid for, unlike the double-decker bus company, which was now my competition.

After exchanging good-byes with the members of my inaugural tour group, I raced up the stairs to my apartment, bursting with enthusiasm for my new undertaking. Dusting off an old laptop I hadn't touched since college graduation, I immediately set to work developing a business plan: defining a mission statement, establishing goals, identifying areas of strength and opportunities for growth. Finally, my strategic planning skills were being used on a project that actually mattered to me.

I settled on a pricing structure designed to lure tourists away from CityLights: ten dollars cheaper than the bus ride for a tour that lasted two hours, featured loads of exercise, and ended at a place to grab some grub. Also, the tickets would be fully refundable, transferrable, and reschedulable. Sophie's Spontaneous Tours were about seeing the best sights the city had to offer, but they were also about flexibility and fully acknowledged the fact that not everything was under our control. Some things just had to be left up to the roll of the dice.

One thing I couldn't leave to chance, though, was my budget. Initial revenue projections for my fledgling business were a paltry fraction of what I'd earned at McKinley, and if I didn't make some major modifications to my spending habits, I'd wind up draining my savings account in a matter of weeks. Armed with my trusty spreadsheet of personal finances and a thick stack of old bank and credit card statements, I analyzed each purchase I'd made over the past six months, determining where I could make the deepest cuts.

Slashing expenditures turned out to be an easy task, since most of my money went to supporting a lifestyle I'd no longer be living. Those latte macchiatos I guzzled to stay alert while hopping time zones? Deleted. The takeout I constantly ordered because I was always on the road? Gone. My available funds increased with each expense I removed from my spreadsheet. While I knew this all meant I'd be forced to take a hiatus from globe-trotting for the foreseeable future, it was the price I was willing to pay to pursue my dream job.

Perhaps my greatest thrill came from knowing I'd never have to pay another dry-cleaning bill. Each month, I'd spent absurd amounts of money to launder my work attire, designer duds I didn't even enjoy wearing; the stuffy blazers and demure dresses felt more like armor than apparel. Since they certainly wouldn't be practical choices for leading walking tours, I happily deleted the dry-cleaning expense from my spreadsheet, then opened the door to my organized closet to survey the neatly pressed items suspended from slim velvet hangers. A double-breasted seersucker jacket. Wool pinstripe trousers with painted wood buttons. An A-line skirt with embroidery ringing the hem. They'd cost me a fortune when I bought them off the rack at Brooks Brothers. Maybe I could earn some of that money back.

One by one, I removed every article of clothing from my closet and, using my laptop's webcam, photographed each item before posting it on all the online resale shops I could think of. By the time I published my final listing, it was well after midnight, and my eyes were starting to close of their own volition. There was still more planning to do, but it would have to wait until morning.

I crawled into bed and buried my face in the pillow, waiting for sleep to envelop me. But instead of peacefully drifting off, I was jolted awake by the heady scent infused in my sheets. The distinct spice of Carson's aftershave prickled my nose, reminding me of his abrupt departure, the terrible words we'd exchanged, the back of his head as he disappeared down 42nd Street. Had that really happened only twelve hours earlier?

Willing myself to forget these vivid images of our final encounter, I turned on my side with my eyes wide open and saw a speck of light glinting off a small, shiny object atop my night-stand: the spare key to my apartment, the one I'd left on my kitchen counter for Carson earlier that morning. Beside it was a crumpled piece of vellum, and even though I didn't need to un-fold it to know it was his five-year plan, I did anyway. I wanted to see his handwriting, the smudged pencil strokes, the tangible evidence of his love for me. Though after the way we left things, who knew how he felt about me now?

\* \* \*

Sleep didn't come easily. All night, I faded in and out of con-sciousness, my brain cycling between excitement for my new venture, despair for my lost love, and anxiety for how drastically my life was about to change. At the first peek of sunlight, I gave up the fight and put on a pot of coffee, ready to turn my full at-tention back to my business. But first I tucked Carson's five-year plan out of sight, in the very bottom of my nightstand drawer. Nothing was going to distract me today.

The next item on my task list was to design my itineraries. My goal was to have several different walking tours throughout Mid-town, each with a rough agenda that remained adaptable based on current events or even the whims of the attendees. Instead of cre-ating all my itineraries from scratch, I decided the most expedient way to get my enterprise off the ground would be to dig up all those travelogues I used to write, back when I took those weekend tours around New York City. I still had them all, waiting for me on the bookshelf of my childhood bedroom.

I threw on a comfortable pair of jeans and a casual top—my new daily uniform for the foreseeable future—and walked downtown to Penn Station. The 8:37 train to Woodbridge was pleasantly empty, since most commuters were heading into Manhattan to begin their days at work. I slid right into a window seat with no one else around me and sank into the vinyl cushion, watching the crowded platform fade from view. But as the train ducked into a tunnel and sped beneath the Hudson River, panic set in. Because for all the planning I'd done, I still had no idea how I was going to break the news to my grandmother.

She'd always thought my love for traveling and tourism was frivolous, dangerous, and foolish. I cringed to envision her reaction when I announced I'd quit my stable, prestigious, high-paying job to hang out with tourists in the city all day. She didn't understand what it meant to me, and there was nothing I could say that would make her happy, no way I could convince her this sudden upheaval in my life was a positive development. Which is why I didn't warn her I was coming over. I didn't want to give her the chance to ruminate before my visit or to prepare some big derisive speech.

Also, I didn't have a phone with which to call her.

So when I showed up on her stoop at 9:30 and rang the doorbell, it wasn't surprising to see the confusion written all over her face. And, of course, since it was my grandmother, the confusion immediately turned into worry.

"Sophie, what are you doing here?" she said, holding the screen door open for me to enter. "Is everything okay?"

"Yeah, I'm totally fine, Gram."

"Why aren't you working today?" She followed me into the foyer, her voice trembling with worry. "Is this some kind of emergency? Has your building been evacuated?"

"No, it's nothing like that. Really, everything's fine." I advanced toward the kitchen with my eyes on the worn parquet floor. "Can I have some coffee?"

"Of course." She approached the kitchen counter and poured the warm liquid into my mug, the same one with the purple cartoon cats. As she measured out the milk and sugar, I took a seat at the table and twiddled my thumbs, looking everywhere but in her direction. Finally, she sat down and placed the mug in front of me. When she saw the sheepish look on my face, her eyes went wide.

"Oh God," she said. "You're not pregnant, are you?"

"No, Gram, I'm not pregnant." I buried my face in my hands, mortified. But if Grandma was already jumping to such far-fetched conclusions, surely the real reason for my visit wouldn't seem so bad. It was time for me to just spit it out. So I lowered my hands, took a deep breath, and said, "I quit my job."

"What?" She pressed her palms against the tabletop. "What do you mean you quit your job?"

"I'm done. I submitted my resignation yesterday and walked out."

"I don't understand. Did you get a better offer?"

I shook my head. "No."

The worry on her face increasingly gave way to anger. "Why would you do that?"

"Because I was miserable," I said. "I've hated that job for a really, really long time. I'd finally had enough."

"How are you going to pay your bills now?"

"I've decided to start my own business."

"Doing what? Consulting work?"

"Kind of," I said, forcing a smile. "I guess you could call me a travel consultant."

"Stop beating around the bush, Sophie," she said, her nostrils flaring. "What are you up to?"

*Here we go.* I took another deep breath before confessing. "I'm becoming a tour guide. I've got it all planned out. See, I'm going to be giving these walking tours around New York, and—"

"A tour guide?" Grandma's face screwed up in disgust. "What the hell kind of a job is that? How much are you getting paid?"

"Well, I won't exactly be making a steady salary. I'll be charging thirty-nine dollars per person for each tour, so it depends on how many customers I get on any given day."

"So you'll obviously be taking a pay cut."

"I certainly won't be making McKinley money anymore," I said. "But I'll be much happier."

"How the hell are you gonna pay your rent?"

I fought to keep my voice even and subdued, despite the tension building in my chest. "Well, I've got enough savings to last me through the rest of my lease. When that's over, I was thinking about looking for something more affordable in Queens." *But never, ever in New Jersey.*

Grandma got to her feet and began pacing around the kitchen, her hand fluttering over her chest.

"Calm down, Gram," I said. "This is *good* news, I promise you."

"This is a mistake, Sophie." Her slippers scuffled against the floor as she trudged from the bay window to the refrigerator to the kitchen table and back again. "You're going to regret this one day."

"No, I won't."

"Yes, you will. Mark my words."

"You know what I'd regret? Not taking this chance. I would regret always wondering what my life could've been like if I'd been brave enough to follow my dreams."

She stopped in her tracks, her veiny hands gripping the back of her wooden chair. "Your dreams?"

"Yes. My dreams. Remember when I applied to college? I was looking at all those schools that offered degrees in travel and tourism." I swallowed hard, afraid to say the next words. But I knew they needed to be spoken. "You threw all the brochures away. You said I shouldn't pursue it. That it wasn't a real job."

"Because it wasn't a real job," she said, throwing one hand in the air for emphasis. "It still isn't. It's a crazy idea. I thought you'd have outgrown it by now."

"You don't outgrow your passions, Gram. I can't live my life making choices simply because you want me to make them. I won't compromise my happiness for you. Not anymore."

I pushed back from the table, causing the chair legs to squeak against the parquet floor, and retreated to the hallway, where I climbed upstairs. As I blinked back tears, I chided myself for getting so upset. I knew this was the reaction Grandma was

going to have. I never expected her to be supportive or understanding.

But I guess it would've been nice if she'd been a shade less
scornful. Or perhaps demonstrated the least bit of respect for my
autonomy, my ability to make decisions about my own life. Then
again, why did I think things could be different than they ever
were before? She still treated me like an irresponsible child who
wasn't trustworthy enough to run her own life. Just like she always had.

I hadn't come to New Jersey to seek her approval, though. I
was here to get my old New York City guidebooks. They were
right where I'd left them, on the four-tier beechwood bookshelf in the far corner of my childhood bedroom. I knelt on
the mauve plush carpet and ran my fingertips along their worn
spines, inspecting the titles. *Walking New York*, *Streetwise Manhattan*, *Urban Adventures in the Big Apple*. Alongside them were
three spiral notebooks—my handwritten travelogues. A wave of
nostalgia washed away my melancholy, and I flashed back to all
the fun I used to have touring through the city. How I used to
dream of leading my own group of travelers around the streets.
*You're making the right decision, no matter what she may think.*

One by one, I removed all the books from the shelf and tossed
them on the striped bedspread. Then I sat beside them, picked
up a spiral notebook—a brown one with pink watercolor orchids
painted on the front—and began paging through it. Right away,
I recognized my immature teenage handwriting, the way I used
to dot my *i*'s and *j*'s with little bubbles. It was so different from
the formal penmanship I'd developed in the intervening years.

Yet there was something so familiar in those written words. Like the feverish joy I'd felt when I'd first committed ink to paper, recording all my experiences, preserving them for the future.

A future that was happening right now.

Floorboards creaked in the hallway, and I looked up to see Grandma hovering just outside the threshold to the bedroom.

"Can I come in?" She sounded uncharacteristically small. It wasn't like her to ask permission; she generally barged in whenever she wanted to. I nodded and made room for her to sit down beside me on the bed.

"What are you doing?" she asked, casting a glance at the messy pile surrounding me.

"Going through my old travel library." I held up the spiral notebook resting in my lap. "I used to keep journals of my weekends in the city. Remember that?"

"Oh yes," she said. "Very clearly."

"You used to get so mad at me for taking the train in by myself."

"I was never mad at you, Sophie. I was worried. There are a lot of dangers out there. The city is no place for a young girl to be gallivanting around by herself."

"Yet I always came home alive. And on time. With no scars. See? You had no reason to be so scared."

She looked down at her lap, where her hands smoothed the fabric of her hand-sewn cotton pants. "I had plenty to be scared of. You have no idea."

Tears pooled in the corners of her brown eyes as she raised them to meet my own. "When you were sixteen," she continued, "you were so much like your mother. You had this fire in your belly. This urgent need to escape from home. Always planning the next journey, always fantasizing about running away. Your mother spent a lot of time in New York, too. Doing God knows what with God knows who. Then one time, she got on the train and she never came back. I was so afraid you were going to end up the same way. Running away to the city. Lost to me forever."

I reached for her hand, and she grasped my fingers firmly in her own. "I'm not lost, Gram. I'm right here. I didn't disappear, and I never will. I'm nothing like her."

"Oh, but you are," she said with the hint of a smile. "You're very much like her. Unconventional. Stubborn. Restless. Your mom was a dreamer, Sophie. And so are you."

Her words struck me like a lightning bolt. I'd always believed I was a planner. The practical, disciplined, sensible one who played it safe, who made smart choices, who never placed a bet with unfavorable odds. As it turned out, I was a dreamer all along. I'd just been fighting my true nature.

Then a terrifying thought occurred to me. I'd spent my whole life striving to be unlike my mother. But all my efforts had been for nothing. *Am I doomed to be just like her, no matter how hard I try to be different?*

As if reading my mind, my grandmother said, "But you're stronger. Your mother, she was troubled. Weak. She had problems galore. I know I don't ever have to worry about you. Look at how independent you've become. So determined. You've got such a good head on your shoulders, such a solid sense of responsibility. If you've got a dream, I know you'll make it come true.

You'll succeed at whatever you put your mind to. I know you won't let anyone stand in your way. Not a man. And not me."

I felt like I'd had the wind knocked out of me. It was all I'd ever wanted to hear her say. I may not have come to New Jersey seeking Grandma's approval, but it sure felt good to get it anyway.

"Sometimes," she continued, "when I look at you, it's hard to remember you're not your mother. Because you're the spitting image of her."

"Really?" I tried in vain to conjure a memory of my mother's face. Years ago, Grandma had kept photos of her scattered around the house, lining the wall of the staircase and arranged on top of the credenza. Over the course of my childhood, they gradually disappeared, without discussion or fanfare, until every trace of my mother's existence was erased from our home. I never asked what happened to them, because frankly, I didn't care; seeing her picture was just a painful reminder of what could've been and what would never be. Besides, I didn't see the point of longing for a person who had so clearly wanted nothing to do with me.

Still, in my darkest moments, I'd think about what she was doing. I would envision her face, coming up with some blurry, distorted picture of what she looked like, a phantasm plucked from the depths of my imagination, an amalgam of random, meaningless facial features. I always pictured someone wholly unfamiliar. I never, ever pictured myself.

"It's been so long since I've seen a picture of her," I said. "I don't remember what she looks like."

Without a word, Grandma stood up and shuffled down the hallway. I stayed put, sitting on the bedspread, trying to catch my breath. She returned holding a tattered shoebox, and when she sat down, she placed it on her lap, with both of her palms lying on top of it. Slowly, she breathed in and out, as if preparing herself for what was inside. Then she folded back the cover, revealing a short stack of photographs. Black and white, color, professional portraits, family snapshots, all the edges yellowed with age. She gently lifted the top photo and held it out for me to see.

"This was your mother on her sixteenth birthday," she said. "Just before she got pregnant."

It was like looking at a memory I'd completely forgotten, because the person in the photograph was me. She had the same high cheekbones, the same little bump in the bridge of her nose, the same wild and curly hair. But when I examined it more closely, I noticed an emptiness in her eyes, a yearning for something that existed beyond her reach. What was she craving? What did she need that she didn't have?

I took the photo from my grandmother's hands and held the edges lightly between my fingertips. "Can I see some more?"

Grandma reached into the box and handed me a pile of photographs. As I flipped through them, the image I had of my mother morphed from a vague, fuzzy form to an actual human being. A rosy-cheeked baby holding a stuffed giraffe. A chubby little girl wearing patent leather Mary Janes. A sullen teenager with an acoustic guitar slung across her back. All of them with my exact face.

"Wow," I said. "I really do look like her."

"I know a man didn't ruin your mother's life," she said. "I know she made her own choices. And I don't regret that she made those choices, because if she hadn't, then I would never have had you. You are the greatest joy of my life, Sophie. You're everything to me."

I lifted my gaze to meet hers, and in her eyes, I saw pain and despair. The same anguished longing that I saw in my mother's sixteen-year-old face. The desire for something more.

"You need more than just me in your life," I said. "I love you, but I can't be everything to you. I'm not a kid anymore. I'm an independent woman. Life is about evolving, Gram. About taking risks and making messes. Even if we're afraid of what might happen."

She didn't respond, but she nodded, ever so slightly. I leaned forward and wrapped my arms around her, buried my face in the loose skin of her neck. My grandmother might not have understood me, and she probably never would, but at least now I knew I had her support.

We spent the rest of the morning together, discussing the details of my business plan and sharing an early lunch, before I packed up my books and said good-bye. At the front door, Grandma hugged me tightly and whispered in my ear, "Call me when you get home. Just so I know you're safe."

Which reminded me: I needed to get a phone.

# chapter twenty-seven

On my walk home from Penn Station, I stopped at the wireless store and signed up for the cheapest plan available, complete with a low-end, refurbished clunker of a smartphone. It was a serious step down from the slim, sexy, cutting-edge device I'd been given at McKinley, but it served its purpose. Namely, giving prospective clients a way to get in touch with me. Now all I had to do was spread the word: As of tomorrow, Sophie's Spontaneous Tours would be open for business.

To that end, I set about establishing an online presence: a streamlined website with contact information, business listings on Yelp and TripAdvisor, Facebook and Twitter accounts to help with promotion. I devised names for each of my themed itineraries, like "Literary Midtown" and "Broadway History," and listed them on my website, along with starting times and meeting locations. Reservations were encouraged, but, in the spirit of spontaneity, not required.

After reviewing my budget, I decided to start by running three tours per day, six days per week, with one day off to rest and rejuvenate. If I could snag at least three customers per tour, I'd earn enough to scrape by without making too big of a dent in my savings account. Given the abundance of tourists walking the streets of New York at all hours of the day, I assumed this was a realistic, attainable goal.

Unfortunately, my assumption was wrong.

It's not like I expected my phone to start ringing uncontrollably as soon as my site went live, but after three separate Craigslist ads and four hours wallpapering Internet travel forums with my Web address, I'd hoped to have sparked at least an inkling of interest in my business. A question, a retweet, some minor interaction to inspire confidence in my endeavor. To let me know that somewhere out there, someone cared about what I was doing. Instead, I was met with hostile silence, as if the Internet at large had reflexively scrolled past every last one of my posts with a collective, disinterested yawn.

To distract myself from the ineffectiveness of my marketing campaign, I did what I always liked to do to calm my nerves: I planned a dream vacation. This time, I returned to Australia, hopping a flight inland to Alice Springs to embark on a virtual adventure through the Outback. There were hot air balloon flights over spectacular desert ranges, camel rides across sienna-colored sand dunes, and open-air campouts under the stars. Just like the fantasy Carson and I shared during one of our last late-night phone calls.

By midnight, I'd designed a complete and comprehensive itinerary for an imaginary journey through the Red Centre. Judging by my empty inbox, though, I'd failed to drum up curiosity in my real-life tour company. Still, I convinced myself this didn't mean much; after all, I was selling spontaneity. Some impulsive individuals would undoubtedly be waiting for me on the steps of the New York Public Library the next morning, right?

I showed up fifteen minutes early for my ten o'clock "Astonishing Architecture" tour, bright-eyed and caffeinated, eager to greet my first paying customers. Half an hour later, I was still standing alone, the corners of my mouth fighting gravity, the effects of my morning coffee fading fast. As the reality of canceling my first official tour began to sink in, I scanned the faces of the stragglers all around me. Some sat on the stairs, others leaned against the lions, and at least half of them looked like they were waiting for someone. Could it be they didn't recognize me? Admittedly, that corporate headshot I'd used on my website was a few years out of date.

"Excuse me," I said to a small group on my left. "Are you guys looking for Sophie?" They blinked in my general direction. "Of Sophie's Spontaneous Tours?" More blinking. Only then did it occur to me that they didn't speak English. Embarrassed, I bowed my head in silent apology and walked away.

"Excuse me," I said, this time to a teenage couple embracing beside the handrail. "Are you guys looking for Sophie?" The girl scowled and shook her head before burying her face in her boyfriend's neck.

I continued on like this until I'd been rejected by every last person in sight, including the one man who kept inching away every time I came near. I guess I couldn't blame him for trying to avoid me. With my nondescript jeans and T-shirt, I certainly wasn't wearing anything that set me apart as a tour guide. He probably thought I was a panhandler. Or a con artist.

When I was still by myself at ten-thirty, it became crystal clear that "Astonishing Architecture" would have no takers. Rather than retreat into the library and hide my shame among the stacks, though, I forced my chin to the sky and started walking, following the path I'd planned out for my tour. I thought it would be good practice to familiarize myself with precise locations along the route while silently rehearsing my spiel, to prepare myself for the day when I had a dozen customers trailing me around the city at once. Surely that day would be soon. Wouldn't it?

As morning turned to afternoon, I persisted in keeping my head held high, even though no one showed up for either of my two remaining tours. Remaining optimistic proved to be more difficult the next day, though, when, yet again, I failed to attract a single customer. That night, I trudged back to my apartment with my head hanging between my shoulders, my gaze fixed to the sidewalk.

The following morning, the shrill ring of my discount cell phone roused me from an anxious sleep. The screen flashed with an unfamiliar area code, and I shot upright, answering the call with a fluttering heart.

"Sophie's Spontaneous Tours. This is Sophie speaking. How may I help you?"

"Hi, yes, I'm interested in your ten o'clock tour."

Success!

"Certainly! That would be the Times Square Trivia tour, one of my favorites." That was true. I loved all my tours, but this one was especially cool; it was loaded with trivia questions I planned on asking the audience while we walked along, making it an extra interactive experience. "Would you like to make a reservation to guarantee your spot?"

I may have been pushing my luck; I certainly didn't anticipate a sold-out tour, especially after the dismal disaster of the past two days. Then again, one could never be too sure. Perhaps I just needed a little bit of time to allow the existence of my new business to propagate throughout the public consciousness. Now that word was obviously out there, who knew how many customers might show up?

"Sure," he said. "Why not?"

Three minutes later, I had my first reservation for two. Rick said his 773 area code was from Chicago, and he and his girlfriend were visiting the city for a long weekend away from home. I gave him specific directions to the starting location in Times Square and a detailed description of what I was wearing. This way he'd be able to find me easily, despite my unremarkable attire.

After I hung up, I swallowed a squeal, rushed through a shower, and proceeded directly to 7th Avenue. Even though the tour didn't start for a while, I wanted to survey the area and review my notes, to see if I could tailor the trivia to my clients from the Windy City. It took me almost a full two hours, but I managed to weave in questions about *Chicago* the musical, variations in regional pizza, and the height of our cities' respective skyscrapers.

While wolfing down a buttered bialy, I walked over to the designated meeting spot at the bottom of the glowing red steps in Duffy Square. My excitement could hardly be contained as I waited for my customers, bouncing on the balls of my feet, smiling at every body-painted exhibitionist and counterfeit Elmo that walked by. But as the minutes ticked past, ten o'clock came and went, with no sign of Rick or his girlfriend. *Maybe they're lost,* my delusions whispered in my ear. So I pulled out my cell phone and dialed the 773 number from my call history.

When he answered, I said, "Rick? It's Sophie." After a moment of awkward silence, I followed up with, "From Sophie's Spontaneous Tours."

"Right! Hi."

"Hi." He seemed relaxed, unconcerned with the fact that he was fifteen minutes late for his trivia tour of Times Square. "So, are you having trouble finding me? I'm waiting right at the bottom of the red steps. By the TKTS booth."

"Nah, we decided to skip it."

"Skip it?"

"Yeah, we wanted to check out Brooklyn instead."

"Oh." The neon lights surrounding me were suddenly shining twice as bright, flashing twice as fast. I pinched the bridge of my nose and squeezed my eyes shut against the dizzying glare. "I didn't realize...I mean, I'm still waiting here, that's all."

"Sorry to flake on you," he continued. "I figured it wasn't a big deal. Your website said you were totally flexible. Spontaneity and all that, right?"

"Right." While I pondered whether spontaneity and common courtesy were mutually exclusive behaviors, there was one thing I knew for sure: The verbiage on my website would have to be reworded. Maybe if I required a deposit for reservations, people would call to explicitly cancel instead of leaving me hanging. Or maybe the best option was to revise my cancellation policy altogether.

Another tour, devoid of tourists. I hung up, dejected, and surveyed the surrounding crowd, feeling like my shame was on display for all to see. Was the person in that Elmo costume laughing at me behind his mask? Were those women slathered in body paint rolling their eyes at my failed efforts? Seized by a sudden need to escape from Times Square, I hurried east on 47th Street and hung a sharp right to head south on 6th Avenue, toward the north edge of Bryant Park. Pushing onward through heavy pedestrian traffic, the clamor of a thousand bodies drowned out the niggling voice in the back of my head. *This was a stupid idea,* it said. *March back to the McKinley office right this instant, get down on your hands and knees, and beg Elizabeth for another chance at your old job.*

The towering specter of One Bryant Park came into view, its silhouette composed of sharp points and razor edges, as if it could slice open the blue city sky. Maybe that was where I belonged. Sitting behind a desk somewhere in that massive skyscraper, one of countless cogs in the machine. Dissatisfied but stable. Not wandering the streets, wondering if I'd make enough money to pay next month's rent, blowing through my savings account like some kind of trust fund baby.

This had all seemed so simple a few days earlier, when I'd been typing out my business plan in the privacy of my apartment. Out in the unforgiving daylight, though, the reality of running my own company was a lot more complicated than a couple of color-coordinated spreadsheets. Planning was supposed to be my strong suit, wasn't it? I'd spent years devising corporate strategies for international businesses. Yet on my own little undertaking, I'd completely dropped the ball.

*This was a stupid idea.*

Standing on the corner of 42nd and 6th, I wrestled with the two warring factions inside of me: the need for security and the desire to follow my passion. I felt haunted by those photographs of my mother, by the look of yearning in her eyes. Maybe I was just like her after all. A restless, stubborn dreamer who ran away from her responsibilities when the going got tough.

I wished there was a way to make this all go away. To snap my fingers and undo the events of the past week. Then I'd still have my steady income, my distinguished career. And I'd still have Carson. Even if our only connection was through fleeting, long-distance phone calls, it would be better than the aching, unending silence that had grown between us in the interim.

But as I stared at the mirrored façade of my old office building, I remembered what it was really like up there on the thirty-third floor. The competition, the nepotism, the emotional discontent. Even if it was an option, even if it meant I'd be with Carson again, did I really want to go back to a job that left me scowling, day in and day out?

In any case, there was no way to change the past. I could only control my choices in the present moment. And right now, even though I was terrified of what the future had in store, I would not resign myself to failure. Rather than run away, I showed up for the remaining two tours of the day, each of which predictably ended with another humiliating half hour of standing alone on the city streets.

The next morning, I woke up early to post some ads on the Internet before heading out for my ten o'clock tour. "Central Park Curiosities" met in the middle of Columbus Circle, at the base of its eponymous marble and granite monument. Strolling through the south entrance of the pedestrian plaza, I dodged skateboarders as they whizzed by, their wheels scratching against uneven pavement. Wooden benches lined the inside perimeter, filled with New Yorkers basking in both the warmth of the mid-morning sun and the cool burble of the surrounding fountains. It was the perfect weather for a walking tour. Too bad I wouldn't have any customers.

As I waited on the stone steps beneath the seventy-foot statue, I tried my best to look casual and blend in with the crowd: hands in my pockets, neutral expression plastered on my face. When I felt a hand on my shoulder, I nearly jumped out of my skin. Two middle-aged women had approached, sporting eyeglasses and salt-and-pepper pageboys. One asked, "Are you Sophie?"

It took me a second to realize they were actually here to see me. That this wasn't some misunderstanding. "Yes. Are you here for the walking tour?"

They nodded in unison. "Forty each, right?"

"Right."

My heartbeat sped up as they fished twenties out of their purses and handed them over. *This is really happening. Two living, breathing customers. Paying me to show them the sights of the city.*

"Thank you." I pocketed the cash and asked, "What are your names?"

"Jan."

"Marie."

"It's very nice to meet you," I said. "Where are you from?"

"Connecticut." They looked down at their feet, inspecting the double knots in their shoelaces.

"Have either of you been to Central Park before?" I was hoping to break the ice, to learn a little bit about them and establish a friendly rapport. If we were going to spend the next two hours together, I figured we might as well get comfortable.

But Marie ignored the question and began to root through her purse, while Jan let out a grunt that could've meant yes or no. Clearly, these two weren't interested in idle chitchat. I stole a quick glance at my phone—three minutes to ten. Maybe Jan and Marie would loosen up if I kicked off the show a little early.

*Deep breath, and...*

"Welcome to Central Park Curiosities. I'm your host, Sophie Bruno, and today I'll be taking you on a tour of some of the more unusual, unexpected sights to see in and around the vast green oasis in the middle of this bustling city."

Marie was still digging around in her bag—what was she even looking for in there?—and from the heavy-lidded blank stare Jan was giving me, she may as well have been sleeping with her eyes open. Nevertheless, I continued on.

"Right now, we're standing in Columbus Circle, directly across from the southwest entrance to Central Park. Take a look at this." I raised my arm above my head, pointing to the statue of

Christopher Columbus perched atop the pedestal. Marie popped a square of gum in her mouth—the journey to the bottom of her purse was now complete—before she and Jan both directed their gaze toward my fingertips, their hands shielding their eyes from the glare of the sun. "This statue of Christopher Columbus is over one hundred fifty years old. It was a gift from Italian sculptor Gaetano Russo to commemorate the four hundredth anniversary of Columbus's arrival in America. But something most people don't know is that this is also the point from which all official distances to New York City from around the world are measured."

They continued to stare at the monument in silence.

"What part of Connecticut are you ladies from?"

Marie snapped her gum. Jan muttered, "Hartford."

"Great. So, when we say Hartford is a hundred miles away from New York City, we really mean—"

"It's actually a hundred and *seventeen* miles," Jan cut in.

"Oh. Okay." *Tough crowd.* "So, when we say Hartford is a hundred and seventeen miles away from New York City, we really mean it's a hundred and seventeen miles away from this spot, right here."

They offered no response. Not a single nod of interest or grunt of acknowledgment. I'd purposely opened the tour with this tidbit of information because Carson had found it so fascinating. But from the looks on their faces, Jan and Marie couldn't care less. Had Carson just pretended to be interested in what I had to say to flatter me? In reality, was I not cut out for this whole tour guide gig?

*This was a stupid idea.*

The sharp crack of Marie's gum snapped me to attention. "Let's cross the street now and head into the park."

As I led the pair out of the circle and toward the busy crosswalk, someone called my name, followed by, "Hey! Wait up!" The voice grew closer and I spun around to see a man with a backpack and a bushy gray beard running in my direction. "Sorry, my train got held up. Is it too late to join the tour?"

"Not at all. Welcome!" Another customer! With this addition, I'd reached my minimum quota of three people, for the very first time. While this didn't erase the fact that my first three days of touring had been a total bust, it was a sure sign of progress. "What's your name, sir?"

"Fred." He pulled a ratty brown wallet from the back pocket of his cargo pants. "Do you take Amex? I've got MasterCard, if that's better."

"I...I actually don't take credit cards, Fred. Sorry." Two semesters' worth of financial planning and operations management courses, and it never once crossed my mind to devise a method of accepting electronic payments. What a colossal failure my business plan was turning out to be.

Fred seemed to agree, because he pursed his lips and widened his eyes in disbelief. "Well, I don't carry cash on me. All I've got is a couple of singles."

"No problem," I shot back, desperate not to lose his business. "I'll be happy to walk with you to an ATM after the tour is over. They're all over the surrounding neighborhoods."

He slapped his wallet closed and shrugged. "Okay."

With the latest crisis averted, the four of us passed through the traffic circle and crossed Central Park West, weaving through street vendors and pedestrians until we came to a stop in front of a massive pylon topped with a gilded bronze sculpture.

"Welcome to one of the busiest entrances to Central Park: Merchants' Gate Plaza," I said, my voice straining to be heard over the racket of a nearby construction site. "As you can see, this area is dominated by the tremendous monument behind us, which honors the American soldiers who were killed when the battleship *Maine* exploded in Havana in 1898."

"Where?" Jan asked, squinting her eyes as if that might help her to hear me better.

"Havana!" I yelled. "Cuba!"

Marie snapped her gum again, the loud pop somehow clearly discernible above the drilling of the jackhammers.

"The sculpture at the top is of 'Columbia Triumphant' riding a seashell chariot, which is being pulled by three mythological sea horses. It's been reported, but never confirmed, that the bronze used in crafting this figure was scavenged from the gunmetal of the battleship itself."

"I'm sorry," Fred said, visibly irritated. "I'm having a hard time hearing you over all this noise"

"Did you say this was donated by Columbia University?" Jan asked.

I jerked a thumb over my shoulder, toward the path leading into the tree-lined trails of the park. "You know what?" I yelled. "Let's go in there. Where it's quiet."

Sure enough, the farther we walked, the greener it became, and the earsplitting noise of the drills and engines faded to a distant thrum. "That's better," I said. "This is about as quiet as it ever gets in the middle of Manhattan."

As if to prove me wrong, Marie snapped her gum, right on cue.

Hugging the west side of the park, we headed north, crossing Center Drive, before heading down one of the pedestrian-only walkways and leaving the crush of humanity behind. As we scaled a gentle incline, I said, "If you have any questions as we walk along, please feel free to ask," but no one took me up on my offer. The only sounds were the pebbles crunching beneath our feet and the periodic crack of Marie's chewing gum.

I showed them Pine Bank Arch, one of the only original cast-iron bridges left in the park. From there, we crossed over Umpire Rock, a huge slab of exposed bedrock named for its superior view of the neighboring Heckscher Ballfields. This led to a casual stroll through the verdant Sheep Meadow, dotted with sunbathers and picnickers, a vastly different view from the livestock that used to graze the area less than a hundred years earlier.

Throughout the journey, my companions didn't say a word. They never asked a question, never wanted me to elaborate on any anecdotes. It was almost like I was talking to myself.

"Next, I'd like to show you one of my favorite parts of Central Park, the Nell Singer Lilac Walk. Now is the ideal time of year to appreciate the fragrance and color of the blooms."

"What about the Pond?" Fred said, his first contribution of

the afternoon. "I was hoping to see that. And the Hallett Nature Sanctuary."

"It's a little far away from us right now," I said. "Maybe we can tack that on to the end of the tour as we head back south."

"I'd prefer to see it now," he pressed on. "I'm just not that interested in the lilacs, to be honest."

"Um...okay. Well, we can certainly change course, if you'd like—that is, if Jan and Marie are okay with it."

They scrunched up their noses. "We want to see the lilacs," Jan said.

"Then let's keep going with our original itinerary, and we'll head down to the Pond after we see Strawberry Fields and Cherry Hill."

Fred huffed, his annoyance apparent in the wrinkle between his overgrown eyebrows. "I thought this was a totally customizable tour."

"It is." I came to a stop in the middle of the path, eager to appease all my customers and put an end to this tantrum before it escalated. "But the rest of the group has to be in agreement."

"That's not what your website said."

Damn that poorly worded website.

"I'm sorry," I said. "I should've made that clearer."

"Then I'm gonna take off on my own." Fred turned on his Teva, but as he started to walk away, I realized we'd never made it to an ATM.

"Uh, Fred?" I called after him. "You never paid for the tour."

He snickered. "Your website said the tours are fully refundable. I'm not paying for this crap."

I watched the back of his balding head grow smaller and smaller as he tromped across the grass, eventually disappearing altogether between a dense group of trees. My cheeks burned; my eyes stung. I wanted nothing more than to run home and hide from my miserable failure.

But there was over an hour left in this tour. Jan and Marie gaped at me, waiting for me to resume my role as their guide. If I didn't get myself together, they'd demand refunds, too. *Deep breaths. You have to see this through.*

"Okay!" I clapped my hands and smiled, as if this whole unpleasant scene hadn't just occurred. "Let's see those lilacs."

Though it was a struggle to keep my voice from quavering, I managed to pick up where I left off, leading my two remaining customers through the middle of the park, passing by Belvedere Castle and Shakespeare Garden. Jan and Marie remained reticent, seeming wholly indifferent to my narration. By the time we reached our final destination in the southeast corner—right beside the Pond that Fred was in such a hurry to see—I was exhausted. Drained, both physically and mentally, from the long walk, the rolling hills, the monumental effort of keeping an upbeat demeanor in the midst of my internal chaos.

But since my website advertised the chance for an off-the-beaten-path meal at the end of each tour, I maintained my smile and asked, "Are you ladies interested in grabbing a bite to eat? There's a German restaurant I like to go to quite often. It's very non-touristy and out of the way."

Marie spit her gum into a tissue and spoke for the first time. "Do they have a gluten-free menu?"

"Uh...I don't think so. But I'm sure there are some options—"

"Better not risk it." Marie nudged Jan with her elbow. "Come on."

Off they went, without so much as a thank-you. With my eyes on the asphalt, I crossed 59th Street and walked south on 6th Avenue. Though the sidewalk was teeming with chatty commuters, one voice thundered above all the others. The voice in my head saying, *This was a stupid idea.*

# chapter twenty-eight

O ver the next few days, business conditions failed to improve. My first week on the job passed by with a grand total of six paying customers—forty-eight shy of what I'd initially planned for. With my realized earnings so far below my lofty projections, it didn't look like I could afford to take that day off to rest and rejuvenate after all.

My self-confidence was at an all-time low; never before had I experienced such doubt in my judgment or decision-making. What a fool I'd been to throw away my chance at long-term success by chasing down an impractical, unreasonable pipe dream. Impulsivity had paid off on vacation. In real life? Not so much.

And yet, as I lay on my bed in my empty apartment at the end of another disappointing day, there remained a very small, very hopeful corner of my mind that implored me not to give up. To keep going, despite the challenges and setbacks. To see this project through, instead of running away. Yes, I'd had an extraordinarily difficult week, but one week would not define the future of my business. I could bounce back from this. I would try again tomorrow.

Then I saw the Yelp review.

> If I could give "Sophie's Spontaneous Tours" zero stars, I
> would. The walking tour of Central Park was poorly planned
> and poorly executed. First of all, the "tour guide" (I use the
> term loosely; she didn't seem to know a thing about giving
> a proper tour) didn't accept credit cards. Who runs a cash-
> only business in this day and age? Beyond that, the route
> she followed was boring and the narration was exceedingly
> dull. Worst of all, the website is riddled with false advertis-
> ing and outright lies. There's no "customization" of the tour
> whatsoever. Save your money and pick up a free map from
> one of the visitor centers in the park instead.

Fred had certainly wasted no time sharing his opinion with
the Internet. And though it was a scathing assessment of my
fledgling small business, it was also one hundred percent true.
My tour was poorly planned, poorly executed, and I didn't know
the first thing about being a proper guide. I should've stuck
to fantasy vacations, to imaginary itineraries scribbled in spiral-
bound notebooks, relegated to the privacy of my bookshelves.

The second thoughts I'd been harboring all week long suddenly consumed me, and that single, hopeful light in the corner
of my mind was snuffed out, leaving only a cold, black dread.
My perfectly ordered life was now a thing of the past, irreparably
damaged by a succession of stupid, irresponsible choices. In a
true sign of desperation, I started thinking of who else I could
blame for this mess.

Maybe my parents, whose absence had made me perpetually
afraid to take a risk. Or my grandmother, who steered me down

a path in life that reinforced those fears. Or, most of all, Carson. If he'd never surprised me in New York, if he'd just listened when I told him our relationship could never go anywhere, if he'd never come into my life in the first place, then everything would've worked out fine. I'd have gone to visit Martin Chu in Hong Kong. I'd have come back to New York with my professional reputation intact. I'd be flitting off to another international destination right now, instead of stuck here in my cramped apartment, staring at a vicious, but accurate, evaluation of what happened when I tried—and failed—to live out my dream.

But the truth was, no matter how much I wanted to pin it on someone else, the blame lay squarely at my feet. I was responsible for every decision I ever made: blowing off Martin Chu in favor of going to Macau with a stranger, walking out of the safety of the office and into the uncertainty of the streets, throwing the sensible stability of my five-year plan out the window. No one forced me to do any of it. I made those choices of my own volition.

I couldn't stand another moment of solitude in my studio, where the silence amplified the weight of Fred's words. So even though the sun had set long ago, and there was no room in my budget for a pint of Bitburger, I made what was most likely another irresponsible decision and went down to Zum Bauer.

Wolf greeted me at the podium with a broad smile. "Sophie! Do you have another tour group for us tonight?"

"No. I'm not..." My voice trailed off when I realized I didn't know how to finish the sentence. *I'm not really a tour guide. I'm not sure what I'm doing with my life. I'm not prepared to talk about this without a beer in my hand.* "I'm just here to see Kat."

He nodded as I made my way to the bar. The heavy happy hour crowds had already cleared out, but there were still several tables full of people toasting to the end of the day. The cheerful faces and raucous laughter grated on my nerves, and all of a sudden, my empty apartment was calling my name. Suffocating in my own loneliness seemed preferable to being reminded that I no longer had colleagues with whom to share a postwork beer or the extra cash to pay for a round of drinks. Just as I considered stealing back upstairs, Kat caught sight of me and waved. "Sophie!" she called, rendering my escape impossible. "Come here, I have something to ask you."

I sat down on one of her handcrafted stools and assumed my fakest smile. "What's up?"

She handed an overflowing pitcher of beer to a waiter at the service station, then wiped her hands clean on a rag stuck in the waistband of her skinny jeans. "What's this I hear about you bringing in a tour group the other night when I was out? Did you take on a side gig on top of everything else you do?"

"Not exactly." I fiddled with a cardboard coaster left behind by a previous customer, peeling away at the damp, frayed edges.

"What's wrong?" she asked.

"Nothing."

She cocked her head to the side and sucked in her cheeks, her expression saying, *You can't fool me.* Like my failure was a visible, permanent stain, tarnishing my entire being. When her expression morphed from mock scolding to genuine concern, I pressed my fingertips to my face to discover it was damp. I hadn't even realized I'd started to cry; I'd just been holding my tears in for so long, it seemed my lids could no longer stem their flow.

"Sorry," I said.

Kat quickly replied, "Stop. You have nothing to be sorry for." She filled a pint glass with Bitburger and set it down before me, but I waved it away.

"I shouldn't."

"It's on the house. You look like you need it. Please, drink."

After a couple of cool, fizzy sips, I finally summoned the courage to tell Kat that I'd quit my job, out of the blue, and my only plan was a half-baked idea about starting my own business.

"Congratulations! That's wonderful!" Kat grinned, wide-eyed, clearly oblivious to how unqualified I was for this job, how unprepared I'd been for the challenge of entrepreneurship.

"It sounds really wonderful in theory, doesn't it? I had all these romantic notions of what it would be like to follow my dreams. To chase joy, just like you did." She raised one corner of her mouth in a sorry half-smile. I continued. "But the truth is, I'm not cut out for this, and now I've completely messed up my life. I don't know what I'm doing and I have no idea how to make things right again." I squeezed my temples and rested my elbows on the bar. "This was such a stupid idea."

"You sound like me," she said. "When I first opened Zum Bauer, I was convinced I had made a huge mistake."

"Really?"

"Oh yes. For the first month or so, I lived in a state of constant anxiety. I didn't have a steady customer base, so my income was unpredictable. The chefs were having a hard time getting my mother's recipes right. And *Time Out New York* gave me a one-star review. They called my restaurant a 'tragic waste of perfectly good Hell's Kitchen real estate.' When I saw that, I cried for hours."

"I can imagine," I said, swiping at my cheeks to erase any remnants of my own review-induced tears.

"There were a few moments when I seriously considered selling the place and going back to the world of fine dining. Just like you, I kept thinking I'd made such a mess of my life."

"And here you are, ten years later. Everything worked out. You're living out your passion."

She nodded tentatively, chewing on the inside of her lip. "Yes. But it took a lot of time and a lot of effort. I quickly learned that passion is worthless without the courage to see it through. So I pushed past all my fears and found a way to make it work."

"How?"

"Well, I reevaluated my budget, hired a new chef, and changed my marketing scheme. But that wasn't the end of it. Even now, I continually reevaluate my plans and change up my strategies. There are good days and there are bad days, and you have to accept that as part of the deal. Running your own business is a never-ending process of reinvention."

"No, that's not what I mean." I took a long sip of Bitburger, while Kat fixed her eyes on me, waiting for an explanation. "I mean, how did you push past your fears? Because honestly, Kat, I'm terrified. When I was at McKinley, I could make big, important decisions so easily. Decisions involving millions of dollars and huge corporations, they didn't worry me in the slightest. I think it was easy because my heart wasn't in it. All I had to do was go through the motions, checking boxes on a task list someone else wrote out for me. But this...this is a huge risk. My dream is at stake, I'm the one who has to write out the task list, and so far, every single thing I've written is wrong."

"Then rewrite the list," she said. "Do it over and over again until you get it right. That's what courage is. Doing what you need to do even when you're scared out of your mind. Changing your plans when they're no longer working for you." She slapped a legal pad and ballpoint pen down on the bar in front of me. "Here, you can get started now."

The top page was covered in handwriting, line after line of indecipherable German text. It appeared to be a list of some sort, or maybe a plan, one that had undergone numerous revisions. Several items were scribbled out; there were notes along the margins in different-colored ink. How many times had Kat rewritten this before she got it right? Or was it still a work in progress?

"You can do this, Sophie." Her voice was soft, gentler than I'd ever heard it before. "Stop being so afraid to fail that you never allow yourself to succeed."

She stepped to the opposite end of the bar, where two new customers awaited her attention, leaving me alone with the paper and pen and the echoing reminder of words I'd spat at Carson only a few days earlier, in the middle of a crowded street. *You're too afraid of failure to try to chase success.* How these words were coming back to haunt me now. Because when your heart is in your work, the risk of failure seems unbearable. And sometimes, the fear of losing it all can prevent you from moving forward.

But I refused to let my worries rule my world. Like I'd told my grandmother, life was about taking risks and making messes, even when we're afraid of what might happen. It was time to practice what I preached. With a shuddering breath, I folded the top paper back over the tattered tape binding to reveal a blank page. Crisp yellow with faint blue lines, at once barren and bursting with possibility. The ideal playground for a dreamer or a planner. Or someone who's a little bit of both, like me.

One by one, I listed out the problems plaguing my business, then brainstormed solutions, listing out the pros and cons of each one. Ideas flowed faster than my pen could capture them, and my hand cramped under the duress of my rapid note-taking. I filled pages and pages with chicken scratch memos, mind maps, and action points, eventually whittling it all down to a single task list. It was nothing more than a jumble of ink scrawls, so much different from the neatly printed pages that would materialize on my desk at McKinley each morning, care of Elizabeth. So much less organized than my color-coded filing system or my perfectly balanced spreadsheets. It was messy and muddled and haphazardly slapped together, but it was one hundred percent mine.

"Looks like you've been busy."

Kat stood above me, her eyes scanning the heap of yellow paper containing my newly revised business plan. I put down my pen and looked around to see the restaurant had completely emptied out; Wolf was wiping down the tables and upending the chairs. I'd been so engrossed in my work, I hadn't realized how much time had passed. Even my beer had gone flat, abandoned before I'd reached the halfway point in my pint glass.

"I think I've figured out how to fix things," I said.

"Good. And if, for some reason, this plan doesn't work, you'll rewrite your list and try again. Right?"

"Right." I tore my pages out of the pad and slid it back across the bar. "I can't thank you enough for your help, Kat."

"It was nothing. We all need someone to talk us down from the ledge sometimes, you know? I'm just glad you're not giving up."

"No, I'm definitely in this for the long haul. There are a bunch of changes I want to make now. Hopefully, they'll help me attract some more customers." I peered down at my notes. "Speaking of which, I have a question for you: Does your menu have any gluten-free options?"

\* \* \*

The next morning, I woke with the sunrise. It was an effortless arousal, since I refused Kat's generous offer of a parting Jäger shot. I simply couldn't risk a hangover; there were too many tasks to check off my list before I set off on my first tour of the day.

First, I signed up for an account with a third-party payment processor so I could start accepting credit and debit cards right away. Then I updated my website, revising all the verbiage to reflect my modified policies and procedures. Reservations now required a deposit and had to be canceled at least two hours in advance to avoid a charge. Furthermore, customized itineraries were no longer a standard offering but for twenty extra dollars per person, groups could reserve their own private walking tour with an individualized agenda. I also included a link to the special prix fixe menu Kat designed for post-tour meals, which included lots of options plucked from the regular menu but labeled according to their dietary restrictions, including vegetarian, vegan, and gluten-free. In exchange for promoting Zum Bauer on my website, Kat agreed to give me 10 percent of all the revenue my tour groups brought in.

Next, it was time to make myself presentable. After a hot shower, I arranged my hair into an aesthetically pleasing configuration of curls while repeating positive affirmations to my reflection in the medicine chest. *You can do this, Sophie. Don't be afraid of failure. Fear is your enemy.* Feeling dauntless from my one-woman pep talk, I flung open the door to my closet. Beaming out from amid the crush of practical dark-colored clothing was my lemon-yellow sundress. It beckoned to me, stirring up memories of the risks I took with Carson, walking the sultry streets of Hong Kong and Macau with little knowledge of what would come next. The last time I wore this dress, I'd felt confident, competent, and courageous, even in the face of the unknown. Maybe if I wore it again, I'd recapture those feelings by sheer osmosis. As an added bonus, the bright color would help me stand out in a sea of garden-variety jeans and T-shirts. I slipped the dress over my head and quickly changed the header on my home page to read, "Look for the woman in yellow!"

After donning a light jacket to shield my shoulders from the chilly spring air, I headed for the post office on 52nd Street to drop off a package—my most expensive Brooks Brothers suit had sold overnight, providing a much-needed boost to my withering savings—and continued on to the copy shop four blocks farther north. The final task on my checklist was to address one of the problems I'd identified in the previous night's brainstorming session: the limitations of my current marketing scheme. With my website and social media presence, I was only targeting people who were regularly plugged into the Internet. But as I'd learned from Carson, not everyone lives their lives with their noses buried in their phones. So I devised an alternative way to reach them.

Twenty minutes later, I emerged from the copy shop with four hundred flyers for "Sophie's Spontaneous Tours." They'd turned out perfectly: Along the top, I'd printed the times and meeting places for each of my tours, and at the bottom, I wrote my phone number in big, bold letters. But the focal point of the advertisement, right smack dab in the center, was the caricature Carson had created of Sophie the Spontaneous Tour Guide. His drawing was the embodiment of everything I wanted my business to be: fun, fanciful, and full of charm.

For the next two hours, I distributed them throughout Midtown, stapling them to telephone poles in central locations and handing them to passersby on the crowded sidewalks. While most people veered away from my outstretched arm, ignoring my hollers of, "Let a *real* New Yorker show you the *real* sights of

the city!" there were a few merciful souls who accepted my of-
ferings with the barest of smiles. Even though they most likely
deposited those flyers in the nearest corner trash can as soon as I
retreated from view, I still took these small gestures of kindness
as a good omen.

At ten o'clock, "Midtown Highlights" was scheduled to meet
right outside the entrance to the Empire State Building. No
one had called to reserve a space, but I still kept my chin up as
I walked down 5th Avenue. I was in this for the long haul; I
couldn't give up on my dream because of one bad tour, one bad
review, or even one bad week.

*You can do this. Don't be afraid. Fear is the enemy.*

At five minutes to ten, I stopped at the curb in front of the
revolving glass doors that led to the lobby of the second tallest
building in New York, the fifth tallest skyscraper in the United
States. Standing beside a potted-plant-cum-communal-ashtray, I
tilted my head all the way back, studying its Art Deco façade.
From this vantage point, it was impossible to see its pinna-
cle. There were only windows embedded in concrete, growing
smaller and smaller the higher they climbed, until they disappeared into the milky overcast sky.

"You must be Sophie."

The sound of my name pulled me back to the ground floor,
where three women stood before me on the sidewalk. They all
looked to be around my age, sporting sensible travel purses and
comfortable walking shoes, their faces alight with eager smiles.
One of them held my flyer in her hands. Seems like that new
marketing plan was already working.

"You look just like the cartoon in your ad."

"I love your dress. Yellow's a great color for you."

Before I could say thank you, they procured three different credit cards from their respective wallets.

"It's forty dollars a person, right?"

"Do you take Amex?"

Biting back a giddy smile, I said, "Of course." As I entered their payment information in my phone, I asked them some questions to break the ice. "So, where are you guys from?"

"Ohio."

"We're on a girls' trip."

"We just got in yesterday. We're in New York for the whole week!"

"How fun!" Though my personal experience with girls' trips wasn't something I'd describe as "fun"—at least, not the "girls" portion of the trip—these three friends seemed to be having a great time. "What's on your agenda? Besides this tour, I mean."

"No agenda."

"Yeah, we're just winging it. Do you have any tips? Especially for nightlife." They eyed each other conspiratorially. "We're looking to get a little wild."

"Ladies," I said, unable to control my grin, "you've come to the right woman."

# chapter twenty-nine

By the end of the following week, business was starting to pick up. Inquiries had increased significantly since I'd revised my business plan, and in the span of a few days, I went from canceling tours because no one showed up to routinely hitting my minimum quota of three people per tour, sometimes even more. Some of this newfound success was due to my revised list of itineraries—I'd eliminated the tours that consistently underperformed, while doubling up on the popular ones—and I'm sure the new crop of positive Yelp reviews didn't hurt either. But when I asked my customers where they'd heard about me, they almost always said, "I saw your flyer." So it was safe to say my new ad campaign was working its magic.

Which wasn't all that surprising. Carson's caricature was so well done, it grabbed people's attention right away. Who wouldn't want to tour the streets of New York with the smiling, curly-haired woman in the picture? She looked confident, courageous, and happy. All the qualities Carson saw in me and translated to the page. I only wished I'd seen them in myself a little sooner. Like he said, though, sometimes people don't know what they want until they see it drawn out for them.

There were a million things I wanted to say to him. I wanted to explain the look on Seth's face when his father hung up on him, to tell him how I'd quit my job, to show him all the wonderful risks I was taking to pursue my new career. My new life. My happiness.

More than anything, though, I wanted to thank him. Because I never would've surrendered to my inner dreamer if he hadn't challenged my perceptions of what a successful life could look like. In all probability, I'd have continued to let my secret aspirations fade away while I stayed at McKinley forever. Climbing the corporate ladder, collecting fat paychecks, but at the end of the day, never feeling fulfilled.

By now, I was sure he was far away, somewhere on a distant continent, finding new sources of creative inspiration. The sketchbook filled with our intimate memories of Hong Kong had been sitting untouched in my nightstand drawer ever since his departure. I couldn't bring myself to look at it, knowing that he might have already found someone else to be his muse. Someone who didn't ridicule his choices, who accepted him as he was. Someone who had the courage to say yes instead of defaulting to the comfort of no.

For the most part, I tried not to focus on my regrets. Obsessing over the past would get me nowhere in the present. These days, I was all about living in the moment. Every day was a new adventure, a new discovery. Even though I'd seen the same New York City landmarks dozens, if not hundreds, of times before, the job never grew tedious. There was something invigorating about watching someone else witness the overwhelming majesty of the Empire State Building for the very first time or noticing how their eyes lit up when you told them they were standing on the exact subway grate that caused Marilyn Monroe's white dress to flutter above her thighs in *The Seven Year Itch*. After this, there was no way I could ever go back to the corporate world.

Not that I necessarily needed to. Once I started reaching—and sometimes exceeding—my quotas, I was no longer operating under a financial deficit. I'd probably still have to find a more affordable place to live, but for now, I was financially stable. Then again, I also knew circumstances could change on a dime. My rent could go up; my sales could drop off. So I allowed myself to remain open to possibility. Anything could happen. I had to be able to roll with the punches. To rewrite my task list, again and again.

Tonight, though, I was reveling in the joy of it all, because business was starting to boom. The last tour of the day boasted my biggest turnout yet, and at the end of a two-hour stroll around Midtown, I marched into Zum Bauer with seven happy, hungry clients trailing behind me. When I approached the host stand, Wolf muttered something indiscernible under his breath.

"I hope you're not cursing me out in German," I said.

"Not at all," he replied with a smile. "You've got a big party. Business is picking up for you?"

I nodded. "Looks that way. For now at least. Do you have any tables for seven?"

He surveyed the dining floor. "I think I can push a few tables together in the back. Let me see. Will you be joining them?"

"No. I'm actually meeting someone else here tonight."

A slender hand came to rest on my shoulder, and I turned to

see Elena's big green eyes shining down on me. With my busy schedule, I hadn't seen her since that morning at my grand-mother's house almost three weeks ago. After texting her my new number, we'd played phone tag for days until we were able to nail down an actual conversation, and when I told her about my abrupt career change, she insisted we meet for a drink.

"Hey," she said. "That color looks fab on you."

"Thanks." I smoothed the front of my lemon-yellow polo shirt. Since I couldn't wear the same sundress day in and day out, I decided to invest some of my earnings in appropriately colored work attire. After combing the sales racks at Century 21, I'd managed to fill all those empty hangers in my closet with yellow shirts, skirts, pants, and dresses. Now customers were able to spot me from a block away.

"Is this the other member of your party?" Wolf asked, making moony eyes at Elena.

"Yes. Wolf, this is my best friend, Elena. We go way back. Elena, this is Wolf."

He extended his hand for her to shake. "Nice to meet you."

"Likewise." Elena returned his dreamy gaze. As he turned and led my tour group toward their table, her eyes stayed glued to his back. One by one, I waved good-bye to all my smiling customers and pocketed tips from a few generous ones who'd had a particularly good experience. After they were gone, I looked to Elena, who still appeared spellbound from her encounter with Wolf.

"You okay?" I asked.

"Yeah," she said, dazed.

"Let's sit down." I pointed to the picnic table next to the front windows. "How about there?"

As soon as I slid onto the bench and lifted my swollen feet off the floor, I breathed a sigh of relief. "It feels so good to take a load off."

"You do a lot of walking in your new job, huh?"

"That's an understatement."

"Well, I saw all your Yelp reviews, and you've got a lot of satisfied customers. Are you enjoying yourself?"

A smile burst across my face. "Absolutely."

Elena smiled back. "That's so great, Soph. I don't think I've seen you looking this happy since... Well, it's been a really long time."

"I think it's because I'm finally feeling good about what I'm doing with my life. I've always wanted to work in the travel industry. I was just too afraid to pursue it."

"I remember when we were in high school, you used to keep those journals of your weekend trips into the city. And that big stack of guidebooks you had for countries all over the world. You had all those dream vacations planned out. Remember?"

"Of course. Traveling has always been my thing," I said. "I still plan out dream vacations. I've actually started posting them on my blog, just for fun."

"Aren't you going to miss it?"

"What do you mean?"

"Well, I know you hated your job and everything, but you used to talk about how much you loved that McKinley flew you all over the world. You said it was the best part of working there. Now you're just kinda...stuck here in New York."

I tapped my fingers on the scuffed wooden tabletop. "Sure. I'll miss jetting around the world. But the thing is, now that I'm doing what I've always wanted to do, I love my life in New York so much more than I did before. All of a sudden, I'm not feeling this need to pick up and run away. Not right now anyway. I'm sure the restlessness will come back eventually. When it does..." I shrugged. "I'll cross that bridge when I come to it."

Elena raised her eyebrows. "Wow. You're a whole new Sophie."

"No, I'm not. I'm just finally letting myself be who I always was deep down."

Wolf approached the table. "I've got everyone situated along the back wall. They've already ordered four pitchers. You must've given them a good tour; they're all in party mode." He looked from me to Elena. "What can I get you ladies to drink? First round's on me."

Elena giggled and touched a fingertip to her lower lip. "What kind of white wines do you have?"

"Our Riesling's on happy hour special right now."

"I'll take that," she said.

Their gazes lingered on each other for a moment before he turned to me and asked, "The usual for you?"

I nodded and he walked toward the bar. Elena watched him leave, studying his easy swagger and the way his muscular shoulder blades pressed against the thin fabric of his T-shirt. Her tongue was practically hanging on the floor.

"Wild guess," I said, "but do you have the hots for Wolf?"

Her cheeks turned a bright shade of pink and her lips curled into a devious smile. "Maybe a little. What's his deal? Do you know? Is he single?"

"I'm not sure. I don't know much about him. But here's a question: Are *you* single?"

"Yes, of course! Why wouldn't I be?"

"Well, when last we spoke, you and Roddy were still on a break. So, if history is any indicator, that means the two of you will be getting back together sometime around next Wednesday."

She set her jaw and shook her head. "Not this time. I mean it. I'm done."

"Really?" I'd heard Elena say she was through with Roddy countless times before. But I'd never seen such resolve in her eyes. Maybe this time she actually meant it.

"I've been thinking about what you said when we were in Hong Kong. About how our relationship was dysfunctional."

"Oh, Elena, I'm sorry about that. It wasn't my place to pass judgment on your relationship. I only said that because I was hurt and lashing out and—"

"But you were right," she said. "We *were* dysfunctional. What healthy couple breaks up and gets back together four times? Then decides to move in together right away? It doesn't make any sense. I mean, I couldn't even be apart from him for a week. How pathetic is that?"

"It's okay to miss someone. Especially someone you love." I understood that now. How it could feel like a part of you was on the other end of the earth.

"I didn't just miss him," she said. "I was obsessed. To an un-healthy degree. Now I've realized that I'm too young to settle down."

Those were quite possibly the last words I'd expected to come out of Elena's mouth. Ever since eighth grade, she'd been jump-ing from relationship to relationship, never spending more than a couple of weeks without being attached at the hip to some boyfriend. I assumed she'd been itching to walk down the aisle sooner rather than later.

"What sparked this epiphany?" I asked.

"Honestly? That whole conversation with your grandmother. My career is basically nonexistent. Yeah, I have a *job*, but it doesn't mean anything to me. I don't want to be a receptionist forever, you know? I've spent my whole postcollege life chasing around after Roddy. It's time for me to figure myself out. Find out what I'm passionate about. So I'm gonna put my love life on the back burner while I concentrate on me. In the meantime, I can date around casually and play the field. Just like you."

*Just like me.* While Elena had been busy tying herself down all those years, I'd been out bedhopping, loudly swearing I'd never allow myself to fall victim to the burdensome trap of love. Yet here I sat, in this dimly lit pub, secretly pining away for a man. The complete opposite of Elena's newfound swinging sin-glehood.

Right on cue, Wolf appeared with our drinks. Elena glanced up at him under her long lashes and tossed her hair over her shoulder. "Thanks."

He placed the Bitburger down in front of me but didn't peel

his eyes off of her. "Let me know if I can get you anything else," he said before retreating to the host stand.

"I see you've already honed in on your first potential target," I said.

"Possibly." She wrapped her pale hand around the stem of her wineglass and raised it to me in a toast. "To self-discovery."

We clinked cups and I took a sip of my new signature drink, the only beer I'd tasted since I'd returned from my trip to Hong Kong. Each time I caught sight of the sweating pint glass, full of golden lager, emblazoned with a Bitburger logo, it never failed to transport me back to Lan Kwai Fong. To the first time I ever saw Carson's face. His thick head of sandy hair. The dimple in his stubbled cheek. Features that would be etched into my memory for eternity.

"So," Elena said, "I was hoping you'd decide to offer up the information without me having to ask, but it seems like you're not going to talk about it unless I drag it out of you."

"What information?"

"That long stupid story? About an artist? You never elaborated."

"Oh."

"*Oh?*" She threw up her hands. "That's it?"

I shifted in my seat. It's not like I was purposely trying to hide the truth from her. I just didn't think I was mentally prepared to recount the tale and relive the whole heart-rending experience all over again.

"Who is he?" she demanded.

I couldn't keep it from her forever. *Deep breaths. You can do this.*

I brought my beer to my lips with a shaky hand. After a long swig and a loud swallow, I said, "His name is Carson."

For the next ten minutes, I confessed everything that had happened over the past few weeks. How we met in Hong Kong and spent the whole week together. How he asked me to stay with him and how I said no. How he showed up on my doorstep in New York, out of the clear blue sky. How we'd made love all night and into the morning and talked about our plans to be together. And how it all fell apart at the end.

When I told her he punched Seth in the face, she said it was romantic.

"What are you talking about?" I said. "He could've gotten me fired."

"But you quit that day anyway."

"That's not the point."

"Look, Sophie, men have very animalistic instincts," she said. "He was merely defending your honor, in the only way he knew how: blunt force trauma to the face."

I peered down into my half-empty mug. Light glinted off the glass like sparkling blue eyes.

"Where is he now?" she asked.

I shrugged, took another sip of beer.

"Is he the one who drew those flyers?"

"Yeah. Have you seen them around town?" My mood lifted instantly. *Damn, those flyers are effective!*

"I have, and they're really cute, Soph. He's a good artist. I actually grabbed one as I was walking through Penn Station. I figured I'd bring it home to show my mom."

"That's weird," I said. "I didn't put any flyers in Penn Station."

"No? There was a huge stack of them right under the Amtrak sign."

My heart began to thud against my ribs. "Are you sure they're mine?"

"No, it must be some other girl named Sophie who's running a different spontaneous tour." Elena rolled her eyes and unzipped her purse. "Let me see what I did with it."

As she rifled through her mess of a bag, I scratched my chin and tried to think of a reasonable explanation for a pile of my flyers materializing in the concourse of Penn Station. Perhaps an enthusiastic client wanted to spread the word about my tours? Or maybe Kat was making extra copies to advertise, since she was certainly benefiting from all the extra business I was bringing in.

"Here it is." Elena pulled a rumpled sheet of paper from her purse and smoothed it against the rough tabletop. When I saw what was spread out before me, my heart leapt up to my throat.

It wasn't my flyer.

Oh, it was a flyer for my business, all right. It had the same phone number, the same schedule, the same "Sophie's Spontaneous Tours" banner written across the top. And it was definitely my own face smiling back at me.

But it was a completely different caricature from the one I'd been using. Instead of the Statue of Liberty hovering behind me, this time I was flanked by Broadway signs and neon lights. And instead of standing on top of a double-decker bus, I was strolling

on the sidewalk, surrounded by tourists who were snapping photos and hanging on my every word. The drawing was every bit
as eye-catching as the other one. It was just different. New.

And I would know those pen strokes anywhere.

Carson was still in town.

# chapter thirty

The new flyers were all over the city. Somehow I must've been blinded to them, but once I opened my eyes, I realized the posters I'd been seeing on the telephone poles weren't the same ones I'd stapled up there two weeks ago. Of course they weren't; in this town, I'd have been lucky if a flyer survived a single night tacked up in public. Clearly, Carson had been replenishing them for me. Not to mention, handing them out in other places I hadn't even thought of, like Penn Station.

So the whole next day, as I conducted my tours, I kept an eye out for them. Like magic, they appeared: taped in the window of the Port Authority, plastered to bus stop shelters and scaffolding. A million copies of my face adorning the streets, imploring its inhabitants to tour the city with me. What's more, I discovered Carson had designed a whole array of new flyers, not just one. There were six in total—at least, six that I found. No wonder business was booming. It turned out I had a lot of help from an extensive ad campaign I wasn't even paying for.

If he was in town, and he knew where to find me, then why wasn't he showing his face?

It was a question I pondered all day, but only during my hour-long breaks between tours. Because while I was working, all that mattered was providing my clients with the best possible New

York experience I could give them. I had to focus, stay in the moment. Shake thoughts of Carson off until later.

Which, admittedly, was not such a hard thing to do, since I loved my job with a fiery passion. Particularly when I led my tour groups down the Great White Way, so named for the millions of lights shining on billboards and signs along Broadway. My favorite time to walk through the area was at dusk, when the marquees really started to shine. People gathered on the streets clutching ticket stubs, their eyes wide with expectation as they filtered into theaters for evening performances. The energy was contagious.

This evening, as I led the charge west on 44th Street, I stopped in front of Sardi's, like I usually did, and gave my little speech about its history. When I got to the part about the celebrity caricatures adorning the walls, the members of my group had some questions.

"Do you know anything about the artist who draws them?" asked a man in the front.

"There have been a number of artists over the years," I said. "But the very first one was a man named Alex Gard, who was compensated for his work in daily meals from the restaurant."

The man guffawed. "That guy sounds like a chump. I bet he could've made a pretty penny."

"Actually," I said, "I like to think it was a testament to how much the artist loved his work. Money didn't factor in. He did it for the simple joy of it."

A woman in the back raised her hand and shouted, "Is this what inspired your ad campaign?"

"No. Those caricatures were drawn by . . . a friend of mine."

"Are you paying him in meals, too?" said the man.

The crowd laughed, and I laughed along with them, but I had to clasp my hands behind my back to keep them from trembling. *Deep breaths, Sophie. Stay focused.*

We continued down the street until the lights of Broadway were far behind us. Pedestrian traffic thinned out, and theatergoers were replaced with residents walking their dogs among ivy-covered brownstones and leafy oak trees. In the span of a block, the city had turned from cultural epicenter to cozy enclave. This was a side of New York the big red tour buses never adequately showed. A hush fell over the group, and we walked silently, taking in the surroundings. When we reached Tenth Avenue, we were thrust back into a noisy, bustling metropolis. Trucks rumbled down the asphalt, laughing couples spilled from the back doors of taxis, and our tour was coming to an end at Zum Bauer.

By this time of night, I was usually so exhausted from hours of pounding the pavement, I could do nothing more but say my good-byes before retreating up the five flights of stairs to my apartment and crawling into bed. But tonight, I didn't feel quite so tired, and I definitely didn't feel like being alone. Not yet anyway. So I joined the group for a nightcap, thinking a pint of Bitburger might be what I needed to take the edge off and help me sleep.

Our party was so large, Wolf had to split us up into two separate tables. I sat at the end of a long bench, next to three Argentinian guys—Emilio, Nico, and Andrés—who were backpacking around the United States. They were handsome and strapping, their faces tan and covered in thick, dark facial hair. Their accents were so hot, they could've melted the whole crock of butter Wolf brought out for the *Brötchen*.

There was a time, not long ago, when I would've conspired to lure one of them upstairs to my apartment. Hell, I might've even tried to nab all three. But now my heart was telling me something different. There was only one man I wanted to be with; I just didn't know where to find him. So I sipped my beer and made casual small talk, trying to distract myself from the feeling that something important had been misplaced. Like my life was an intricate puzzle with a single missing piece.

"How long have you guys been touring the States?" I asked.

"Almost two months," Emilio replied. "We started in California and worked our way east."

"It's all over on Monday, though," Nico said. "That's when we fly back to Buenos Aires."

"Back to the real world." They clinked glasses and exchanged solemn glances.

"Well," I sighed, "all vacations must come to an end."

"Not for you!"

"Yeah," Andrés chimed in, "your whole life is one vacation. Bringing people on tours and traveling the world. What an amazing job you have."

"I don't travel the world. All my tours are based right here, in New York."

"What about all those itineraries on your website?"

Emilio was referring to my blog. There was a link to it off

my main site, but before now, I wasn't sure anyone was actually reading all those dream itineraries I'd been collecting since I was a kid. A South African safari. A cruise around the Baltic Sea. A camping adventure through the Outback of Australia. Putting them up on the Internet made me feel like I was setting my wishes free into the world with the hope that one day they might come true.

"Those aren't actual tours," I said. "They're only fantasies."

"That's too bad," Nico said. "They seemed so real to me."

"Yeah," Andrés added. "When I saw your sample walking tour of Old San Juan, I almost booked a flight to Puerto Rico on the spot."

"It just wouldn't be feasible. I mean... I couldn't."

*Could I?*

I knew what my instincts were telling me: that the mere idea of traveling the world as an independently operating tour guide was a completely ludicrous idea. Then again, a few weeks ago, I would've thought that quitting my job at McKinley was outside the realm of the possible, too. So what was stopping me from taking Sophie's Spontaneous Tours around the globe?

Like a flash of lightning, the answer popped into my head: *Nothing.* Nothing was stopping me. I had no obligations to fulfill, no deadlines to meet. The only roadblock between me and the realization of my dreams was myself.

The wheels in my head started spinning. Kat had told me that running a business was a never-ending process of reinvention. That if I wanted to remain relevant and successful, I'd constantly have to evolve and adapt. If I wanted to make this a reality, there were so many logistics to consider. Not the least of which was how to get the word out to potential customers.

"So, is that how you found out about my tour?" I asked. "Through my blog?"

"No, we found you through the flyers at the hostel."

"Yeah. Some guy in the lobby dropped them off and said you were a great guide," Emilio said.

"Hostel?" I repeated.

"Yes, the Times Square West on Forty-Sixth and Tenth."

"Forty-Sixth and Tenth?" At this point, I knew I sounded like a parrot, but I had to repeat the words out loud to really believe them. That hostel was only two blocks north of here. *Could Carson really be so close by?*

Suddenly, I was on my feet. Not even my half-finished Bitburger could take the edge off now. Every cell in my body was telling me to run to this hostel, right away, as fast as my legs could carry me.

"This has been a great tour, everyone," I said, nearly tripping over the rungs of the chair as I tried to disentangle myself from the seat. "I really have to run now, but you guys sit and stay for as long as you want and enjoy yourself. Wolf will see to anything you need."

I turned away and sped toward the door, waving behind me at the people who were still shouting their good-byes. I realized I could be walking away from some healthy tips, but money didn't factor in. All I could think about in that moment was finding Carson.

On my way to the front door, Kat waved me over to the bar,

her brows furrowed in concern. "Is everything all right?" she asked. "You look a bit frazzled."

"Everything's fine. Better than fine. At least with the tour. But there's somewhere I've gotta be right now."

"Say no more," she said. "Go. Wolf and I will take care of the tour group if anyone needs anything."

"Thanks a lot," I said, already pushing the front door open. "I'll see you tomorrow." Then I was out on Tenth Avenue, running uptown, a hundred nervous butterflies beating their wings inside my stomach. My legs vaulted along the sidewalk, and by the time I reached the front door of the Times Square West Hostel, I was in a full sweat. I was also grinning from ear to ear, completely convinced I would find Carson there. So when the clerk behind the front desk told me there was no Carson Greene listed in their guest registry, I made him check again.

"Sorry, ma'am," he said. "No Greenes have been here all week."

"Well, what about the week before?" I clenched my clammy hands into tight fists.

"Ma'am, I can't give out that information."

"Well, have you seen him around here? He's about six feet tall, sandy hair, blue eyes."

The clerk's patience was wearing thin. "I see hundreds of people every day that fit that description."

He turned to face his computer, finished with this conversation.

*Shit.*

Frantically, I looked around the lobby, hoping in vain to find some clue that might lead me to find him. All I saw was a wire rack of tourism brochures and a half-empty vending machine. I didn't see my flyers posted anywhere. Not even on the community message board.

Perhaps it had been naïve of me to think I might track Carson down so easily. Still, I couldn't help but feel a crushing sense of disappointment. And a growing sense of frustration. He knew how to contact me. He could come see me whenever he wanted. So why was he hiding out?

All the nervous energy I'd been running on all day drained from my body in one fell swoop. I flopped down on the threadbare tweed couch in the center of the lobby, hoping to catch a second wind before walking the two blocks back home. As I scanned the advertisements and announcements posted on the community message board, I wondered if Carson had really ever been here. Maybe those nice Argentinian guys had been mistaken as to where they saw the flyer. Maybe they'd just seen it on a telephone pole or in Penn Station. Maybe they'd received it from one of my other customers.

Hinges squealed as the front door opened. I peered over the back of the couch to see a gaggle of young women walking in, chattering away in Australian accents.

"That walking tour looked fun. Do you wanna do it tomorrow?"

"Maybe. But I'm more interested in the hot guy who delivered the flyers last night."

"Oh, I know. Do you think he'll turn up again tonight?"

"I hope so. God, he had the sexiest blue eyes."

My heart raced anew as the girls plunked themselves down onto the beanbag chairs behind the couch. I sank down low into the cushions, hiding myself from view while I eavesdropped on their banter.

"Let's wait here for a little while and see if he shows."

"Maybe we can invite him to go out with us later."

"Hey, I call dibs on him, sweetie."

The sound of their giggles was muffled by the blood rushing through my ears.

Carson had been here.

Which means he'd probably be here again.

And I wasn't leaving until I saw him.

# chapter thirty-one

Time ticked by, each minute more painful than the last. And I'm not just referring to the torture of listening to the nonstop babble of the women on the beanbag chairs. I'm talking about physical pain, too. Like the crick I'd developed in my neck from sitting in an awkward, half-reclined position on that ratty, saggy couch. I suppose I could've sat up to alleviate the discomfort, but I didn't want them to see me; I kept hoping to discreetly overhear some other snippet of conversation pertaining to Carson. So far, though, they'd only shared stories of their lives back in Melbourne, and I made a mental note to research the Yarra Valley when I got home. From their anecdotes, it seemed like it might be an interesting tourist destination.

I had no idea how long I'd been waiting there, but from the death stares being lobbed in my direction by the front desk clerk, it was safe to say I'd overstayed my welcome. My hope of meeting Carson tonight began to wither and die. *Maybe tomorrow,* I thought. And the ladies on the beanbag chairs agreed with me.

"Well, girls," one of them said. "I hate to say this but I think we might want to abandon our quest for the hottie with the flyers tonight."

"Yeah, it's getting kind of late, isn't it?"

"Oh, let's wait just a few more minutes!"

"This is New York, sweetie. Hot guys are a dime a dozen. Come on, let's get ready to hit the clubs."

The chairs rustled as they stood up, and when the clack of their footsteps faded away, I pushed myself up to a seated position. Rolling my head from side to side, I massaged my neck, kneading away the muscle spasm. When the clerk vigorously cleared his throat, I figured it was probably my cue to leave. Besides, it was getting late, and I had a full day of touring to tend to tomorrow.

With a heavy sigh, I hefted myself to my feet and turned toward the exit, just in time to hear the hinges on the door squeal once more. In walked a guy about six feet tall, with tousled hair and piercing eyes. In his arms, he held a stack of photocopies. Halfway to the community board on the opposite end of the lobby, he stopped in his tracks, staring at me.

"Sophie," he said.

"Carson."

"What are you doing here?" he asked.

"I think a better question would be, what are *you* doing here?"

I gestured to the flyers in his hand, where a brand-new caricature stared back at me. This time, I was standing in the middle of Bryant Park, with the Josephine Shaw Lowell fountain trickling off to the side, and my old office building soaring in the background. "How many of these have you made by now?" I asked. "Seven?"

"Eight."

"And you've been posting them up in here?"

"Yeah. I hope that's okay. I saw you were putting them on

telephone poles and stuff. But, in my experience, you'll really get the best exposure to tourists if you place them in touristy places. Like hotels or hostels."

"Or Penn Station."

"You saw them there?" he asked.

I nodded. He chewed on the inside of his cheek, seeming insecure, almost defensive, like he wasn't aware of how significant his efforts had been. How much he had helped me, without even knowing it.

"Do you like them?" he asked.

"I love them." I took a step closer to him. "Truly. They're amazing. Thank you so much for doing all this."

He let out a breath he'd been holding. "I was happy to do it. You know, when I first saw your flyer around town, I had to do a double take. Then I started seeing them everywhere and I thought, man, she's really doing it. She's taking the chance. I wanted to be able to support you. Even if it was only in this small way."

"This is not a small gesture, by any means. If you've been in town this whole time, though, why haven't you just come back to see me?"

"Because I wasn't sure you wanted that. Not after the way we left things."

I took yet another step closer, drinking in his spicy, familiar scent. "You were right, Carson. About everything. My whole life I've been caught between what I thought I needed to be and what really made me happy. I finally decided to give happiness a chance."

He raised his hand and caressed my cheek lightly with the backs of his fingers. I surrendered to the sensation, the blissful comfort of being here with him, of finding that last missing piece of the puzzle I needed to feel whole.

"That's all I wanted," he said. "For you to be happy. To live the life you've always dreamed of."

I wrapped my arms around his torso, feeling his warm, solid body press against me. Our lips grazed, exchanging tender, delicate kisses. Kisses that spoke of their own accord. *I love you,* they said. *I've missed you. I'll never leave you again.*

"I'm sorry," I whispered against his mouth.

"For what?"

"For accusing you of not following your passion. For saying you're afraid to be a success."

He paused a moment before he said, "Well, maybe you had a point."

"No. I had this narrow vision of what it means to be successful, and I shouldn't have tried to force that on you. Success doesn't mean making a lot of money or pursuing a prestigious career. Success means being happy. As long as you're happy, that's all that matters."

Carson pulled away from me slightly, heaving a weighty sigh. "If I'm being totally honest, Sophie, I'm not happy."

His words hit me like a freight train. He was an independently wealthy artist, with the freedom to wander the world on a whim, to sketch whatever his heart desired. He answered to no one; he made his own rules. For him, every day was a different adventure. Without a doubt, he lived a life most people, including me, only dreamed about. "What do you mean you're not happy?"

He licked his lips and tilted his head back, searching the ceiling for answers. "I've been thinking a lot about what you said. How I'm just floating around, with no direction, no purpose. How I don't set goals for myself because I'm too..." His voice faltered for a moment; then he cleared his throat and started over. "Because I'm afraid of failing. I've been doing that for a long time, ever since I dropped out of art school. Now I'm starting to feel like my life is sort of meaningless. What am I here for? What am I doing?"

I patted his chest, right where his tattoo was concealed beneath his shirt. "You're seizing the day."

"That's the problem," he said, placing his hand over my own. "I'm not seizing anything. I dream and I dream, but I never *do*. I'm stagnant, standing still, while the rest of the world passes me by. I've always been so scared of turning out like my parents, obsessed with this idea of living in the moment. But life's about growing. Trying and failing and trying again. Seeing how you put yourself out there and took this chance just reminds me of all the chances I haven't been taking."

He lowered his gaze to meet mine, and I recognized the raw emotion in his eyes: the torment of never feeling good enough, the fear of never finding peace. Then he continued. "Remember my old roommate, Johnny, from college? After you and I talked the other day, I decided to look him up. Turns out he lives in New York. We met for a drink last week, caught up on our lives. He's still hustling with his artwork, trying to book shows and sell his sculptures and stuff. But he's also got a day job at a graphic design firm, and he really likes it. I was thinking ... something like that might be good for me."

I widened my eyes, unable to contain my excitement for his sudden burst of ambition. "That's a great idea, Carson. You could totally pull something like that off!"

His lips curled into a small smile. "You're the only person who's ever believed in me, Sophie. Who thinks I can be somebody great someday."

"You already *are* somebody great."

"But I know I can be more. I see that now."

"I don't need you to be more than you already are," I said. "But if you feel like something is missing from your life, then I want to help you find it. Just like you helped me."

"Whatever you did, you did it all by yourself. I was only ever cheering for you from the sidelines."

Carson pulled me close again and kissed me, sending a shock through my tender, flooded nerves. I yielded to his soft, open mouth, and as he gripped my waist, the flyers slipped from his hands and spilled to the floor around our feet. A low moan escaped from the back of my throat and echoed all around us. The fear of never seeing him again had quickly been replaced with a fierce need to touch him, to taste him, to hold him and never let go. For a second, I could've sworn we were in Wan Chai again, standing at the edge of the waterfront promenade, with briny breezes blowing off Victoria Harbour and settling over my prickling skin.

It wasn't until the front desk clerk emitted a phlegmy, deliberate cough that I realized we were still standing in the lobby of this grubby New York hostel. When we peeled our lips apart and glanced in his direction, he was shuffling papers and purposely averting his gaze.

"We'd better leave," Carson whispered, bending over to gather the flyers from the floor. I straightened the front of my now-rumpled shirt and watched him as he approached the community message board to tack up an ad for Sophie's Spontaneous Tours. As he pressed the pushpin into the cork, he glanced back at me over his shoulder. I caught a glimpse of the dimple in his stubbled cheek, and a tingle rippled through my stomach.

Out on the sidewalk, I asked, "Where are you staying?"

"Just down the block." He pointed to a brick town house on the other side of the street. Striped awnings shaded its first-floor windows, and barrels of pink peonies flanked its shiny red door. "It's a little boutique hotel."

"No more hostels for you, then?"

He chuckled. "You were right, the Grand Amadora may have spoiled me. I feel like I'm outgrowing that whole six-snoring-guys-to-a-room thing anyway. This place I'm at is really nice. All the best amenities. Private bathroom. Comfy king-sized bed."

I hooked a finger in the front pocket of his shorts and pulled him to my side. "I can't wait to see it."

"Don't you wanna go back to your apartment?" he asked.

"Hell no. It's always more fun to do it on a hotel bed."

His laughter echoed along the narrow side street and he curled his arm around my waist. With my face nuzzled against his chest, I said, "I was so afraid I'd never see you again."

He pressed his thumb under my chin and raised my eyes to meet his. "I said I'd follow you anywhere, Sophie. And I meant it."

I thought back to the idea that had come to me after my conversation with the Argentine backpackers. To take Sophie's Spontaneous Tours on the road, leading fellow adventurers out to explore the unknown.

"Would you follow me around the world?" I asked.

Carson answered with a kiss. A kiss that said, *I will follow you wherever you go.*

Never before had I seen so many stars.

I don't know if it was the stillness of the summer evening, or the dry desert air, or the fact that we were seemingly hundreds of miles from anything resembling modern civilization. But the sky was so clear and expansive, I must've been able to see every single celestial body in the Southern Hemisphere. Whole galaxies appeared in majestic, milky swirls. It was the first time I'd ever actually witnessed a star twinkle. Childhood nursery rhymes were brought to life before my eyes here in the Australian Outback.

"So, which one of these constellations is the Southern Cross?" I asked.

Carson studied an astronomical chart using the dim glow of his headlamp. He kept turning it around in his hands, trying to line the image up with the real-life view on display through the skylight in our tent. I snuggled closer to him, resting my head in the crook of his armpit, thankful that I'd sprung for the two-person sleeping bag.

"I'm not totally sure," he said. "It's too dark to make out the fine print."

"I should've installed that interactive sky map on my phone before we left Alice Springs."

Carson tossed the paper aside and clicked off his headlamp. "Who needs to know exactly what we're looking at? Let's just enjoy it for what it is: beautiful."

We lay there, side by side, nothing visible but the millions of stars sprayed across the sky. A dozen different night creatures clicked and croaked around us in the bush camp, making me happy to be safely zipped behind impenetrable canvas and nylon mesh. Carson's body heat warmed me; I hadn't expected it to be so chilly this evening, especially after hiking under the scorching sun all day. I stretched out my sore limbs, feeling the effects of our earlier trek through Kings Canyon. It was an arduous four-hour journey, but it had been worth the physical exertion to be able to perch on the edge of a cliff and watch the sunset bring the fiery red sands of the desert to life.

"What time should we wake people up in the morning?" he asked.

"No later than five."

"So early?"

"Well, it takes four hours to drive to Uluru from here, and we want to get everyone there with plenty of time to walk around the park before the camel rides begin."

"What camel rides?"

"I didn't tell you? Nick and Ilene were talking all excitedly about this camel farm in Yulara. So I contacted the farm yesterday and set up a forty-five-minute camelback tour for tomorrow afternoon. When the rest of the group found out about it, they wanted in. I thought it sounded fun, too. So I booked ten tickets, for all of us."

"You're such a good tour guide. Always giving people what they want, even at the spur of the moment."

I poked him in the side. "Hey, I'm not just a tour guide anymore. I'm also a certified international—"

"Tour director. Yes, I know." Carson kissed my shoulder and hugged me tight, one big strong arm wrapped around my torso. "How could I have forgotten? Those first sixteen days you spent away from me were torture."

I giggled, but in truth, those sixteen days in August were the exhilarating start of a whole new life for me. I'd spent them at the International Tour Management Institute in San Francisco, obtaining an official Tour Guide and Director Certification. Once I'd made the decision to take Sophie's Spontaneous Tours on the road, I figured I'd attract more clients if I had some serious credentials. When I finished my training and added that little ITMI badge to my website, requests for more information on my services started pouring in. Since then, I'd led a group of travelers on a customized tour of Japan, from old-world Kyoto to trend-setting Tokyo, and I was in the process of organizing two more trips based on sample itineraries I'd posted on my blog; seems I'd finally get to behold the wonder of Machu Picchu at sunrise after all. Whenever I wasn't traveling the world, I was still running my walking tours through the streets of New York City, which were now routinely selling out.

Although Carson had promised to follow me anywhere, we both knew that wasn't always feasible, especially after he enrolled in a design program at the School of Visual Arts. His specialization was creative advertising; all those flyers he created for my business sparked a fire within him, compelling him to use his art in ways he'd never before allowed himself to imagine. To be sure, he still sketched his heart out, filling notebooks with the wild and varied sights of New York. He even started a club at his school called "City Sketchers," in which he and his fellow students gathered together in various public locations with their sketchbooks and pencils in hand. What's more, he and Johnny were searching for gallery space to host their first joint exhibition: sketches and sculptures, side by side. He said he hadn't felt so connected to a creative community since the days of his old high school art club.

With all these changes, Carson was starting to feel like he'd found a purpose in his life. Goals to work toward, so he wasn't floating around with no direction. While I led these international tours by myself, he stayed at home in New York, chasing his own dream, but cheering me on from the sidelines.

This trip to Australia was special, though. Carson had postponed his original voyage down under to be with me, so I couldn't very well plan a spectacular three-week excursion through Oz without him. Instead, I timed it to coincide with his winter break from classes, which started right after Thanksgiving. It turned out to be perfect timing, too, since I found a team of eight adventurous Americans who were interested in a tour through the region as well. This was my life now, combining work with pleasure. I was able to see the world, share it with other people, and make a living while I did it.

There was one upcoming trip that I was planning for free, though. Right after the New Year, I was going to spend five days touring Miami, because Grandma had finally decided to take the plunge and visit her good friend Sadie. During a particularly cold early winter storm, Grandma had called me up asking for my advice in buying her a plane ticket down to Florida. I booked one for her, as well as one for myself, and then I spent a few hours designing an amazing itinerary for the both of us, intent on giving her an experience she would never forget. Maybe she'd like it so much, she'd consider moving down there herself. It seemed like a long shot, but I'd learned that the world is an uncertain, unpredictable place. Anything was possible, as far as I was concerned.

"We should decorate our bedroom ceiling with those glow-in-the-dark star stickers," Carson said.

"No."

"Why not?"

"Because they're cheesy."

"Come on," he said. "We keep saying we're gonna fix up our place and then we never get around to it."

Carson had a point. We'd moved into our cheap one-bedroom in Queens almost two months earlier, but ever since, we'd both been too busy to spend time making the place feel like home. In fact, we still had several unpacked boxes piled up in our hall closet.

"Wouldn't it be great to re-create this view?" he continued. "We could fall asleep looking at these stars every night."

"I already like what I fall asleep to every night." My hand squeezed his midsection and I nuzzled farther into his side, my nose grazing his chest. I kissed the branches of his tree and felt my skin tingle as he slid his fingers up the length of my body. When he buried his hand in my tangle of curls and pressed his lips firmly to mine, I reluctantly pulled away.

"We shouldn't do this here, out in the open," I said.

His voice was a deep, hungry growl. "There's a reason I pitched our tent so far from the rest of the group. The closest camper is a good thirty feet away."

I lifted my head slightly to peer out the side of the tent. There was nothing beyond but blackness. No noises except for the continuous cacophony of desert wildlife.

"Okay," I said. "But keep your voice down."

He snickered and rolled on top of me. "Don't worry, I won't make a peep."

Our mouths met once again, and as I lost myself in his tender caresses, I couldn't help but smile. Because I had it all. A fulfilling career. A passport full of stamps. An unwavering love.

I couldn't have planned it any better if I tried.

# acknowledgments

First and foremost, I owe a mountain of gratitude to my brilliant agent, Jennifer Johnson-Blalock. Thank you for plucking me out of the slush pile, for seeing promise in my words, for bringing out the best in me, for always being in my corner, and for encouraging me to drink that last mai tai. Thanks also to everyone at Liza Dawson Associates for being so supportive.

My editor, Christina Boys, helped make this book better than I could have imagined. Thank you for your deep understanding of Sophie and her story, for your enthusiasm, for your insight, and for your guidance as I learned to navigate the world of publishing.

Thanks to everyone at Center Street, especially Jody Waldrup and Diane Luger, for your beautiful design work and for being so accommodating. You've truly created the cover of my dreams. Also, a big note of appreciation to Carrie Andrews for her meticulous copyediting skills, and Bob Castillo for bringing it all together.

Without my teachers, I would have never developed the skills necessary to finish an entire novel. Thanks to Shari Goldhagen, Michael Backus, Leigh Michaels, and the staff of Gotham Writers Workshop, for showing me how it's done.

Thanks to all my early readers and amazing friends who offered valuable feedback and endless encouragement: Jenn Amini, Mary Birnbaum, Margaret Chantung, Dora Fisher, and Emily Morton-Owens. An extra huge thanks to Eleanor Nystrom, for eagerly reading every single version of this manuscript ever written (and there were a lot). Also, a big shout-out to the members of RWA San Diego, for welcoming me with open arms and being such a helpful, kind community.

Marci Blaszka and Jessica Schwarz have provided me with over two decades of unyielding moral support. Thank you for loving me enough to be honest with me and for cheering me on, no matter what. You're the best friends a woman could ask for.

Finally, thank you to Emilio, who believed in me from the moment I said, "So I signed up for this writing class." Thanks for pushing me off the cliff so I could learn to fly. I love you and Andrew more than words can say.

## about the author

KRISTIN ROCKAWAY is a native New Yorker with an insatiable case of wanderlust. After working in the IT industry for far too many years, she traded the city for the surf and chased her dreams out to Southern California, where she spends her days happily writing stories instead of software. THE WILD WOMAN'S GUIDE TO TRAVELING THE WORLD is her first novel. When she's not writing, she enjoys spending time with her husband and son, and planning her next big vacation.

# reading group guide

1. In the opening scene, Sophie is abandoned by Elena on the first day of their girls' trip. What would you have done if you were in Sophie's shoes? Do you sympathize with Elena? Why or why not?

2. Why is it so important for Sophie to always have a plan and a goal to work toward? Why does she abandon it so easily when she first meets Carson?

3. Carson's technophobia is rare in today's world. How do you think this influenced his burgeoning relationship with Sophie? Do you think Sophie found his technophobia to be a strength or a flaw? Why?

4. Sophie and Elena have been best friends since childhood. Why do you think their friendship has endured through so many years and so many changes in their lives? Do you have any friendships that have stood the test of time? If so, how are they similar to or different from Sophie and Elena's friendship?

5. In what ways does Sophie's relationship with her grandmother push her to be better? In what ways does it hold her back?

6. Discuss the significance of Sophie's favorite book, *The Wild Woman's Guide to Traveling the World*. What are some of the ways in which she identifies with it? How does it influence her throughout her life?

7. Do you think Sophie would have stayed in her job at McKinley if she'd never met Carson? Would she have ever followed her dream of becoming a tour guide? Why or why not?

8. How does Sophie's practical, disciplined nature work to her advantage when she starts her new tour business? How does it work against her?

9. Where do you see these characters in five years? Do you still see Sophie and Carson together? Is Sophie's Spontaneous Tours still in business? Is Elena still a swinging single?

10. Travel is Sophie's biggest passion. Talk about some of your favorite travel experiences. Where are some places you dream about going but have yet to visit?